OUT OF THE WORLD

Cultural Memory in the Present

Hent de Vries, Editor

OUT OF THE WORLD

Peter Sloterdijk

Translated by Corey A. Dansereau and Gill Zimmermann

STANFORD UNIVERSITY PRESS
Stanford, California

Stanford University Press
Stanford, California

English translation © 2024 by the Board of Trustees
of the Leland Stanford Junior University.
All rights reserved.

Out of the World was originally published in German in 1993 under the title *Weltfremdheit*. © Suhrkamp Verlag Frankfurt am Main 1993. All rights reserved by and controlled through Suhrkamp Verlag Berlin.

Printed in the United States of America on acid-free, archival-quality paper

Library of Congress Cataloging-in-Publication Data

Names: Sloterdijk, Peter, 1947– author.
Title: Out of the world / Peter Sloterdijk ; translated by Corey A.
    Dansereau and Gill Zimmermann.
Other titles: Weltfremdheit. English | Cultural memory in the present.
Description: Stanford, California : Stanford University Press, 2024. |
    Series: Cultural memory in the present | "Originally published in German
    in 1993 under the title Weltfremdheit." | Includes bibliographical
    references.
Identifiers: LCCN 2023037113 (print) | LCCN 2023037114 (ebook) | ISBN
    9781503633292 (cloth) | ISBN 9781503639003 (paperback) | ISBN
    9781503639010 (ebook)
Subjects: LCSH: Philosophical anthropology. | Metaphysics. | Ontology.
Classification: LCC BD450 .S5467 2024 (print) | LCC BD450 (ebook) | DDC
    128—dc23/eng/20240102
LC record available at https://lccn.loc.gov/2023037113
LC ebook record available at https://lccn.loc.gov/2023037114

Cover design and art: Daniel Benneworth-Gray

My friend, I too have relatives, for I am, as Homer has it, "*not born of an oak or a rock, but of human parents.*" —*The Apology of Socrates*, 34d

Contents

	Preliminary note	xi
1	Why is it happening to me? Guesswork concerning the animal that stumbles upon itself, that makes great plans, that often does not move from the spot, and that sometimes is fed up with everything	1
2	Where do the monks go? On world-flight from an anthropological perspective	38
3	What are drugs for? On the dialectic of world-flight and world-addiction	60
4	How was the "death drive" discovered? Toward a theory of the soul's end goals, with continual references to Socrates, Jesus, and Freud	85
5	Is the world negatable? On Indian spirit and Occidental gnosis	115
6	What does it mean to take oneself over? Experiment in affirmation	148
7	Where are we when we listen to music?	164
8	How do we stir the sleep of the world? Conjectures on awakening	183
	Notes	215

Preliminary note

> If it were possible that someone could be positioned outside of the world, then the world would be invisible to him, like a point without extension.
> —Nicolaus Cusanus, *De ludo globi*

With the title *Weltfremdheit* I headline a series of attempts to make an ancient gnostic motif fruitful for a modern theory of man. In this respect, the following considerations are free variations on the question that Thomas H. Macho and I addressed in the reader and workbook on gnosticism titled *World Revolution of the Soul*, published in 1991. Readers can see for themselves that there, as well as here, it is a matter not of theological or spiritualistic restorations but of attempts at a historical ontology of human facts. It would probably not be easy to decide whether what counts in the following pages are the approaches to a theory of discrete nothings—attempts at a non-Parmenidean discourse of being, or the anthropological statements concerning the moved man, kinetic variations on the Augustinian motif that our heart is restless. If asked where the author's motives are most betrayed, I would point to three passages in this book: in the first chapter, the sections that deal with self-foundlings and inspired people; in the fifth chapter, the section that comments on the gnostic, Brahmanic, and Buddhist answers to the question of how humans get into the world; and in the eighth chapter, the preliminary meditations on states of awakeness and the primitive communism of attention in its world-historical metamorphoses.

The delightful, perhaps a-bit-too-German-sounding word *Weltfremdheit* names an attitude, as primitive as it is inescapable, of ancient minorities and modern majorities toward a whole whose agreeability does not survive the test of history unscathed. How easy it was to love the world when one knew little about it. How simple it was to be a worldling in an epoch when the cosmos was little more than a bigger hut—at most the starry sky over the city. How quixotic [*weltfremd*] our cosmophilic and world-innocent ancestors now seem to us, the worldly and historically-experienced contemporaries of the late twentieth century. The high-cultural era appears to us in retrospect as the period in which a still-disputed divorce proceeding between man and world began—an epoch of alienations and scatterings. One might see the classical philosophers as attorneys who, in the trial between man and world, brokered the settlement in various forms—not least with the help of gods, those thirds who let themselves be construed as the common ground of the first two. Meanwhile, the metaphysical world-age seems to have run out, and into the philosophers' shoes have stepped the psychoanalysts, who think of the world as clinic and human beings as providential patients. Thus, the relations between the parties are placed on a new inharmonic basis—for who has ever heard that patients are supposed [13] to love their clinic? Residency, arranged as comfortably as possible and for as long as necessary—such is the order of the hour. In the horizon of these new conditions already looms the recognition that clinical residencies cannot be financed in the present style for much longer. The following investigations could be read as an expert opinion on the structural reform of the world-residence system.

In essence, the book *Weltfremdheit* does not belong to cultural criticism, still less to moral philosophy. Its science is certainly not sad, but its gaiety is restrained. What it treats is a phenomenology of a worldless or world-averted spirit. This unfolds, as it were, a great world-theater seen from far offstage. If one were to characterize these studies as being of *anthropological* interest, that would be correct with only one qualification. The heroes of the story are not men but the rhythms and forces of world-rise and world-set in which men appear.

OUT OF THE WORLD

1

Why is it happening to me? Guesswork concerning the animal that stumbles upon itself, that makes great plans, that often does not move from the spot, and that sometimes is fed up with everything

> Anthropology is that interpretation of man that already knows fundamentally what man is and hence can never ask who he may be. For with this question it would have to confess itself shaken and overcome. But how can this be expected of anthropology when the latter has expressly to achieve nothing less than the securing consequent upon the self-secureness of the *subiectum*?
> —Martin Heidegger, *The Age of the World Picture*[1]

1. Self-foundlings

On the northern edge of the Alps and the southern edge of the Scandinavian glacial zone, amid gently hilly or flat grasslands, lie great chunks of rock whose origin has always seemed mysterious. The folk tongue calls these randomly arrayed megaliths *Findlinge*, perhaps to express the fact that hardly anyone at the sight of such an object can help feeling that they are standing before a remarkable find. Whoever encounters a *Findling* faces an object whose nature or mode of occurrence implies conspicuousness. Conspicuous is what is not understandable in terms of its surroundings. Perhaps the name also echoes the feeling that they were abandoned by some faraway stepmotherly mountain, like mineral foundlings [*Findelkinder*], whose human equivalents used to be laid by unfaithful parents on the steps of churches or at hospital entrances.

Enlightenment doesn't stop at stones; needless to say, the geological research of our century has solved the mystery of the *Findlinge* and explained their origin to us in detail. We know that the rocks were transported during the last ice age from the mountains to the plains, where they remained erratically after the glaciers melted, witnesses of a history that reaches beyond any human memory.

Why talk of stones when the subject is mankind? There seems to be no path from the mode of being of stones to that of people. To be sure, the Egyptians, if the impression they left does not deceive, took pains to convert men to stones; people were also named after stones; in fact, the church is supposed to have been built on a human rock. Nevertheless, it remains that the stone "is," whereas of man and only of him can it be said that he "exists." Ovid's hint at the end of his poem of the world-ages, that the current human race descended from the stones sowed by the original parents Deucalion and Pyrrha after the fall of the iron race, can no longer expect any contemporary understanding. He who sows stones shall reap people—this is not a possible sentence of modern anthropology.

[16] The only reason to come from stones to humans stems from the foundling-effect, which undeniably also occurs in human subjects. It may not happen often, but it does happen that humans pause in the midst of the landscape of things and become aware of their egos. Suddenly they stumble upon the incomparable fact that they are "there"—a circumstance that is the opposite of a physical find but that nevertheless strikes self-consciousness like an abrupt occasion for finding. Unfortunately, the word *existence* has been so worn down by the palaver of the century that it no longer really serves to designate this abyssal conspicuousness of a person's own being-there. The concept of existence has long become a mere academic token—wherever it turns up, it has a nostalgic effect, like a postcard from the Paris of the 1950s. It hardly still points to the unexpectedness, illegitimacy, and uncanniness that can be characteristic of ecstatic self-finding. What remains of it is a philosophically pasteurized anxiety and alterity. What this word truly wagers was captured by—to name one example—Ernst Bloch, in a spoken

autobiographical remark that seems as valuable to me as his entire system. One day, as a child of perhaps ten years, out of the blue he felt his ego; it rushed into him like a thunderbolt that he was truly and irrevocably himself, and that he could no longer escape himself and his body alive. Such terrifying enlightenments occur only episodically. No discourse and no practice leads to this panicked self-experience of being-there. The unprepared ego bumps into itself as an unconditional finding. [17] The self-foundling [*Selbstfindling*] experiences itself in this moment as the uncanny being that positively is not a thing and that cannot be understood in the light of things. I am not one of the things—that means: I find no refuge in the inhuman anymore. I am—and now I know it—no stone, no plant, no animal, no machine, no spirit, no god. With this sixfold denial I circumscribe the uncanniest of all spaces. Whoever is human lives in a place that absolutely stands out to itself. From then on I am only the scene of a question. My life is a theater of trembling over the fact that I have to be different from everything that enjoys the comfort of being a thing among things, a being among beings. Why is it happening to me?

One of the characteristics of this experience of being in I-ness [*Seins im Ichsein*] is its suddenness. A rupture in the brain cinema that takes itself to be thinking, and there gapes the abrupt presence of the basic questionableness for which even the richest concepts: Being, reason, God are only conventional images. One could speak of this unexpected gaping as a trapdoor through which I fall—if only I could say whereto. One often marks the direction of falling by pointing to oneself, whereas it would be more correct to admit that the direction of the fall remains unclear—one falls into the inner non-thing, into the subjective galaxy. Who could say where it leads? If the human were a being that searches for itself by nature, then self-discovery would be less alienating. But the scandal of the human being is that it can find itself without having looked for itself. One can be twenty-three or thirty-one or older and discover, while crossing the street, [18] or when ones keys drop on the floor, that one exists. From this there is no secure shelter. Neither theory nor alcohol can guarantee a foolproof contraception of Dasein. *Safer thinking, safer drinking*—that doesn't help in every case. Even someone who regularly jogs in the woods, and from age thirty onward has regular doctors' checkups, cannot preclude that existence will break in during the night. Whoever this happens to joins those individuals who have been shattered by wonder—the self-foundlings "in an uncanny landscape in which it is impossible to orient oneself"—I transpose a famous formula of Wittgenstein from the context of the investigation of language into that of the interpretation of Dasein. Under the self-foundlings, too, the glaciers have melted away. Enigmatic to themselves, each one lies uneasily and randomly in the landscape—a breathing monument to a prehistory that escapes its own memory. I sit on the table and exist; I see a chestnut tree's root and I feel a choking in my throat: existence. How lucky that "I exist" is not a thought that must accompany all my ideas. When will it be over? Self-foundlings stand amid the landscape of fellow human beings like siblings of the megalithic heads on the Easter Islands, apparently permanently unwilling to reveal the secret of their origin to any investigation. Whatever we are dealing with here, they are no positive plastics—more like negatives of such, omissions in the circle of things, gaps in the continuity of beings, holes in being, groundlessly agape—for themselves and their kind as conspicuous as they are unintelligible. One has bumped into oneself and can make no use of it.

[19] All this seems to call for psychoanalysis. For modern rationality, it is unacceptable that precisely the central organ of enlightenment, the developed, project-oriented ego, should be inherently affected by an unreasonable uncanniness. Was the psychoanalytic concept of the ego not invented ultimately to ban the uncanny to the outer edges of the autonomous life and to contest all its claims to a place in the center? It is characteristic of the psychoanalytic conception of man that it cannot accept the groundlessness of the self-foundling's finding. For it, even the phenomenon or episode of sudden self-finding must be grounded in the subject matter—where matter itself here means the history of the subject's ego-formation, with its stages and crises. Psychoanalytic concepts of individuation refer to this history—here I am thinking more of Margaret S. Mahler than C. G. Jung, more of the vicissitudes of the second birth in the extrauterine "separation" of children from the mother than the archetypal dive trip of the Jungian analysand, who is supposed to traverse his shadow and integrate it. We discover the most significant indications of a real reason for the groundless self-finding of individuals midway through life in Otto Rank, the student of Freud who first developed the psychoanalytic interpretation of myth into a real archaeology of the subject. Thinking that he was nothing but a faithful student of the master, early on he unhinged the schematism of classical analysis. By the

year 1909, Rank had already begun to drive the prehistory of subjectivity far beyond [20] the specifically Freudian Oedipal drama. Rank's paleontology of the ego goes back to the border that separates the intrauterine life of the human being from the postnatal world-light and day-light. What Rank began to develop at that time signified no less than the birth of heroic subjectivity out of the spirit of concealed attempts at infanticide. This makes us prick up our ears, because insofar as heroes, from a historical perspective, represent the prototype of subjectivity, their stories belong to the prehistory of even the most prosaic life that today says "I."

Rank's short text on the *Myth of the Birth of the Hero* seems at first glance to be only one of the countless psychoanalytic interpretations of myth that float around in the no-man's-land between profundity and irresponsibility—and which, incidentally, have not bothered anyone for a long time. In truth, Rank begins the breakthrough of mythological analysis through the layer of secondary symptoms and their interpretation. He ventures for the first time into a real history of the still weakly structured self and lays open contents of the primary process.[2] These are not yet the dramas of gifted children that later became famous; Rank also doesn't speak directly about the invisible infant mortality that today in the First World is much higher than the visible infant mortality of the Third World. Rank's great discovery orbits the drama of the child brought to the brink of death who escapes an archaic attempt on its life as if through a miracle, and later sets off on a path to change from a survivor of abandonment into a living subject in full possession of the truth of its origin. [21] The heroic stories compiled by Rank are, without exception, about self-foundlings in the literal sense of the word. Their common template is the abandonment of newborn children in wild mountains or dangerous rivers. Most often the heroes were objects of murderous intentions on the part of the father and the mother—sometimes it is alien political forces that forced the mothers to abandon the child—the Moses and Oedipus legends come to mind. These stories also have in common the fateful figure of "fortune in misfortune" ["Glück im Unglück"]. Through a miraculous stroke of fate, a helpful being intervenes—a surrogate mother willing to sacrifice herself, a goat, a wolfess, a midwife, a water bearer, a pastor, a childless couple. These providential helpers rescue the foundlings from certain demise; they bring them into their caves, their houses, their palaces, to nourish them, give them clothes, and names, and raise them until adulthood. After this *holding*[3]—beyond the blood relation with its terrifying truth—begins the third act of the hero's life, which overtly drives the heroic individuation forward. Through some catalyst, the subject-to-be is led to the trace of its "true provenance" and of its faraway murderous "own blood." The hero picks up the scent that guides him back to the site of the original crime. He thus returns to the scene of his abandonment, his violent estrangement. But there, according to the mythical text, he discovers his real destiny. He becomes the exemplary proprietor of the titles that were initially withheld from him. He rises to become the successor of the father or the ruler in all functions, [22] in one famous case even to the point of the sexual possession of the mother, upon which Freud placed so much emphasis that he elevated Oedipus to the first rank among all heroes, even if sleeping with the mother is the exception, while the treacherous abandonment by the mother—or at least the near-fatal violent separation from her—is the rule.

Now it seems as if the hero's early endangerment is what first poeticizes his life and equips him with the compulsion to elevate himself. The foundling who retrieves his lawful rights becomes a charismatic ruler, the leader and pioneer of the collective, even the savior. One is tempted to see a causal relationship here: just because the hero was first the victim of abandonment, he has the motivational talent to later become an autonomous perpetrator [*Täter*]. Listeners to his story hear a prophecy of the later deed born of the earlier suffering. In that sense myths are not infrequently prophetic. As stories of heroic self-discovery, they predict that victims become perpetrators, and that those who in the end find themselves and set themselves into their rights are recruited from among the abandoned.

At the core of heroic subjectivation we thus discover, following Otto Rank's suggestions, the drama of a very early, all-permeating insult. What drives the hero, the charismatic, or the prophet to find himself, is the silently endured, still-active memory of an absolute objectification. Life revealed itself to him before all reflection as an unmitigated totality of pain. For the hero, [23] no specific part of his being hurts, except: all. There is no spot that is not in distress. The motor of heroic ego-formation is full self-elevation out of full sunkenness in the ocean of helplessness. The hero is the man who comes ashore from the sea of despair. In him, the adventure of civilization begins as the colonization of egoic solid ground—the inhabiting and throning of a new continent: autonomy, power, will, and knowledge. That is why heroes are the psychological pioneers of culture; they clear the jungles of impotence and confusion. In the wake of the early heroes, it becomes possible for humans to secure themselves by routinely learning what is humanly possible in their time. On this view, heroes are not just subjects of force with sonorous names; their ego is not simply an appendage of their energy. Rather, heroes, with all their force, are nothing other than heroes of being an ego, champions of self-elevation to ability and to the conquest of their own names. As such, mythical heroism is always protagonistic—its essence is the First Fight against a First Defeat. But this also remains, albeit tacitly, my, your, his, her, their, our fight. The fight is so universal because the experience of despair in imposed objectification encompasses much more than just the murderous abandonment of infants in hostile elements. Ever since humans became numerous, there have been many forms of casual attacks on children's lives, and just as many forms of self-recovery and self-discovery along non-heroic life paths. Countless individuals look back in diffuse ways [24] at deep and early abandonments without mounting a heroic counterattack.[4] A survival syndrome ubiquitous in trace elements forms the nervous substructure of higher civilizations. To it belong the needy and the addicted, the manipulable and the irritable, the biding and the refusing, the furious and the moody, the salvation-hungry and the dreamers. All of them, to varying degrees, show traces of archaic self-objectifications. Because of them, and because they grew numerous, resentment could become, as Nietzsche recognized so sharply, a superpower—for resentment is the sentiment of subjects who have fallen among the things. These individuals are given to themselves like a difficult dowry; for them, the gift of life remains swathed in a diffuse catastrophe. Resentment reflects the crankiness of an existence that is thrust ever again into the consequences of its initial violent abandonment. This also means that the ego of heroes and prophets is primordially related to that of migrainic and hypochondriac subjects. Are hypochondriacs not then athletes of ill temper, heroes of horror at oneself? What are the labors of Hercules but the official counterpart to the hypochondriac's twelve struggles against the treacheries of life? Must not death be vanquished again and again in both the heroic and the hypochondriac sequence of acts? While the positive monolithic hero unfolds his power in a counterstrike on the initially unfriendly world, neurasthenic subjects remain [25] in their out-of-tune life as if in an eternally undecided battle. The hypochondriac ego clings to itself like the desert anchorites to their cussed naturalness. In a sixth-century legend it is said of John Climacus, the Christian psychagogue who consumed himself in ascetic practice for forty years in his desert hut near Thola, that he shared his cell with a sea monster, "this heavy and wild body."[5] Contemporary subjects, whether heroes or hypochondriacs, share their four walls with an even wilder monster, the uninhibited and future-pregnant brain.

2. The determined, the called, the inspired self

An influential tradition explains the origin of human self-consciousness from shame. Ever since the biblical myth of original sin and the expulsion from paradise, becoming a subject has been associated with becoming aware of nakedness; from this emerges, "as if spontaneously [*von selbst*]," the urge to hide the genitals, that is, the monuments of painful differentiation. Through the disgrace of being naked and different, sexuality becomes conspicuous and conscious to the subject. In beings who have become conspicuous to themselves, shame is the impulse to withdraw into inconspicuousness, invisibility. The ashamed wants to get off the stage on which his or her banishment from the plenum of being was exposed. Accordingly, shame—along with guilt and separation—would be the oldest and most powerful instance of the self-reference through which individuals form an image of themselves. In this image, the deepest traits of being-there are marked as an existing lack. The ability to be ashamed remains the proof of human freedom for Kant. Thus, Kant thinks that depictions of the naked human body require the fig leaf[6] in order to spare the moral subject from remembering the tools that fabricated it, without being asked and with an uncivilized gasp.

In feeling guilty or ashamed, man turns on himself as the object of a comprehensive negation. Because every determination implies negation, we find the self-ashamed human in a primal scene of self-negation; this entails a first, and if not first, then at least early, self-determination. Determinations, understood thus, are not only logical operations but passions—imprints, tattoos, and primary programmings of the soul. From the first beginning of their determination process, subjects start to grasp themselves as objects of suffering and negation. Whoever doesn't wish to sink into the ground lacks one of the essential experiences of subjectivity. Only a theory of self-destruction and suicide could provide insight into the general human fate: [27] to be for oneself an object of partial or global negation. The suicide shames himself to death by his own hand, self-administering a determination by completely negating himself. In Japanese suicide culture, the *negatio* is expressly developed into an extreme performance of *determinatio*—hara-kiri or seppuku is the thrust of the knife from the center into the center, from the negator into the negated. Thereby the determined-determining subjectivity celebrates a precarious triumph; it appropriates shame as its own act and does not cede total self-negation to an external force. In extreme cases, it becomes evident that high-cultural subjectivations are impossible without the erection of a relation of violence in the interior of the subject. What holds true for shame and the age-old turnings against oneself is, however, even for turnings to the world and heroic voyages and missions. The violence within the subject emerges as the passion for destiny and self-determination on the open world stage. In this sense, becoming-human rhymes exactly with aggression and self-projection. Thus can ardent followers of destiny become a *force majeure* for themselves and others.

How can a historical anthropology be about heroic, prophetic, inspired individuals? Is there not an unbridgeable methodological gap between a vulgar theory and a noble object? Can an unsuffering, unheroic, and uninspired theory approach that high plateau of heroic passion and prophetic inspiration that undeniably belongs to human facticity? [28] Should there be a passion of anthropological observation that rivals the self-determining tension of those who have demanded the extreme of themselves? With these questions I want to suggest that a noble anthropology may become possible if the methodically vulgar study of man finds a way to surpass itself with regard to the noblest exemplars of the species. Anthropologists must enhance their ability to describe human beings to the point that they can speak of heroic and prophetic subjects from a perspective other than that of a valet or republican. A historical theory of humankind that would not underbid the human condition faces the task of a contra-heroic observation of heroism and a contra-prophetic description of prophetism—whereby the theorist of humankind, without being a hero or a prophet, qualifies as the third in the band of those who seek to understand and represent the extreme high end of the spectrum of human phenomena. Traditionally this third is called the philosopher. Without a philosophy that perceives the human in his height—or his hypertension—we are condemned to remain mere onlookers at humanity, which means being anthropologists in the disparaging sense Heidegger gave to that word. Therefore anthropology *must* become a philosophical one—or else it insists on remaining vulgar, that is, null with respect to noble and eminent objects.[7]

[29] At the core of a noble anthropology we find a language-theoretical discipline that for the vulgar intellect ipso facto cannot exist: a linguistics of inspiration. Starting from the theorem that the human is the animal that predicts itself, it studies the speech acts with which people announce coming people. This formula makes clear that the self-prediction of human being must be understood not as solipsistic, as in a soliloquy, but rather as *fait social*; humans experience what they can be out of a perpetual storm of announcements, appointments, and callings. Humans announce humans by speaking, even in the loftiest tones, of human possibilities. It is language as *melos*, as *mythos* and as *logos* in which people tune their kind to become human. Whoever follows the invitations spoken from the higher human possibilities becomes caught up in the human *Bildungsprozess*. In being imbued with such speeches, individuals experience the impulse not to remain a mere hearer of the word but to become its enacter [*Täter*]. All along, hominization was a process in which eminent speakers suggested models of human being to their fellows—exemplary tales of ancestors, heroes, saints, artists. I call this demiurgic power of speech the promise [*Versprechen*].[8] [30] The human must be promised the human before he can test out his own potentials. One who has never heard the histories of gods, heroes, saints, prophets, and artists will hardly want to or be able to become a god, a hero, a saint, a prophet, an artist. There must have been talk of "great men" in the third person before an individual can arrive at the idea of becoming such a subject himself.

The linguistics of inspiration deals with these transitions. It is plain to see that the critical point of manic subjectivations is the transition between he and I—or, in the case of female inspiration, between she and I. Apparently, the decisive processes of hominization are tied to a grammatical riddle. Charging the subject with the manic propulsion-system requires counting down from three to one; a third person must inspire the first. How is this possible? As a rule, the manic *countdown*[9] occurs only if I am the *you* of a poet, prophet, or founder who moves me, elects me, and favors me with his address. I assume only the inspired position as the hearer of a voice that elects me as myself, predicts me to myself, and promises me my own-most ability to be [*Seinkönnens*].¹⁰ From time immemorial, the outstanding humans were the great addressees—hearers who took seriously what was predicted and promised, in some cases more seriously [31] than their narrators and educators had intended it. Would Alexander the Great have become what he was had he never heard of the Homeric heroes? Would Karl XII of Sweden have been tempted to lead a hero's life in modern times without first reading Plutarch? Would Francis of Assisi have become legendary had he not been an enthusiastic imitator of a man he took to be greater than all men, indeed the greatest of all men: the god-man? Indeed, would this god-man have become possible had not 1,200 years earlier a certain Jesus utterly invested his I in the Rabbinic stories of a coming Messiah who would bring freedom to the Jewish people? Just as heroic subjectivation is conditioned by the story of a hero, which functions as an announcement, so too do prophetic and messianic subjectivations presuppose stories of prophets and saints, who were spoken about before individuals with their own *I* could fall into their role. In view of such effects, one must permit the question of whether the spiritual history of humanity is not carried forward by the fact that individuals always seek anew the risk of falling into the role of the announced, the promised, the declared-possible Great One?¹¹ The core of prophetism [32] is not the prediction of the future, or moral exhortation, but rather the announcement that one day, maybe soon, a prophet or a messiah will reappear—maybe you.

The risk of letting oneself be decisively inspired can be taken only where a current excitement leads to the deactivation of mental reserves; then, on the narrator's side the irony and on the listener's side the admiring skepticism fade away. Now speakers emerge who are no longer narrators or mythologues but baptists and appointers; through them, the offer of manic subjectivation is sharpened into direct address. *Tua res agitur*. This is no longer about art but about salvation, not about entertainment and contemplation but about decision and redemption. Severe speeches in crisis renew the promises attached to the inspired life with its sacrifices and blessings. While literature blooms only when it's not a matter of all or nothing, mania in its sacred or profane versions requires a climate in which subjects are prepared to go to the extreme. Seriousness divides not only spirits but also inspirations. We know: irony cheapens everything, and the aestheticization of life bets on the thesis that ultimately nothing can be entirely serious and grave. Mania, in contrast, is in its element only in the emergency; its beacons are the difficult, the severe, the single necessity. Thus, it is no wonder that heroes and prophets permanently hover in the self-imposed danger of being swallowed in the vortex of self-overload. Whoever seeks the emergency will perish in it. But what are the grand narratives about [33] if not the successful resistance of such dangers by eminent subjects? The purpose of telling about great men is to establish that certain individuals, under the most extreme pressure, were able to withstand the imminent demise of the ego in overwhelming clashes of self-determination. In a certain sense, all storied heroes are, like Odysseus, divine sufferers or patients. Without patience, no narration. The heroic histories narrate subjects whom no outer-worldly opposition could rob of their purposefulness; because the hero keeps his goal in mind to the end, the narrator, too, remembers the path and the deeds along it until the end. Thus, the hero and his poet together defend the honor of unconditional effort against the indolence that changes intention halfway or forgets it. Hagiography, in contrast, reports on individuals who turn their backs on the frivolous, sensual, ambivalent common world [*Mitwelt*] in order to orient themselves, amid an "age of consummate sinfulness" and in spite of all complacent worldliness, exclusively toward the godly. Together the saint and his hagiographer defend the honor of radical interiority against drifting about in external affairs. Finally, the stories of prophets remember individuals who did not let the alien, cynical, ambivalent discourses in their environment muddle their mission to say what was dictated to them as truth. The prophet and his scribe defend the honor of the non-arbitrary decisive language against the baseless chatter of the indecisive multitude.

As the crisis heats up consciousnesses, the stories produce a suction in their hearers that [34] places their ego in the position of the subject being talked about. In the drama of actualization, the storied subject is supposed to become the real present agent; as if from within, the subject springs onto the stage of being—the theater of the greatest acts and meanings. Where he was, I shall be. But the inverse of this sentence would also apply: where my previously trivial ego was, he shall splendidly enter the stage. The crisis is the wardrobe where the inspired costume change takes place.[12] I exchange ego for higher self—so goes the perennial ad for manic soul-searching; manic subjectivity emerges through possession from above. "I live not, but Christ lives in me," writes Paul exemplarily in Galatians 2:20. But those who change from Saul to Paul, from the uncalled to the called, from the indeterminate or falsely determined to the man with true determination—cannot simply be said to have been twisted or violated; their missions are experienced as elevated lives, however high the price of the passions may be. Therefore, to draw a fairer if also riskier picture, one would have to say: the called one leaps with his entire being through the burning hoop of the possibility of becoming a hero, saint, or prophet himself. Such a subject exists only as leap; indeed, one must recognize that his inspiration remains entirely the possession of the leap.

Oswald Spengler has reconstructed, with intense empathy, the critical moment [35] of Jesus' messianic individuation in the midst of apocalyptically agitated Palestine two thousand years ago. He reminds us that Jesus was thirty years old when "the awakening came upon him." At that moment Jesus went to John the Baptist and let him baptize him in the river Jordan "and became his disciple." His consciousness, according to Spengler, was at that time hardly different from the Mandaic apocalypticism that predicted the coming of Barnasha, the Son of Man; this of course wouldn't have been understood as the national messiah of the Jews but as the bringer of world-ending fire and paradise:

> That "he" would come now and end this so-unreal reality was his great certainty, and for it he stood as a herald, like his master John. Even the oldest of the gospels that were integrated into the New Testament are still permeated with that time in which he in his consciousness was nothing more than a prophet. But there comes a moment in his life when the notion, then the certainty comes over him: you yourself are it. It was a secret that he at first hardly admitted to himself, then admitted to his friends and companions, who now shared with him the sacred gospel in silence until they finally dared to reveal the truth in the fateful walk from Jerusalem before all the world.[13]

Here Spengler could have introduced two elements that are indispensable to understanding the critical moment. [36] First, the fact that after the decapitation of John the Baptist, Jesus no doubt came under an inner pressure to succeed him—inasmuch as the baptism in the river Jordan must have constituted an indissoluble bond between him and the baptist. Then, that disquieting scene of self-revelation in Caesarea Philippi, which exposes the secret that the messiah, not least through the disciples' confession of him, was in the fullest sense of the word "determined" to become what he was to become. I quote the sixteenth chapter of the Gospel of Matthew:

On his way through the far north Jesus came into the coasts of Caesarea Philippi. There he asked his disciples, saying, "Whom do people say that I am?" And they replied, "Some say that thou art John the Baptist; some, Elias; and others, Jeremiah, or one of the prophets, returned from the realm of the dead." He saith unto them, "But whom say ye that I am?" And Simon Peter answered and said "Thou art the Christ, the Son of the living God." And Jesus answered and said unto him, "Blessed art thou, Simon Barjona, for men have not revealed it unto thee, but my Father in heaven has put it in your heart. And I say also unto thee, who you are: Thou art Peter, and upon this rock I will build my church; and the gates of hell shall not prevail against it.["] ... But he ordered his disciples not to tell anyone that he was the Messiah.

The dialogue has lost none of its power almost two millennia later. Despite the obvious [37] Matthean tendency to counterfeit in favor of the Jerusalem Petrine line regarding the legitimacy of Jesus' succession, the structure of the drama clearly shows: awakened by a wink from the master, Peter, the enchanted enchanter, plays the fateful partner in the play of messianization; he holds up the burning hoop—"you are God's commission"—and Jesus leaps through to his destiny by accepting the identification and saying "I." This is the real primal scene of "Christendom." Here the word overtakes the flesh in order to lead it into the holy catastrophe. *Omnis determinatio ist negatio*. The rest is half written in the Passions of the canonical gospels, the other half in the missionary and criminal history of Christianity.

It has become customary to characterize the ideological movement of modernity as a detachment from the Christian determination of man via secular or humanistic self-determination programs. This is reflected in the fact that, since the eighteenth century, the discipline of anthropology has emerged as a new form of anthropodicy. In it, "the" human begins to take itself empirically and to research its nature on the basis of its "own" appearance. This also expresses a new ethos that wants nothing other than for the human to now take itself absolutely humanly. Being the image of God increasingly becomes an embarrassing idea from the theological nursery of the genus. From now on, the adult of modern times is content to emulate the best of its own species—even and especially if [38] these are not images of god but *only* humans. Anthropology is the science of the condescension of man to mere humanity—a self-confident condescension, of course, which fundamentally already knows how man ought to take man. Thus, from the outset anthropology itself is designed to become human, all too human. It accompanies and causes a development at the end of which Nietzsche will be able to say that we—the humans who are experienced with the human—are tired of humanity.

What Nietzsche had in mind in his vision of the dawning age of the last men is the seemingly unstoppable descent of man from the old manic heights to a universally self-satisfied, semi-depressed mediocrity. The last men are those who celebrate man's underbidding of man as his fulfillment. Who could deny that the media age has led to a triumph of dispirited vitality—oriented toward the model of athletico-musical borderline debility? The last man: the bystander with a microphone. Nevertheless, the process of civilization is not a linear decadence; the dynamics of life still encompass more than just the manic initial forces burning out to the final disenchantment. No doubt every wakeful European sees this descending line on which first God becomes man and then man becomes a smurf. But modern people can also have a manic rising sign that climbs when the zeitgeist is falling. For Nietzsche, the sentence "God is dead" signals the bet that people after *Ecce homo* can learn to manufacture their own inspirations. The word *Übermensch* is a cipher for the transition of mania into the age of its artificial reproducibility.[14]

[39] I would now like to briefly suggest that the most instructive form of the announcement of great men in the age of the human image goes back not to the doubtless significant drafts of Herder and Kant, but to Johann Gottlieb Fichte. He is the only of the great authors of the founding years of anthropology before and circa 1800 who fought the condescension to empirical man from the very beginning. Whereas Kant and Herder are for good reason taken to be the fathers of descriptive anthropology, Fichte is falsely regarded as the author of a modern prophetic—one could also say manic and agitating—anthropology. His little-read treatise *The Determination of Man*—one notes the double meaning of *determination*—contains an underappreciated draft of a theory of the inspired human.

Fichte first of all subjects the empirical ego, which believes itself to be dependent on nature and the external world, [40] to a hellish journey into complete self-loss by showing how each of my states is produced by the foreign rule of an infinite chain of natural and social determinants. Whatever I previously imagined myself to be disintegrates into a mere haunting. In every moment of my being-there, I now realize, what is really there is not me, but rather the nature in me—the not-I, the external, the dead, in my place. Along the path of seeking myself in nature, I dissolve into an abyss of illusion and alien determination; I am nothing, the energy is all; *energy* here is not a synonym of life but simply means death in motion as distinct from death at rest. And this death am I, so far as I stand in nature and put a being before myself and let it rule.

Now so-called epistemology intervenes. It resists the loss of self in external determinations; it sets itself the goal of shattering even the last semblance of objectivism and determinism so that I can no longer misunderstand myself as a determinate thing among determinate things. For if I present myself to myself as a determinate something without seeing through this determining operation as my own deed, then I have reified myself, forgotten myself, negated myself, and delivered myself to death. I have handed my life over to a sham life. Fichte never tired of making these fatal diagnoses to his readers: that through undetected self-objectifications they have already thought themselves dead. The penetrating call-structure of Fichte's lectures—like a gnostic barker he thinks thoroughly in the appellative—is based in the urge to blast open the slavish worldview of melancholic majorities and the dreamy worldview of elite aesthetes. [41] Both groups, the materialists as well as the idealists, drift in a more or less comfortable irreality. Against these irrealities the "determination of man" aims itself like an apocalyptic sermon on the will to realization; it rifles through the materialists' and idealists' respective unrealities and drives them to the edge of the decision to live; the single theme of this philosophy is the resurrection of man from the dead which he already is. Existing, then, means calling oneself out to a radically active life. This, however, is not an originary operation that strives back into some ancient saintly womb or lets itself be overwhelmed by a pre-given Being—rather, it is nothing other than the leap into the inspired upswing of pure will. The spring of this origin bubbles always now only— and what comes forth from it is a beam of absolutely benevolent aliveness.

The sentence "where he was, I shall be" seems to apply to Fichte as well. "He," however, is no longer merely the hero of mythical narration or messianic oration. All that I have hitherto thought about myself—and thus have thought about "he" or "she" as whom I present myself—succumbs to the demand that it cancel and consume itself in the vital, active, and absolute life that exhausts itself in goodness. The ego that I am to become is not the one

I have previously imagined as myself but rather the godly life in my stead. Fichte as philosopher of religion installed himself without further ado to the left of God, [42] the right being already occupied for obvious reasons. In his case, though, the left wanted by all means to know what the right was doing. Jesus is of interest to the self-aware philosopher not so much as a savior but as a naïve colleague who acted correctly on the fly but would have been unable to give a reflective account of why his actions were correct. Thus, for Fichte there is a thoroughly collegial Christology—with stark Johannistic tones, from which horrified contemporaries saw the atheist's cloven hoof sticking out. The naïve and the reflective acosmists are colleagues in the act of recalling fellow human beings from their self-reification to drive them into the abyss of the triumphant god within—no doubt a thankless task. Both of them feel the sarcastic inertia of the worldlings who would rather go a little further with the liberal devil than surrender unreservedly to a good god who takes everything.

Fichte, one might say, raised mania to the rank of a science and a technology; according to his own claim, he discovered the procedure by which every consistently thinking ego can drop into the inspiring ground of the world, that is, into an absolutely world-awake life, to then throw itself forth as a divine medium in deeds of spontaneous goodness. Along with directions to the blissful life, the Fichtean art of thinking contains instructions for the annihilation of the stubborn, sluggish ego in favor of a godlike, dynamic, strong-willed imagination of cosmogonic spontaneity—a thought that foreshadows Nietzsche's immortalistic voluntarism. [43] Fichte's "god through me" of course cannot help but always behave in an exceedingly noble and decent way, while the Dionysus summoned by Nietzsche stands out unpleasantly in his godlike lack of restraint. Incidentally, one can see in the contrast between Nietzsche and Fichte that even modernized, self-reflexive, and certified manias occur in the plural, and that the war in heaven continues, even if there are no longer gods in the old style. The clash of gods and titans has become the clash of manias and morals. Fichte already seems to suspect that amoral inspirations, too, will theoretically retrofit themselves, and so with great clairvoyance he hurls his declaration of war on the "fanaticism of perversion" into the future; one might call this a prelude to the task identified as the "critique of cynicism"—initially as a critique of the pride of false prophets and narcissistic self-made gods:[15]

> Just as... one who is inspired by God wishes... that God only radiate back to him how he is in himself, so too, conversely, one who is inspired by himself wishes that... from all sides... only the image of his own unworthiness radiate onto him. (*Die Anweisung zum seligen Leben, Werke* 5:547)

For Fichte, great logician of domesticated manias, the "world" is tasked only with being a radiating-back or affirmative mirroring of what [44] the subject radiates into it. He at least admitted, in a manner as deeply sensible as ambiguous, that the initial radiation cannot originate in the individual's proprium. Only shone-through can the ego shine by virtue of an older, deeper, more productive incandescence; a well-formed ego is at bottom nothing but the glittering in the eye of God.

Fichte's reflections open out into a technology of autogenous ascension; with its help, the subject should detach itself from the illusions of earthly gravity. After the desperate passage through self-loss in the external causality of nature and the equally desperate attempt to procure meaning and stability through reflection on absolutely certain but totally contentless knowledge, the subject is finally ripe for the leap into the moral self-calling that initiates self-creation. For this explosive endeavor Fichte uses the disappointingly conventional expression "belief." A "belief" is supposed to be what delivers the self from gravity and, even if it cannot yet move mountains, promotes it to a real Being for the first time. Ultimately, the reader, ignited by the author, is supposed to reach the summit of self-inspiration and to be able to say with the book-ego:

> I am thoroughly my own creation... I will be not Nature but my own work; and I have become it by having willed it." (*Werke*, 2:256)

> It disappears before my eyes and sinks into the world that I only just now marveled at. For all the fullness of life, for all the order and prosperity that I see in it, it is still only the curtain that conceals an infinitely more perfect one. [45] My belief moves behind this curtain... It sees nothing determinate, but it expects more than it will be able to grasp within time.

> So do I live and so am I, and so I am unalterably and consummately for all eternity; because this beyng [Seyn] is not recognized from the outside, it is my own true beyng and essence. (*Werke*, 2:319)

Looking back at the Fichte event, one can venture the claim that a brave new world of enlightened enthusiasms has begun. Be it mania, it also has method. Letting oneself drop into God or into an active ground of drives is from then on divulged as the secret of the enterprising life. Since the year 1800 modern humankind lives, without officially recognizing it, under the law of thoroughly reflective manias; with this, post-critical conditions are generated in principle. The neo-manic or neo-mediumistic ego-constitutions of the past two hundred years remain unintelligible as long as one doesn't know about the new disinhibitions of the ego toward god or power or determination.[16] Whoever wished to intervene in the world-game on a higher level had to partake in the now-half-aerated manic secrets of human history; accordingly, ambition, will, and success are only superficial expressions for the basic relationship, [46] that it is "a god" that lets himself go within me and likewise that it is "a god"—one could also say an "anonymous energetic ground" or, with Wagner, a delusion—that builds up powers of will and knowledge in me to the point of actualization. If one takes Fichte's and Nietzsche's fundamental insights together, it becomes clear how the world of actualized enthusiasms generates itself; the power of realization springs from the point of indistinction between vision and unscrupulousness. In manic élan, the clarity of knowledge and the darkness of risk merge in a coincidence of near-irresistible energy.

In no issue is modernity more blind than in the question concerning the driving forces of eminent men. In the epoch of greatest unleashings, there is also the greatest willful ignorance regarding the sources of subjective power. It seems as though the sheer magnitude of the game drives countless people into wanton distractions and into a freely willed stultification that lets itself pass for enlightenment. The neo-religious shuteye that lets itself be carried by dark causes works just the same in this regard.

To the philosopher who would like to consider himself an accomplice of mankind at the heights of human facticity, the following task presents itself: to be the third in the manic league—and at the same time the skeptical witness. Faced with a multifacetedly and contradictorily inspired humankind, the role falls to him to act as a comparativist of manic campaigns. This becomes all the clearer in a time that is characterized by a renaissance of monotheistic energies, which remains incomprehensible to many—to remain silent for the moment about the synthetic manias of the Californian and neo-oriental types. [47] Surrounded by prophets, fortune-tellers, and proclaimers of all kinds, philosophy becomes, *nolens volens*, an expert school for "comparative fanaticisms," to cite Amos Oz's quick-witted remark. In view of the manic wing of humanity, tasks of exorcism enter the house of philosophy—today more than ever. One must ever again drive out compulsive spirits to clear space for the free spirit. The differentiation of inspirations is the most serious task of intelligence. It knows, by virtue of its office, to speak neither of nihilistic despair nor of being overpowered by self-authorized energy gods. Without succumbing to mania itself, philosophy must harbor the dangerous knowledge that the history-perturbed world can be grasped only from the center of the manic cyclone. Inspirations have hitherto only overflown the world in various ways; the point, however, is to come to the world.

3. The encircled, the hardened, the depressed self

> Man is often enough fed up, there are whole epidemics of this state of being fed up . . . ; but even this nausea, this weariness, this fatigue, this disgust with himself—everything manifests itself so powerfully in him that it immediately becomes a new fetter. His "no" that he says to life brings a wealth of more tender "yeses" to light as though by magic.
>
> —F. Nietzsche, *On the Genealogy of Morality*, Third Essay, §3

It is distinctive of the human fact that experiences of manic subjectivity are esoterica open only to a numerically insignificant group of individuals, [48] while the popular everyday knowledge of the embarrassment of being an ego deals with gray states in which one's experiences are burdened with heavy loads. For most people, according to biblical wisdom, all that remains at the end of a long life is the acknowledgment that it was trouble and work. The ability to drop into the powers of upswing belongs to the experience of the fewest; to that of the majority, encirclement by conditions and relations that fill the horizon. In historical times, the vast majority of people have reason to believe that they belong to a species of animals condemned to overload. *Animal laborans*—that is the genus concept that the majority bears in their bones like a painful complicity [*Mitwisserschaft*]. Consequently, for the many, a story of human evolution from monkeys must make more personal sense than one of divine incarnation.

In Kafka's tale *A Report to an Academy*, an ape only recently converted to civilization explains to a petit bourgeois audience the history of his hominization. As a genetic novice, the monkey is able to recognize the peculiarity of the human condition more sharply than any habitual member of the human race. Looking back upon his animalistic life, his free "apedom," the humanized animal surmises what he gained and lost in the cage of the Hagenbeck fishing ship on the trip from the primeval African forests to the European cities. [49]

> I had always had so many ways out, and now there was none. I was trapped. My freedom of movement couldn't have been more restricted if they had nailed me down.... I had no way out, so I had to invent one: otherwise I was doomed.... and so I stopped being an ape...
>
> I'm afraid that you may not understand exactly what I mean by a way out, which I mean in the most ordinary and fullest sense of the phrase. I am deliberately avoiding the word freedom, because I don't mean this grand feeling of freedom on all sides. As an ape I may have known it, and I've met humans who yearn for exactly that.
>
> No, I didn't want freedom. All I wanted was some way out—right, left, wherever it might lead. I kept my demand small, so that if it turned out to be a delusion, the disappointment would be no greater. Anything to get on, to get out!... Looking back, I think I must have sensed that if I wanted to live, I needed to find some way out, and I must have understood that fleeing would not accomplish this. I no longer know whether such an escape was possible, but I believe it was—surely escape is always an option for an ape.
>
> ... A lofty purpose began to dawn on me. No one promised me they would open the bars if I acted like them.... I repeat: I never felt any desire to imitate people; I imitated them because I was looking for a way out; that was my only reason.
>
> ... Ah, one learns when one has to, when one is looking for a way out; you learn with no holds barred.... [50] Through an unprecedented exertion I managed to acquire the education of your average European, which might not mean a thing in itself, but at least it helped me out my cage, at least it provided me with this way out, this human way.[17]

Like a talking mirror, an envoy from the animal side, the ape presents to his audience the new, the true determination of man: man is the animal that couldn't get out. What we call man is in truth the aporetic, the hopeless creature. He is the being that must make itself into something other than it is in order to endure its lack of a way out. Incarnation itself is only to be understood as the exit that the exitless animal has cleared for itself in its forward flight. In this respect, humans are, from the ground up, creations of forward flight, children of metaphor, of metamorphosis. As long as they, in pursuit of a way out, make every effort to alter themselves, they perpetuate the species' history as exit work. Perhaps one would do well to read Kafka's insights as a late Jewish replica of the truths of Greek tragedy. Here as there, man's position is recognized as one that becomes serious through dilemma, aporia, imprisonment in exigencies and loyalties that are mutually exclusive and yet must share the same space. If being-there [*Dasein*] means being trapped, so too it means inhabiting the trap as *world*.

[51] In fact, the development of the genus follows a principle of progress in consciousness of non-escape. If we overlook the process of civilization from its modern results, we get the impression that man's encirclement by man is gradually coming to a systematic conclusion. From the beginning of high cultures, the generic process emerges more and more as a history of man's circumvention by man. The Marxian thesis that all history is of class struggles loses its false emphasis as soon as we consider that "class struggle" may be only a provisional title for a more basic process: for the encircling movements of complex hierarchical societies in which so-called ruling classes impose a state of siege upon the ruled. Today, the foreseeable conclusion of this process sheds light on past developments. Since humans became sedentary during the "neolithic Revolution," no further great event could compare to the one that increasingly consummates itself before our eyes. In Neolithic times began the self-encirclement of the human, who feels forced to stand firm on what is henceforth a sacred and cursed ground. To the degree that human life becomes "grounded," it comes under the terror of a new logic; possession by the concepts of genealogy, affinity, and property takes over; from here on, the intellectual history of mankind resembles, for long stretches, an inventory of possession systems; the inevitable consequence of [52] the early grounding self-encirclement was the chaining of men to the galley of provenance and origin, whose rudder is held by the principles of genealogical thought—in the first place, the principle that there must be principles, logical sovereigns and their dominion over the second things, the logical vassals, tied to causality and reprisal, ancestral series and karmic chain, inability to escape the past and the dead, the preponderance of kinship and territoriality over sympathy and freedom of movement. If one wanted to characterize the essence of traditional societies with a basic gesture, one would find it in the submission of all the living to the words of the dead: wills and testaments.

The process that got underway with the Neolithic revolution progressed with relentless fecundity toward the class societies of advanced civilizations, which until the dawn of modernity managed to persist under a kind of self-centering or encirclement within themselves on the various continents. From 1492 on, the European expansions opened the age of globalization. Half a millennium after the voyage of Columbus, we discern where the all-encompassing strategic, informatic, and demographic self-encirclement of humanity can lead on a planetary scale. For the first time, the rhetorical singular "humanness" corresponds to a tendentially real, albeit extremely uncanny state of affairs. What seems to prevail in the deep structure of the civilizing process amounts to nothing less than that humanity, at least in its highly modernized fraction, now completely leaves behind the world-age dominated by the genealogical principle.[18] [53] Under tremendous crises it feels its way forward into a synchronic mode of being in which contemporaneous strangers on Earth become more important to one another than their hitherto-identity-bestowing own ancestors. Whereto the existence of a horizontally networked humanity in a realized planetary synchrony will lead man—that is unforeseeable even by the greatest anthropological imagination.

The inability to evade, which emerged due to agrarian grounding pressures and proto-urban neighborhood constraints, is obviously closely related to the development of a new kind of inner time-consciousness. In its wake, tendencies toward a radical introversion of life could gain "ground": now the spaciousness of contemplation must provide compensation for the depressing constriction that the world-conditions—in city and countryside alike—impose on the lives of the many. When Oswald Spengler once remarked:

> One of the last secrets of humanity, and of freely-moving life in general, is that the birth of the ego and anxiety about the world are one and the same,[19]

he emphasized somewhat too one-sidedly the ego-forming discovery of the world's vastness. From a historical point of view, anxiety about the world is also a claustrophobic answer to the rising pressure of encirclement to which individuals were subjected in old class societies and early cities. [54] That is why it's plausible that the idea of salvation first appealed to city-dwellers while the agrarian countryside always stuck to the belief in rebirth. Ever since cities and states became the unsurmountable horizon of life for many, people have taken an interest in what religious historians know as metacosmic metaphysics or apocalyptic thought; closely related to this are the intertwined phenomena of soteriology and nihilism. Only under the "terror of history" do ideas of abolishing the world-condition start to attract radical minds at all. A new type of quixotic [*weltfremd*], world-fleeing, world-overflying people enter the scene. They think all at once about great negations and transformations of all things; an unknown passion for the nonexistent, the other, the beyond, and the unworldly take possession of these pioneers of history. Now, salvation, liberation, and enlightenment become the mottoes of revolutionary new supracosmic and anticosmic orientations. How else could the *ekpyrosis* awaited by the apocalyptics hold out the feverish prospect of the imminent abolition of the world qua totality of doom? The idealistic two-world doctrines of the Platonic type also lifted world pressure by suggesting to adepts that they withdraw from cosmic encirclement into metaphorical and inner heavens. From the ethos of messianic re-creation of all creation sprang the promises of a new heaven and a new earth. Even modern Marxist chiliasm wouldn't settle for less than [55] the great technical reconstruction of the star Earth into the home of a humanity finally liberated from world angst. All these ideas, by their age and their persistent recurrence, testify to a continuum of revolutionary tensions: for more than two thousand years, the encirclement of the human by the human produces violent breaks with the control systems of mythic thinking about origins. The leap into modernity takes place some two or three thousand years ago at the moment when a human raises its head to the proto-blasphemous thought that not all is good that comes from the old, the ancestral, from god and gods. There begins the long agony of the well grounded. Where the pressure of discomfort with the given world rose highest, the history-making, manic future tense established itself for the first time. Ever since, a historically powerful part of humanity is on its way—or should we say on its way out?—into the future as the space of all improvements. In this sense, futuristic utopianism would be the manic counterpart to the depressive forms of damaged life in time.

The exits inward and forward in time are not the only—indeed, not even the majoritarian—responses of highly cultured people to the encircling pressure of their worlds. Perhaps one should refer the formula *omne animal triste* not to the post-coital blues but to the inescapable condition of most intelligent beings in advanced civilization if they observe their situation without illusions. To understand how humans cope with the misfortune of being encircled, one must study the formation of resigned, hardened, and depleted modes of life. [56] When people cultivate styles of survival in chronic misery, they obey the imperative to align their self-image with the sight of a prospectless world. It then seems to be in their interest to reduce the risk of having a soul to a minimum. As a result, they sidestep their own intelligence, their own sensibility, and their shared wakefulness as if it were an inner safety hazard. That man endlessly underbids man[20] may be a modern formulation, but it describes an archaic, or at least ancient, fact.

If Shakespeare's wisdom is to be trusted, then man, by virtue of his cowardice, is the creature in whom misfortune reaches old age. The "respect" that causes this is the fear of death, which "makes us rather bear those ills we have / Than fly to others that we know not of." One should not go so far as to impute to the depressed in general a love of their misery; nonetheless, miserabilism is one of the anthropological constants on the shadow side of high cultures. Where it predominates, it must be assumed that countless people prefer a known misfortune to an unknown fortune at any given time. Man in revolt remains the exception; *Homo patiens*, the rule. Wherever one looks, men appear more as patients than as rebels, more as minions than as subjects, more as inmates than as outbreakers. It wouldn't be this way without [57] developmentally deep-rooted causes. Being housed in the factual world teaches people—especially in cultures with high domination and encirclement factors—from the earliest infancy to endure and accept more than is good for them; at the same time, it is good for them in the survivalist sense if they learn to endure more than would be acceptable in terms of a life of freedom. Structures of withstanding belong to the encircled existence as pressures of self-control belong to advanced civilization. Thus, along with the flight into future becoming, the flight into sufferance and endurance is another prototypical response to the increasing hostility of world-conditions. When individuals in struggling and desolate populations voluntarily commit to inuring themselves, they of course bring a trace of freedom into the game, as the will to hardness appears to be one step ahead of the destiny that forces one to harden. Willed and affirmed hardness intercepts the hardship that awaits the overburdened, and only in the case of unsuccessful self-hardening does depression overtly emerge. This usually happens when subjects secretly yearn for life in a milder climate. One becomes depressive who carries weights without knowing why. Then life becomes too heavy for itself, since it can no longer rely on its anonymous basic hardness [*Grundhärte*]. The depressive meets burdens not with cheerful positivism but with an array of ruinous effort. Thereby the strained doubly inflict the hardnesses of life on themselves, creating the basis for depressive debilitations. When these are in motion, the subject fundamentally [58] does not want what it must want but objects to the existential workload with a part of its being. It is therefore unable to develop the *amor fati* that arranges all vicissitudes of destiny on an inner line and allows no fully exterior coercion, no completely alien fate. Whereas in depression the subject consumes itself in the hopeless attempt to want the unwanted. Depressives are clinical stoics in whom failed revolutionaries hide.

Obviously, in the early phase of high-cultural subject formation, younger men in particular feel pressured to produce their indispensable basic hardness on their own. This compulsion is inevitable because high cultures must intensify the contradiction between childhood, which is under the sign of mothers, and adolescence, in which masculine dressage becomes law.[21] Sparta will forever be remembered as the monument of a masculine culture who systematically exaggerated their hardenings, despite, or rather because of, the fact that there were far more internal than external reasons for such a degree of hardness. One must imagine the "Dorian state" as a military leather scene; it functioned as a cross-generational gay community whose members restrained one another from collapsing under what they put one another through. The homoerotic primitive idealism guaranteed a climate in which a man could enjoy the cold altered state [59] of assimilation to the imperturbable image of the warrior; thanks to the bond between idealization and hardening, the men were able to experience and appropriate the desensitization as their own accomplishment. In certain athletic subcultures these mechanisms survive to this day—with the difference that today women too compete openly for the premiums of hardness. Michel Foucault's retrieval of the so-called techniques of self-care of Greek and Roman late antiquity wouldn't have been possible without an inner participation in the mechanisms described. Foucault discovered the psychohistorically important fact that from antique cultures onward, hardening started to become an individual matter. What since the Greeks has been called *askesis* is essentially the explication of work on basic hardness; it is grounded in the attempt to surpass involuntary burdens with voluntary efforts in order to hold open a space of play for volition and high feelings. This contains the psychological insight that life without reservoirs of power tends to descend to vegetation at the limit of exhaustion. The loss of basic hardness and of *amor fati* must be paid for with the risk of depression. From such a perspective, the hardness premiums of homosexual primitive idealism were nothing other than ancient men's mutual insurances against the dangers of so-called effeminacy and of erotic melting. As in the suicide tradition of Japan, the power of self-negation in Western antique *askesis/ascesis*—which presents itself as love of toil, *ponos*—is simultaneously mobilized as a capacity for self-determination. He who strains himself to the limit becomes not a victim but a perpetrator of toil [*Mühe*]. [60] Herein lies—alongside the indisputable Greek aestheticism—a psychological basis of antique gymnastics as well as modern sports. In the twentieth century there is an athletic modernism that could directly invoke Greek rules of the art of living: "more is less," "heavier is lighter." It is increasingly imperative to stage the inevitable struggle of making the real workload bearable.

Looking back on such considerations, it becomes clear how questionable the oft-heard thesis is, that high-level individualization is a specifically modern development. If one thinks individuation together with the active production of basic hardness, then a downward tendency prevails in the civilizing process as it approaches modernity. The ego-boundaries between modern individuals are in many respects more weakly developed than among members of traditional societies.[22] Individuation in modern times means, rather, to engage in the ambiguity of the self. We see it as progress if we succeed in overcoming the now-unwelcome primitive heritage of self-hardenings and self-definitions with an elastic form of selfhood. How much this deviates from ancient positions becomes particularly evident in the figure of the ancient hero Prometheus. In his capacity as rebel, fire thief, and engineer of men, he might well have become an emblem of modern subjectivity.[23] But as a hero [61] of the impossibility of evasion, chained to the boulder, nibbled by a vulture, bearing the unbearable, he has become fundamentally alien to individuals of the present. No way leads from his heroic suffering to the modern discontent with civilization. Even Sisyphus, in spite of Camus, belongs to a sunken world. What lies between the ancient heroes of suffering and modernity are stoicism and psychoanalysis—the two life philosophies of dampened resignation that have closed the deal with the inevitable hardness of the world, known in modern subjective terms as frustration. Stoicism brought the sufferings into the house and declared a permanent silent reluctance to be the base of social life. Stoically enlightened is the individual who accepts that he cannot escape and, better, doesn't want to escape from the conditions that cannot be altered but only endured. However, it remains an open question whether popular stoicism will have the last word on the hardships of life. Maybe today we are experiencing the last generations of adults whose self-image is characterized by stoic motifs. After all, even Sigmund Freud claimed a stoic constant for patients of the twentieth century when he wrote in 1915, regarding the first world war: "To bear life remains, after all, the first duty of the living."[24] [62]

4. The diving, the breathing, the pneumatic self

Insofar as, according to Plato and Aristotle, wonder is one of the primal motives of philosophy, a theory of humankind, as soon as it becomes philosophical, should take note of the threefold wonderment that corresponds to the major conditions of selfhood discussed here. From the manic life, exalted by successes, a wonder erupts: that *I* of all people should become the bearer of such election and illumination. "No one rises so high as he who knows not wither he is going," Oliver Cromwell is supposed to have said; when else was the bewilderment of the distinguished person at his eccentric position more clearly expressed? On the other hand, the oppressed and disenchanted existence will be filled with wonder in the form of the question whether this gray mass is really all there is. This is echoed in the popular sarcastic quip, *"Is there life before death?"* For mystical consciousness, however, it is characteristic to feel wonder, as it were from the edge of the world, that the world is there at all. "Not *how* the world is, is the mystical, but *that* it is."[25] [63]

A discussion of the facts of human life, however brief, cannot be finished as long as there has been no talk of so-called borderline experiences. Anthropology, whether noble or trivial, cannot avoid taking into account psychopathic varieties and mystical hybridizations of human subjectivity. Both borderline cases are indispensable to an overview of the field of humanness. There is no consciousness of reality that does not place itself in contrast to mania and transfiguration. To a certain extent, every member of the human genus already has normative ideas about the domain of humanness and what exceeds it. Even more so, an anthropological view of the human field cannot avert its eyes from what is happening at and beyond its borders. But a theory of "altered states" with philosophical ambitions will not be content to leave the field of borderline experiences to psychiatrists, ethnologists, and mystics.

The standard psychological anthropologies have one thing in common with the everyday understanding of the human condition, namely, that they must always start out from the finished individual in his baptized separation. Indeed, even the phase theories of developmental psychology usually begin with the individual in the state of physiological separation from the mother. To be theoretically significant, a human must at least have "made its appearance," become visible and noticeable as a born and individuated special and unique being. [64] But *de facto*, for psychology as well as everyday awareness, the human being "is there" only from the moment of the second birth, when the dissolution of the postnatal symbiosis with the mother makes it possible to speak of an effective individuation.

It is typical of the mystical awareness of self and world, however, to attest to states in which birth, umbilical severance [*Abnabelung*], particularity, and individuation are totally unknown. In this respect, mysticism generally seems to be possible only as a symbiosis—but not one that *in actu* aims for a being-in-the-Mother, but rather a being-in-something-entirely-open.[26] Back and forth between the standpoints of ego-isolation and symbiosis moves the specifically philosophical form of research. It remains independent of both poles as long as its movement back and forth succeeds in thematizing the difference between severance and non-severance. The autonomy of philosophy is thus the result of a double complicity: it does not shut its eyes to the real occurrence of mysticism, but it also cannot avoid taking note of the accomplished facts of separation, of becoming-ego, of individuation. Even a mysteriophile philosophy must for the time being unreservedly affirm the position of umbilical severance. Therefore, even a philosopher, were he to occasionally glance at his own navel, would observe firsthand the separation scar that commemorates the event [*Ereignis*]—unless an occupational farsightedness prevents him from doing so. [65] Thus, for him, as for all mortals, it is too late to bring the "standpoint" of non-separation into play. The history of separation turns out to be one that is always already underway. The mere attempt to think non-separation leads into absurdity from the start—for it takes for granted what is not granted: namely, that nothing had happened to cause individuation. At the same time, philosophers in particular must admit that until recently, the greatest or perhaps most important part of their profession consisted in thinking the totality or wholeness in which every ego or particular being is also supposed to be able to know itself as an unseparated and contained one. Where classical philosophy was most itself, that is, in its theories of total reality or the Absolute, it could not avoid taking the standpoint of containment and thus of a certain non-separation. Insofar as it tries to be a theory of totality, it also already thinks, rightly or wrongly, of the absolute container or the universe that both produces and embraces the world-beholding I. Wherever thinking doesn't diminish itself, it is chased and sometimes caught by the shadow of the thought of All-Oneness. Although the psychic and physical life of man presupposes that he leaves the womb behind him, existence is at the same time directed toward finding and maintaining a being-in, hence a womb-relationship, with someone around him, even while wide awake.[27] [66] The movement of coming-to-the-world in general is by nature the metaphorization or transposition of the self from the mother womb to the world-womb—where the latter has the uncanniness of being a "vessel" that, because of its vastness, does not so much hold individuals as let them fall. All holistic consolations notwithstanding, the world-womb can never be said to be completely closed [*zu*], completely round and dark and harboring. The absolute container—better to say: the surround that forms the sphere of all being-in—is no longer a mother's womb.[28] Because human beings are existents in the literal sense of the word, that is, those who stand out and are held out, coming-to-the-world means for them: being in a transition, a suspension, a passion. The severity of the passion is determined by the degree of womb-difference, which can be milder or more severe. Hereupon a climatology and an ambiance-theory and mood-theory would have to operate with ontological intent.[29]

[67] An anthropologist may be temporarily affected by contemplations of this kind but not definitively carried away by them. It is in the logic of his profession that sooner or later he will pose the question of how a human being must be organized so that as adult subjects humans can still come into mystical womb-relations with a totality. As indicated earlier, subjectivation is a process of increasingly determining individuals from respectively achieved states of determination. An individual would thus be a living diary or a "mystic writing pad" in which his or her history of experience is recorded

like a neuronal chronicle. The more that is already there, the more likely it is that new experiences will be possible only as captions for pre-existing entries. Individuals are therefore living memory foils of themselves. Each of them is both the archive and the archivist of his individuation-history. Therefore, each of them has the chance, at least hypothetically, to turn away from the acquisition of new information and to sink into inner archival work; colloquially, such work is known by the thoughtless expression "self-awareness." Whoever goes into his own "archive" takes advantage of the peculiarity of human memory, that not only information or "contents" are stored but also memories of the informing scenes or situations in which the "contents" were registered.

But to what extent are mystical states the matter of this inner archive? Do not countless mystics bear witness to a condition that is unique in its emptiness and freedom from all representations—[68] in any case, different from everything that one "remembers"? Just here lies the key to the mystical effect. Under certain conditions, human awareness remembers its own condition prior to the inscription of language-bound information. Thus, to express it no less paradoxically than it is in the nature of things: one of the peculiarities of memory is the ability to recall its state when it did not yet have to remember anything; if this paradoxical case actually occurs, then the memory of the state must conjure up the state itself;[30] with the descent into the oldest secret compartments of the inner archive, the archivist transforms into the document; his selfhood assimilates itself to the empty pages that stand at the beginning of the documentation of personality. To this extent, the mystical memory of nothingness is a natural, if also mostly inaccessible dowry of the human brain. The void is innate; representations are acquired. Thus, it is characteristic of lucid mystics that they recognize so-called enlightenment as the self-evident starting point of every conscious life. A genuine mystic will never understand how anyone could not be enlightened.[31] When the paradoxical memory of nothingness [69] takes hold in a brain, the latter's state goes back *before* the information reservoir in which the world is stored in language- and image-bound concepts along with the typical informing scenes. The "content" of memory is in this case a state that can be described as an awake, cognition-free sojourn in a clear medium or a nothing, with the addendum that this nothing is experienced from the "position" of being-in and so can equally be interpreted as fullness. However, because the state itself is prelinguistic, the question whether emptiness or fullness better characterizes its true nature is irrelevant. Where unity takes place *in actu*, problems of representation and hermeneutics are far away. Such appear only when we have to connect the language-free state to linguistic processes. One could call this transition *the* communication problem of mystics. They all know the insurmountable awkwardness of using signs, which serve to make distinctions, to evoke a state that is untouched by distinctions. The principle of phenomenological consciousness-research, that every consciousness is consciousness of something, runs aground in the mystical depolarization of subject and object—unless we also accept the state-memory of nothingness as "something."

What do anthropologists gain by exposing themselves to such considerations? [70] After demanding that the philosopher—the non-condescending anthropologist—prove himself an accomplice of the uplifted as well as the depressed life, we will now not fail to posit in him a certain degree of complicity with manifestations on the mystical wing of the human condition. Whoever claims to be interested in the human as a natural and historical being should not ignore that hints of such states of consciousness have been handed down for at least three thousand years. In Asia, winks from the mystical side have become culturally hegemonic; in Europe, they remained the affair of notable minorities. In particular, Neoplatonism has repeatedly attempted to reclaim the mystical idea as an inner issue of reason itself; some of the West's greatest thinkers have argued for the thought of All-Oneness as a legitimate imposition on thinking subjects.

Thus, if memory is the organ of history, we must admit that the memory of having-nothing-to-remember also counts to a well-understood historical consciousness of humankind. The pursuit of deliverance from the terror of history is indeed one of the best documented motifs of the historical life of the species. In this sense mysticism can be interpreted not only as the antithesis of prophetic consciousness but also as its most acute form: it proclaims the possibility of a convalescence from history and a transition into the happiness of no-longer-historical existence; it foretells of humans who have overcome the terror of time and escaped the [71] causal mechanisms of history-making misery. In fact, from a critical moment onward, the history of man is also a history of breaking up with found life-forms. For millennia, the thought has been virulent that individuals who have been born into awful conditions can be set free through a mystical second birth. The traditional alternatives to the trivial life in the world of work and unhappiness, for their part, make up a long list. This includes the desert and the cloister, trance and contemplation, drugs and ascesis, the hermitage and the pneumatic community, Taoist alchemy and hesychastic rapture, the mortification of the flesh and the unleashing of the senses, the garden of Epicurus and the gardens of Zen. Nowhere does the paradoxical historicity of the human being become more evident than in the venerable old age of these tendencies and disciplines. As countless modes of flight seek ways out of time, in the meantime they themselves form a mountain range of facts that crisscross the historical human world. Historicity is thus ambiguous from the ground up; it exists only as a composite of the histories of history-making and histories of cessation.

It is characteristic of mystics to reverse the basic tendency of psychic development from the liquid to the solid. Insofar as mystical teachings are at all suited to establish schools, they can best be interpreted as diving schools; in them, composed subjects learn to pass from the solid into the liquid. While heroes on their way to individuation have nothing else in mind than to get solid ground under their feet, [72] mystics are out to dissuade individuals of their fixed ideas about their so-called own paths. If heroic egos are entirely aimed at making a name for themselves through deeds and struggles, mystics are oriented to the task of finding the state of final surrender and inaction, which grants immersion in a divine anonymity. Thus, heroes and mystics embody complementary modes of movement; each represents a wing of human depth-mobility, insofar as humans cannot be otherwise than as surfacing or diving, coming into the world or going out of the world.

When an individual acts as a diver, it forfeits its distance from the world as a well-organized objectivity and risks immersion in a "fluid" medium. Accordingly, diving can be taken as a general name for all exercises of transition from the confronting to the medial way of being—whereby *confronting* refers to a behavior that emphasizes being-opposed, whereas *medial* refers to a behavior in which being-in takes the lead. If being-opposed creates a "horizon," being-in dissolves the subject in a sphere. A parable passed down from the Greek Orthodox poet-monk Symeon the New Theologian (949–1022), illustrates these connections perfectly:

If a human descends into the ocean up to his knees or to his hips, he can see the water all around him. If he dives into the water, he will no longer be able to recognize anything outwith; all he knows is that his whole body is underwater. That is what happens to those who immerse themselves into the vision of God.[32]

[73] For understandable reasons, many humans feel strong aversion, if not panic, at the mere idea of such a state. They intuitively associate the idea of "diving" with the threat of drowning and suffocating. Others feel a voluptuous suction emanating from these notions, to which they happily hand themselves over. In this light, one must say of a diving teacher that he hasn't mastered his trade until he knows how to steer past panic and vortical tendencies alike. Psychic diving requires the formation of an inner water-solubility in which all traces of the confrontational subjectivity disappear. Solubility means an ability—pure, equidistant from addiction and escape—to let oneself be immersed.[33]

It should come as no surprise that the game of transferring oneself to the total surround has not only mystical effects but erotic implications as well. In "Letter from Madame Emilie Teste," Paul Valéry offered a study of the metaphysics of enlightened marital masochism. The expression "enlightened" here means that we're dealing with relations not of sexual but of psychic penetration. In her letters, Madame Teste expresses herself only half mystically, thus psychologically informatively, about her strange relation to her monstrous intellectual spouse:

His mind contains my own, as a man's mind contains the child's or the dog's . . . Never do I feel my soul without bounds . . . But surrounded, and enclosed. My goodness! How difficult it is to explain . . . I do not mean at all *captive* . . . I am free, but classified . . . Well, to one person I am transparent, I am seen and foreseen, just as I am, without mystery, without shadows, without possible recourse to the unknown in me—to my own ignorance of myself! . . . I may say that at every moment my life seems to me a practical model of man's existence in the divine mind. I have personal experience of being in the sphere of another being, as all souls are in Being.[34]

Valéry makes clear that being beaten and being constantly seen through amount to the same thing; in both cases the subject answers submissively to a sadistic wish to penetrate. From this perspective, masochism appears as the deformed twin of mystical diving—deformed insofar as, in consenting to being completely engulfed by worldly conditions, it carries distortive traits of violence and addiction; masochism is the feverish cooperation in the overpowering of the self by the other. Remaining within the metaphor, masochists would be divers who let themselves be beaten by the water in order to be dissolved in it. A freely immersed consciousness wouldn't even know what it means to abuse itself. The proverb says that one who sleeps does not sin; even more rightly one could say that one who dives is not looking for experiences. With a pure ability to let oneself be surrounded, ultimately the question of the occasioning medium would become irrelevant. In the context of certain initiatory exercises, it may begin with actual water; indeed, the wide array of practices of baptism and diving in the most different cultures suggests the universality of "birth of the soul from water" motifs; elsewhere, solid enclosures in tombs, dark chambers, caves, and saunas may initially play a role in triggering mystical womb memories. But the suffocating materiality of the mediums must be abandoned as soon as the diving subject is able to experience presence in general as a flowing surround.

[76] Insofar as it is important to differentiate mystical diving from its masochistic and suicidal doppelgangers, it becomes necessary to formulate a psychopathology of spirituality. Within it, a theory of the perversions of philosophical reason and of the use of understanding in general would be developed simultaneously. Here it may suffice to emphasize that in non-psychopathic variants of mystical inner experience, the motif of diving is always balanced by a respiratory or pneumatic component. The essence of mystical immersion is not anticipatory self-annihilation but deeper animation.[35] More breathing, less opinions. We can hardly become fish and fetuses again—and the Taoist practices of so-called embryonic breathing remain sealed to Europeans for the time being. What will immediately make sense, however, is the rule that one must always combine diving with breathing. Breathing provides emergence in the midst of submergence; it guarantees defascination in the midst of the fascinating. The free breath ensures that mystical being-totally-in-an-element retains the meaning of being-totally-in-the-open. Where it is lacking, religioid masochism takes over with its hunger for submission to a wombly power. Diving into surroundedness leads to the experience of freedom when the surrounding [77] wraps itself around life as a ring of openness. The free breath is the guarantee that we are surrounded by non-confinement [*Nicht-Enge*]. A pneumatic anthropology recognizes the animal that is determined to dive into the air and what lies within it.

Although the mutual conditioning of diving-, breathing-, and thinking-habits is an old intuition of philosophical doctrines of the soul, it was hardly ever made into the object of systematic investigation.[36] The character building of humanity begins, according to everything we know today, not first in the phase of postnatal world-relations but already in the fetal space and with the dramas of the first breaths. The fact that traces from both of these primeval spaces of experience are imprinted into the intellectual or logical physiognomy of the subject has drawn little attention. Show me how you dive and breathe, and I'll tell you how you think. Breathing and diving are in a certain sense somatic preludes of the faculty of judgment, because, on a protological level, diving is coupled with affirmation and fusion, while breathing is coupled with negation and separation. Where early disturbances have engendered a diving-inhibition, there is a restriction of the affirmative function that reaches down to the somatic level; hard upon this follows a difficulty in saying yes; if on the other hand, a restriction of breathing predominates, negation is damaged—[78] manifesting as the difficulty to say no.[37] These two defects on the primary or protological level entail almost inevitably distortions and compensations on the secondary or logical and discursive level. The world-pictures corresponding to such basic distortions exhibit typical disproportions. Whoever has to compensate for diving deficiencies tends to produce thought-forms with a counterfeit originary-mythical quality and with a forced holistic pathos; if, in contrast, negation-debility is what is compensated for, then the subject often presents in the posture of cognitive force behind a shield of intimidating criticism. The affirmation-weak life will repress at all costs the feeling of groundlessness and deficient participation that was inscribed in it during earlier imprintings—even if it must pay the price of logical masochism; it is recognizable by its compulsion to hyperbolic submission under representations of a majestic, all-encompassing power of being. Where, instead, a primary negation-debility leads to a simulation of critical powers, everything revolves around the repression of the fear of being overwhelmed by intrusive and terrifying realities; the price for this is logical sadism, that is, excessive submission of being to analysis and negation.

Who could deny that these powerful tensions have discharged themselves for millennia in the dramas of the high-cultural use of reason? Every single individual life is run through by the fronts of the titanic battle [79] between yes and no, participation and separation, relation and schism. What

Heidegger in his gnostic-toned meditations called *die Irre* (error)—our ineluctable movement in the signpost-poor landscape of existence—stems not least from the insecure embodiment of affirmation and negation on the path of coming-to-the-world. Is man not the animal that cannot live with the truth but equally not without it? Ambivalence accompanies it already in its easiest and earliest gestures. Perhaps what man would need to make the best use of his in equal parts terrifying and promising intelligence would no longer be philosophy, at least not in the sense of the traditional *philosophia prima*, but rather a philosophical orientation amid the primary processes. Anyone who could have confidence in such a possibility would qualify to take *errant unerrant* as his motto.

2

Where do the monks go?
On world-flight from an
anthropological perspective

> The total movement is composed of an infinite number of repetitions; each moment convinces the next that we will never arrive. . . . Can it be that eternity and hell are the naive expressions of some inevitable journey?
>
> —Paul Valéry, *Monsieur Teste*

1. *Metoikesis*—Resettlement of soul

Sometimes nothing is more ironic than civil obedience—this is one of the lessons that can be drawn from the platonic report on the execution of Socrates. The sage has just rejected Crito's plea to postpone the drinking of the poison for a while; a last opulent supper, a last coitus—for he who has resolved to leave, these are things for which it is not worth deferring the accepted course of fate. Certainly, for sensuous people such things have a charm that can remain in full force up to the last moment; but for the philosopher, the sublimator, the master of dying, corporeal things have long ceased to solicit the eternal once-more. Why stock up where there is nothing left—Socrates' final teaching [81] decides against the absurdity of deferral. But since even proper behavior during one's own execution requires a piece of knowledge, the sage lets the deliverer of the cup of hemlock instruct him in the art of being a correct *moriturus*. In the report that Plato puts in the mouth of the young eyewitness Phaedo, it says:

When Socrates saw the man he said: Now, my friend, as you are familiar with these matters, what do I have to do?

Nothing at all, he said, except drink, and then walk around, until your limbs start to feel heavy. Then lay down. Then the poison will take its effect. And with that, he gave the cup to Socrates.

He took it and, think to yourself, my beloved Echecrates, happily, without shivering or changing colors or grimacing his face, but in his wonted manner, Socrates, looking at the man firmly, said to him: what do you mean, is it permitted to pour a dedication from this drink? Is it allowed or not?

We only mixed just so much as we believe will suffice.

I understand, he said. But to send a prayer to a god, that is indeed permitted.

And rightfully so, so that the resettlement from here to there may befall felicitously.

Therefore I now pray and so may it come to fulfillment.

After these words he took the cup to his lips and drank it up smoothly and peacefully. (*Phaedo*, 117 a–b)

[82] I have quoted this section of the Passion of Europe's archphilosopher in Hans-Georg Gadamer's translation not for stylistic reasons only. Gadamer has done more than replace the creaky pseudo-Greek of Schleiermacher's standard translation with a credible and elegant prose. He has listened more closely to the original wording and thinking of this crucial passage and thus finally translated the word *metoikesis* properly as "resettlement" instead of the pale and incorrect Schleiermachian "wandering from here to there." We now see: the expression *metoikesis* conceals Socrates' final theorem. The movement-metaphor "resettlement" allows a doctrine of the essence of mankind to appear for a brief moment—a proposition that, if formulated explicitly, might read: the human being is an animal destined to relocation. Perhaps a philosopher had to make his own passing-away the object of theory before this thesis could enter the scope of the thinkable and sayable. Once uttered, nothing could seem more self-evident: from the ground up, we are in fact *metoikoi*, migrants, transit-existences—*gueules de métèques*, strange faces. Transitions from one *okos* to another define the form of movement called "human life" from start to finish. Of course one must keep in mind that, for Socrates, the substrate that can relocate, which changes its place of residence in dying, is not the total psychophysical human but only the soul, which, after the subtraction of the body, can finally afford a large, or one would like to say proper, house. The word *metoikesis*, rehousing, resettlement,

translation into another form of being-with-oneself, [83] understood as a metaphor of death and title of the final metamorphosis, contains a reference to the depth-mobility of human existence, which entails more than a displacement on the same level and in the same element. Whoever moves with Socrates "from here to there" is not a tourist or a commuter but an element-changer, a migrant between different states of aggregation or dimensions of being. In this view Gadamer's correction is more than just a philological clarification. If one focuses on the corrected expression more closely, one must get the impression that here a dormant category awakens to explicit life. From this moment on, philosophy has one more fundamental concept.[1]

The discovery of *metoikesis*—of the great transition from one vital element into another—reaches far beyond the context of the Socratic death scene. For when Plato speaks here of a resettlement or change of house, he doesn't intend only a consoling euphemism for the irreversible extinction of a human life; rather, the chosen expression belongs to a discourse about the soul in which it is depicted as an immortal and at the same time wandering element- and sphere-traversing force. Because resettlement is a term of this great psychology, the expression points with a fundamental conceptual gravity to the deep kinetics of the soul, which must be thought as a spiritual vitality of irreducible transformational dynamism. The word *metoikesis* implies the approach to a [84] general theory of transformations in an anthropological perspective. The essence of the philosophically interpreted soul includes a three-phase process of entry into the physical world, passage through it, and exit from the same. Pre-existence, existence, and post-existence are the three great stages of the being of the soul that *metoikesis* has to mutually mediate.[2] Thus, while the original context of the expression *metoikesis* may give the impression that it is exclusively a metaphor of death, a second glance reveals that the word is not only a metaphor but also a concept, and also, it not only refers to the final transition but rather concerns the twists and turns of humankind's depth-mobility as a whole. So too the arrival in the world, the housing in what is [*Einhausung ins Seiende*], represents a case of *metoikesis*, and insofar as humans are to be understood as natal, incoming, and arriving beings, one must recognize them as translating and element-changing animals. Are humans not fishes who have taken to breathing through lungs and interpreting the cosmos? In the light of an adventistic anthropology, "resettlement" is the peculiarity that breaks humans out of the sequence of animal forms and condemns them to the ontological adventure, thus to being-there in the movement of coming-to-the-world. As beings of translation, humans become awake to the world; as beings of transition, they build for themselves the metaphorical and metaphysical languages in which totalizing views are expressed; [85] as element-changing animals they develop their characteristic tensions in an elsewhere, which they inevitably picture as an area that they seek and long for; as element-insecure subjects, humans develop themselves into metaphysical problem animals that sometimes go mad over their embeddedness in the world; as beings that can be mistaken about their element, they set in motion efforts to create a remedy against certainty, to be in the wrong place and not in one's own element; as problematic natures among the spawn of evolution, the history-making strenuous animals gain bewildering experience with the weight of the world and must seek out their way between the truths of levity and of gravity. If we were to reach a more exact insight into those searching movements, these considerations would arrive at their goal; they would give an idea of how an anthropological explanation of the possibility of world-flight should be formulated. That certain individuals began to offset themselves from their culture's world-model and to coin slogans of the great refusal of cosmic normality—this can be understood more easily if we interpret the history of the last three thousand years as the emergence of general human resettlement potentials [*menschheitlicher Umsiedlungspotentiale*]. From India to Ireland an ascetic belt stretches over the earth—scene of a forceful secession from the standards of cosmic normality. Beyond positive and negative anthropologies, the outlines of a science of polyvalent humankind appear in a doctrine that regards the natal mortals as element-changing beings. History would then be understood as [86] the drama that unfolds in the giant battle for the true location and true element of human life. The gigantic clears space for itself in the human interior from the moment in which the metaphysical distance-animal [*Entfernungstier*] evolves from the sedentary presence-animal [*Daseinstier*] of the millennia before the invention of state and writing. How to think this emergence? How to place ourselves in this natural history of the unnatural and supernatural? How the negation of the given by the instated becomes a world power. These are all questions that would have to render our self-consciousness historical, if one only knew what "historical" meant.

2. The principle of desert

So where do the monks go? It should have become clear that the titular question's reference to the monastic phenomenon is connected with this historical puzzle; if in the following I record some remarks about the anachoretic revolution of the fourth century as well as some other forms of retreat from the world, it is always in view of the emergence, typical for high cultures, of a pervasive *metoikesis*-problematic. My thesis is that the monastic breakouts from late-antique society represent a rational organization of the problems that necessarily result from an aggravation of metaphorical tensions under monotheistic conditions. Anchoritism and monasticism are practices of self-translation into the all-encompassing, all-surpassing "other element" [87] that begins to force itself on the souls of that time under the resolute singular "God." The two great secessions from the old world, hermitism and coenobitic monasticism first become possible and necessary in an epoch that saw fit to develop cultures for the separation of the elements in the human being itself—it is the epoch of the transition of pagan societies to imperial monotheism. The anachoretic revolution indicates at what cost the Christianization of the masses could alone succeed; the great masters of mortification in their caves and graves, on their columns and trees, demonstrated the efforts necessary to monotheistically reshape souls that emerged from tribal cultures and pagan communities. Only in the desert could the monarchy of God unfold into the new psychagogic law, and everything that would become powerful in the later history of European ideas of the unity of personality was prepared in the Egyptian and Syrian deserts in centuries-long struggles to concentrate on the one necessity.[3] Not only in name is monasticism an effort of the alone and the isolated to correspond with the One of the world's heavenly fundament.

The desert principle gains strength at the moment when Christianity has ceased to be a religion of resistance; only after the end of martyrdom does the psychagogic and psychopolitical potential of monotheistic human-forming techniques unfold in its full seriousness. The inequality between the One God and the lonely soul is subverted through lifelong asceticism, finally producing the saint [88] who stands before all eyes as an equation and parable of the impossible. Thus the desert becomes a metaphorical institution. The first Christian icons are not painted on tablets but carved from reluctant human flesh through transfiguring self-mortification. Therefore, these athletes of divine mimesis, warriors of the One, soul workers and icon-sculptures in their sleepless enclosures, belong to the exertion-history of the western subject—even if modern workers have trouble admitting to themselves their at least indirect descent from these emaciated anti-producers.

From the perspective of an anthropo-poetics that understands becoming-human from the process of an original building of metaphors, the anchorites and monks who begin to inhabit the deserts of Egypt, Syria, of Sinai and Palestine in the fourth century are the martyrs of a metaphoric principle. This harnesses the subject for the audacious translation: it demands from its actors that they transfer themselves out of the dark, worldly life-forms in which they hitherto dwelled, into the *entirely other*, the bright element that will be named God and that speaks to human ears only from burning bushes, if at all. The path into the desert was the most radical poetic act to which humans could possibly rise. As living metaphors for God, the early monks retreated into the inhuman Element to experience, with their own body, or rather *against* it, what being-in-the-fire means, what being-in-the-spirit means, what being-already-there means. [89] The Syrian prayer-master Isaac of Nineveh, a Nestorian monk of the seventh century, articulated in thought-provoking images the praxis of monastic passage and transition toward the Entirely Other:

> The soulfarer in his navigations tacks his eyes to the stars, sets the course of his skiff according to them, and hopes that they show him the way to the harbor. The monk sets his eyes upon the prayer: it alone guides his way to the harbor to which his course is destined. Incessantly the monk sets his gaze in prayer, so that it shows him the island on which he might land without danger, in order to take provisions on board before again setting sail, seeking for yet another island. This is the path of the hermit, as long as he is of this world. He leaves one island for the sake of another: the different spiritual experiences which he encounters are so many islands, until he finally guides his steps toward the city whose inhabitants are no longer traveling and where everyone is fulfilled by that which he has. Blissful are those whose journey through the great ocean passes by without disturbance.⁴

For Isaac the question of where do the monks go is answered in a twofold way; on the one hand, without a doubt, the hermits had in mind the city of heavenly standstill, the Jerusalem of the blessed, as their absolute goal; on the other hand, to reach the city of Last Things, "in this world" they are forced to go onto the sea, jumping from island to island, to traverse the ocean. [90] Whoever has doubted the world-building power of rhetoric finds in this passage reasons to decisively change his mind. In the speech of the monk the ocean has become a metaphor of the desert, just as the desert was earlier translated into the antechamber of heaven. The hermit in his dry cave as seafarer; the praying man in the cell as navigator to the furthest shore; the enclosed monk as island hopper on the way to a postmortal America—who could fail to grasp that the thought in these simultaneously stereotypical and desperate figures of the monks' jargon touches on the riddle that the element-changing being presents to itself? Nautical metaphors bring to light the passion that seeks a language for the paradoxical life-movement out into the desert. They want to halt the drift of care-creating and secularizing coming-to-the-world and to resettle to the entirely alien city that, from Augustine to Bloch, bears the irresistible name: home. For the metaphorical extremists, the desert becomes the psychonautic space in which one's desire to translate oneself completely into God is put to the test. The divine judgment of the desert is carried out in either felicitous or failed transfigurations.

Make no mistake; the desert saints are no poets; they are athletes of a metaphoric discipline that demands to make god-men out of world-men. This transition "from here to there" implies that the world, as the separating third party [*Dritte*] between God and human, is weakened unto nullification. No "resettlement" without the sublation of the triangulation *human-world-God* into the dyad of God and human. [91] The ontological meaning of anchoritism thus lies in its attack on the third as such. World as the epitome of "interest" in the Latin sense of the word functions as the epitome of that which obstructs the God-soul short-circuit, with which the death-appetitive tendencies of the psyche play their game. Being-in-the-world always-already has the sense of a temporary detour through the element that produces "adherence" and attachment by arousing cares. Inasmuch as coming-to-the-world can be interpreted kinetically as a long arc toward the positive casting of exteriorities, its basic gesture is one of a detour or deferral. Aside from [*vor allen*] monkish resistances, to live in the world thus means insertion into sorrows and passions that bind the self to inner-worldly tasks, to set oneself out into the desire that runs toward states of power and pleasure, to integrate oneself into the chain of life that makes us into intermediaries between ancestors and descendants. Through wishes and attachments the psyche is shielded from the deadly overhaste that has no more heart for the things of this world, to speak with Fichte. If this protection is suspended, then the soul will, so to speak, elope; it then wishes, at literally any price, to return from the triadic relationship with impure and ambivalent worldly objects and states to the pure charismatic unity of two [*Zweieinigkeit*], in which God and soul beam at each other. One's own body is the first to suffer the demand [92] for glory, holiness or emptiness. "The soul is that which rejects the body," said Simone Weil in our century; the sentence could stem from Evagrius Ponticus, from Macarius the Elder, from Pachomius or from Symeon the Stylite.[5]

With the anachoretic revolution that conceals the Oriental foreplay to the revolution-history of the West, the attack of dyadic extremism against all forms of triangulating world-constructions begins. In the west, the young Augustine supports these world-critical movements with his severe paring back of Christian epistemic interests to the pair God and soul, inwardly turned to each other:

[93] REASON
    So what do you want to know?
AUGUSTINE
    All that I pray for.
REASON
    Please sum it up shortly.
AUGUSTINE
    To know God and the soul: that is my wish.
REASON
    Nothing more?
AUGUSTINE
    No, nothing but that.[6]

One must always return to this famous dialogue, which Augustine wrote in the winter of 386/387, shortly before his baptism in Milan—even if only for its unexploited possibilities of cosmoclastic development. Expressed laconically and conclusively, the pious interest of the Christian philosopher is, from the ground up, to prevent the world from stepping in between God and the soul. This provides the ontological formula for the motif of world-flight. Because classical psychotheology—the matrix of endogenous extremisms—commits all its forces to a world-reducing ontology of inner space,

[94] it may not give credit to the tendency to construct an intrinsically valuable thirdness or worldliness. Bad enough that men, though created in the image of God, have undergone the fall that makes them sinners in this world. An autonomous interest in the world, from this perspective, would mean enabling the tendency of the Godforsaken, peculiar life to strengthen itself through experience and system building. World-flight is therefore only another name for radically dyadic introversion—something that lovers have always known about, aside from the philosophical or mystical traditions. For the great escapists of all times, it is obvious that one must love God more than the world and man—even if there were no God. The Augustinian *deum et animam* formula to the vastness of the front [*Front*] that carries out the psychotheological turn that culminates in the anachoretic excesses of the Near East. The anti-triadic trait in psychotheology implies the program of an ontological change of dimensions; the cutting of the number of dimensions from three to two refers to an anthropological change of elements. Through the omission of the world, so believe the old masters of deworlding, one can complete the passage from solid to liquid, from stubborn exteriority to the interiority of permanent dissolution in the other element.[7]

[95] Now one sees more clearly what the principle of desert means for the ecology of spirit. Whoever goes into the desert seeks out the worldly location that is uniquely suited to the minimization of the world. The desert is the option of acquiescing only to the world's unavoidable remainder; the least evil place in the evil world is that which is most hostile to life. The desert forms only a translucent film of being holding the souls back from immediate disappearance into the ultimate ground [*Grund*]; it is the real almost-not-being that demands no interest for itself but stands open like an empty cosmic therapy-room for the staging [*Inszenierungen*] of the soul. It is the pure projection-space in which the experience of self and God, including what foils and interrupts it, can be brought to emergence. The alliance with the desert as a sort of transitional thirdness that tends toward zero thus represents a pact with a growth-hostile principle. Inasmuch as growth represents the world-characteristic par excellence, the refusal of it also severs the root of the expansivity of worldly interests.[8] Thereby they dry out the birth-friendliness of worldly misfortune that the force of continuation of evil sinks together into itself, the influx of forces into the reproduction of old miseries comes to a halt. Where nothing grows, spurious Becoming is also

deprived of its foundation. [96] In its place, the desert offers itself as a stage for exclusive adventures into fusion [*Verschmelzungsabenteuer*]; these lead, if one believes the aretalogies or glorious speeches concerning the stars of the desert, through sufferings and euphorias to an ever-higher grade of purity, to an ever more empty and sublime form of drunken soberness. If it is the virtuosity of the saints to challenge the desert, then it is the virtuosity of the desert to be amply gruesome in order to induce or elicit or call forth a salutary desperation; wherever she gives her best, there the desert becomes the bad-enough mother.[9] By giving nothing more than barrenness, scantness, she gives the sovereign emptiness. The desert is hostile and strenuous enough to agitate individuals to a permanent commitment to the extension of the struggle for divinization; it is raw and inhumane enough to exterminate all tenderness for fleeting things. As a zone on the margins of the inhabitable world, it can house the paradoxical movements that want no other status than that of disappearance.

In this empty field,[10] which seems to await signs and miracles since long ago, the first outbreakers from the antique social cosmos inscribed their hyperbolic gestures. Like no other space the desert indeed invites one to act out psychotheological imagery. There, men who at some time in their childhood have absorbed the lectures [97] concerning the captivity of the resistant bodies by the will, move about through the driest areas of Palestine for decades with real fifty-pound iron chains around the hips. They lock themselves for many years into huge graves to prepare themselves for ascension through Christ—and if this is postponed, this is only because of the lethargy of the flesh, in which the nights pass in hard battles with sensual simulacra and the midday hours in the struggle against demons of heat. Famously the life of St. Anthony filled the image arsenals of European nightmare culture up to modernity with inexhaustible impulses. The emergence of gruesome images became possible because the deserted space framed the specter of associating and projecting souls like therapeutic brackets; above the delirious holy patients, the neutral attention of God floats as a saving ear. In this regard, the desert experiment had to lead to a spontaneous discovery of what the nineteenth century calls the unconscious; whoever was there knows more about the area out of which temptations [*Versuchungen*] and symptoms emerge.

If the human decides to go into the desert, he elevates his life into the state of metaphysical alertness—awakeness is everything. The metaphor of keeping oneself alert for the lord translates for these extremists of orthodoxy into an unprecedented battle against sleep, which is for the most part reduced to a few hours and in many cases only sitting, even hanging attached to ropes in vertical position. The saints spark themselves up like living eternal lights who illuminate the desert nights with their awakeness; thus, they correspond to the fixed stars, [98] whose light radiates from yonder into the black space of creation. John of Moschus, the poetic eulogist of anchoritism, saw in the people of solitary prayer out there a blooming "spiritual meadow," and when that meadow laughed, as accords with the rules of rhetoric, its laugh already bore witness to the glamour of the overworld. In contrast, in the literal desert, over centuries people wept more than ever before or after in the history of humanity. Without the gift of tears, hardly one of these athletes could have been capable of elevation into the higher grades of dyadic unity. Tears were at all times held in the highest regard as means and signs of purification by the world-escapists. Together with persistent prayer, that inner monologue of the dyadic monad, tears were incomparably well suited to liquidate the world-blockage and to flush away the separating layers between "God" and soul. If prayers and tears have become identical, nothing is left of the subject but a supplication to be allowed to abandon itself; the supplication makes to its god the unspeakable confession that it wants to be nothing but a part of him; even the anchorite's desperation belongs to God; in his final weakness the desperate one encounters non-being before the beloved. Then the anchorite wants to not be his own anymore, and above all to have no will of his own and no world of his own. For the sake of becoming unworldly [*Entweltlichung*], the monks forbid themselves laughter; many spent their whole lives naked, like animals in ecstasy; others abandoned the use of shoes, some even the use of first-person possessive pronouns. John of Cassian said about the undergarments of the Egyptian monks: "The cutoff sleeves [99] should remind them that they are cut off from all deeds and works of this world. The linen garments say to them that they are dead to all life on earth."[11]

How far the concern for the destruction of all worldliness reached among the holy solitaries reveals itself above all in the mythlike episodes of anachoretic literature, which, from the fourth century onward, submerges the whole Near East in a climate of desert fanaticism. In the life of the Syrian Symeon the Younger, from the seventh century, it is reported that, after receiving baptism as a two-year-old, the future saint fell into a trance, during which he recited for seven days: "I have a father and I have none; I have a mother and I have none"—a recitation that revealed an early appointee in the full bloom of holy asociality; whoever is able to reject having a father and mother on this earth at this tender age is sheltered from the very beginning against the dangers of getting stuck in naïve world-partiality. Thus, no wonder if this family-critical child prodigy goes into the mountains at age seven, sitting on top of a prayer pillar while losing his baby teeth. Here everything that could lead to the development of an individual worldliness is deactivated in the earliest stage of psychic development; world-flight goes directly into an early precaution against all tendencies toward positive world-inhabitation [*Welteinhausung*]. One could say that world-flight itself means the whole world to such individuals. [100] In these excesses looms an increasingly perverse ultimate triumph over thirdness. That modern people were not the first to find this highly strange is testified by the word of a Syrian ruler, who is supposed to have said to the record-breaking self-torturer Simeon: "Now all that remains for you is to pick up a sword and kill yourself." With child anchoritism, we seem to have reached the extreme outer limit of these primary masochism-dominated life-forms: this even a "defense of childhood"—by means of ascetic excess. That Simeon became the victim of his own talent for acting out religious metaphors literally is shown by his further history. The mass of humans who surged around the pillar of the precocious master of mortification became so pressing that Simeon the Younger at the age of twenty decided to flee even from his spectacular world-flight on the pillar. He hid from all humanity in the mountains for ten years; only then did he let himself erect a new twenty-meter high pillar, on which he endured as athlete of standing, of praying, and of sleeplessness for forty-five more years, until his death.

Without a doubt, Syrian Stylitism constitutes the punch line of the anachoretic revolution. The show-ascesis [*Schau-Askese*] on a pole that juts vertiginously into the sky is the clearest and most monstrous gesture that could be found for the figure of speech "becoming near to God." The inventor of this new ascesis, Simeon the Elder, was one of the furious literalists who took it to be impossible that, in talk of God and divine things, anything could be meant non-literally, and thus could be an object of an interiorizing and translating interpretation. [101] Out of his refusal of metaphorical understanding, the most radical of the anchorites enjoins a literal enactment of psychotheological thought-imagery. The poorest in spirit become the most inventive in ascesis. For them, there is no latitude for understanding in the "word of god," let alone a place for inauthenticity or irony. Therefore, the anachoretic revolution is also a literalist one. Precisely where it shows its extremest consequences, it makes clear that the resettlement of the soul is a metaphor whose seriousness can transcend all concepts. On it depends "the human place in the cosmos"—more precisely: the resettlement of the human, who in earlier epochs held himself to be the child of the world's center, to the world's most subliminal and gruesome periphery.

Simeon the Elder, to whom Hugo Ball raised a monument even in our own century, traversed the most complete trajectory of anachoretic eccentricity. The son of poor shepherds, soon after his entry into a monastic community, stood out for his extreme ascesis. His heedlessness of a rope rotting in his flesh provoked the horror of his brothers. After leaving the monastery, he immured himself in a narrow stone hut to fast like Christ and simulate the lowest tier of worldlessness, an intrauterine submission usually only promised for the afterlife. Later he chained his foot to a heap of stones on the summit of his mountain of trial. With increasing spiritual perfection, he sought elevated places on which he, [102] surrounded by the world, presented the triumph of his detachment. The biographies of the saint tell us about a series of pillars of increasing height on which he performed his elevation before the eyes of all of Syria. At the beginning, he is supposed to have stood vigil, prayed, and fasted on the platform of a pillar of no more than five meters, standing on one leg and sleeping for an incredibly short time while seated. It is said that he took food only once per week, prayed for days with hands raised high, and mastered the art of keeping his eyelids open day in and day out without a blink. He practiced these asceses at the same spot later on pillars of six, then eleven meters, until at last, at seventy years old, he died on a twenty-five-meter pillar in the year 459, constantly surrounded by a "human ocean" of admirers from all regions of the world who absorbed the presence of this record-breaking man and miracle healer into themselves like a proof of God. It speaks for the attractive power of this saint that in his eccentric conduct a universalizable fascination was at work. Whoever observed the enraptured man for a couple of days could convince himself that it is humanly possible to be in this world and, at the same time, already elsewhere. For Simeon and his contemporaries, something was evident that the moderns no longer admitted so easily: that this Elsewhere can signify only "God himself." On the basis of the fundamental position of modernity, [103] the elsewhere can be addressed only in a non-theological language—let us say it straight out: in an anthropology of acosmicity [*Akosmizität*]. However, as long as individuals have not lost the sense for the magnetism of this other state, they are, then as now, ready to pay the price for the proof of its possibility.

The desert tourism that developed from the fourth to the seventh century in Egypt and the Near East testifies that personal observation of the world-averted men was a life-changing experience for countless contemporaries. Looking at the anchorites provided, as it were, a plan view of the invisible secret of the dyadic mode of being; one saw with one's own eyes the enraptured men vigilantly standing in their caves, partially petrified like peaceful statues of themselves, partially feral like animals surrounded by an aura of holy despair; one observed the tanned half-skeletons as they endured their heavy raptures in the altered state [*Rausch*] of dehydration; one eagerly followed the continual adorations and prayers of the saints, who in the course of desert decades seemed to have exercised themselves up into the soliloquies of God. In them, the universal warriors and sucklings of God, the capacity of the soul found its overwhelming measure somewhere between transfiguration and terminal weakness. Without the God-intoxicated men in the desert, the religiously ambivalent masses on the cusp between the heathen and the Christian worlds could hardly have grasped what it means, as a human being, to strive for the correspondence between the spiritual and the absolute One. Although it may seem inappropriate that the anachoretic *face à face* with God could become a spectacle, [104] even the mere external appearance of the immersed offers to the pilgrims, the patients, the spiritual tourists, a "proof of the spirit and the power." The preconceptions of the observers meet with the ecstasies of the athletes at the worldless vanishing point which creates space for many kinds of absence from all that is the case.

As the scene of the great secession and as the laboratory of dyadic-monadic transformations, the desert was the cityless city, the worldless world; through the continuous influx of those unfit for worldly service, the seemingly most inhuman of all places became an utopian asylum; in it, the acosmopolitans of all nations united in the most subversive group. In the no-man's-land that promised nothing and everything, the First Acosmic International was constituted. Cloister communism developed itself in the desert into a consummated fact—and into a specter haunting the excluded secular society.[12] Thenceforth *desert* is just another word for the world-shadow in which people meet insofar as they neither interpret the world nor change it but rather wish to omit it.

3. The Western redirection—World-flight forward

One could contend that the complex that we think of as Western civilization is founded upon a refutation of the desert principle. [105] This judgment took place over a series of steps that can be read as a retraction of anachoretic extremism. Of these steps, three should be mentioned here: the repression of the solitaires in favor of monastic communities; the strengthening of the labor dimension in Western monastic rules; the Protestant storming of the monasteries [*Klostersturm*] and the proscription of the *vita contemplativa* by the modern bourgeois society of production. The antimonastic self-conception of modern society, even where it retains denominated or informal forms of religiosity, is so deeply rooted that in the twentieth century most people take the word *world-flight* to designate an illness—escapism.[13] *Contemptus mundi* is itself a term of contempt for modern subjects. Traces of monastic life persist only as systemically irrelevant leftovers from feudal times; they still exist, like castles, cathedrals, scriptures with expensive golden initials—relics of an outdated psychohistorical formation, objects of heritage preservation and learned piety. One reads contemplative texts the same way one listens to old music played on old instruments. In order to "work" on oneself and on things, no one after the French Revolution needs to believe in the necessity of cloisters. European monasticism ends on cheese boxes. The twentieth century is so distant from the cells that it doesn't even remember what the modern world once had to establish itself against. Secular society refuses Western monasticism, which in turn had refused the Orient and the desert. Under these conditions, the question of where the monks are going [106] seems to lose its meaning. The modern West has no monks, and latter-day monks have no desert.[14] Secular civilization has established itself so securely as the universe of need fulfillment that it's as though the irruption of renunciants into civilization never occurred. The self-oriented world is so suffused with the certainty that it is all that is the case, that *fuga mundi* and efforts to reverse the fall can appear within it only as bizarre ideas.

Therefore, whoever wants to ask about the restructuring of monastic acosmism in the bourgeois world must take a different approach. In fact, one of the ontological accomplishments of modernity is that it defends the sovereign worldliness of the world against hasty Orientalisms and against the world-swallowing abysses [*Abgründigkeit*] of radical dyadic psychotheology. It could achieve this only by absolutizing the Third. Modernity is the world-age in which the world is everything that is allowed to be the case. That is why modernity is essentially the time of media, the time of communications, the time of self-mediation. Only late and retrospectively do we grasp the price of the operation of absolutizing the world, since only through progressive modernization can it become clear what it means to live in a world that has absorbed its former transcendences into and over itself. The world must now become the all-mighty medium,[15] which in its own self-production [107] must bring forth divine effects and spiritual effects or their equivalent. Paul Tillich has conceptualized this in his text *The Religious Situation* from 1926, when he characterized the autonomous worldliness of modernity as "the spirit of inwardly-resting finitude." World is the epitome of what can be understood from itself; part of the essence of the modernly conceived world is that its finitude seems to be rich enough to ease the parting from the hard "transcendence" of the old metaphysical type. The mistake of Tillich's formula, the pseudo-metaphysical term "resting," has been corrected by Falk Wagner in his study *Geld oder Gott* [*Money or God*] 1980, in which he, drawing from Luhmann's systematic media theory, grounded the worldliness of the world upon the dynamics of absolutized communication; this, however, has nothing restful about it, but is, as indicated elsewhere, a permanent mobilization. In the epoch of absolutized communications, the unity and autonomy of the world depends on the universality and uninterruptedness of mediating streams. In the face of such a world it would be difficult for even a god to provoke attention, since, to reveal himself, [108] he would have to connect himself to the net and become *message*—a task that could hardly be accomplished in the old style of incarnation. The world-language of modernity is a medial materialism that includes dematerialization; thanks to the godlike superconductivity of money, it accomplishes the connection of everything that is formatted as information and commodity to everything else. If the worldliness of the mediatized world has a weak spot, it can be found where the velocity of communication processes produces unwanted side effects; especially the strongest communicators are exposed to the fiercest feelings of derealization; but it is unbecoming for a world that is supposed to be all that is the case to appear to be a media phantom [*Medienspuk*] or a construct in hyperspace; in this decade, the new postmoderns counter this nausea of acceleration with world-piously intended deceleration therapies, which want to counter the inhuman speed of money and media operations with human-scaled tempos. Everywhere slowness makes a career as the functional equivalent of transcendence; it has the advantage of avoiding the humiliation of assaulting an intelligent public with massive speeches on god and the soul. At the same time, the new *Go Slow* movement involves a substitution for the lost ascesis—it underlines the practiced worldlessness of the exhausted. As a world-suited *remake*[16] of god and soul, [109] slowness is almost as good as the originals—and who knows if those are not already counterfeits?

Insofar as being human in modernization primarily means self-mediation and self-connection, the good old metaphysical God and Soul can only be theorized catastrophically: as disconnectings, as interruptions of mediation, as shock, as pause. The edge runner-theologian Tillich explicated this unequivocally with his expressionistic God-metaphors; according to him, God is still possible in the self-centric cosmos only as an invader; only as a breaker and concussor can he prove himself the Other of all that communicates and connects. In this, Tillich stands in line with his rival Heidegger, who hid his final Catholica in a theology of trembling.

Analogously, certain psychologists of the twentieth century have placed the ontological location of the soul in the interruption—in neurotic symptoms, convulsions, syncopes. In the age of connectability the chances of the "soul" lie in nervous catastrophes; since Nietzsche, they prefer the Dionysian dialect, if they do not pursue strategies of silence. "Soul" is that which does not mediate itself. Psychosis becomes the emergency case of soul in the age of its dissolution in world effects. Souls now only exist insofar as they are forced to announce themselves by the danger of their downfall. *Save our Souls*—the final word of old European psychology? [110] Catherine Clement, the disciple of Lacan, in her book *La syncope: La philosophie du ravissement*, 1990, has provided a summary of the modern psychology of shattering and interruption. So far hardly acknowledged, this book has a plausible chance of emerging as one of the most insightful documents of philosophical psychology under the conditions of radical modernity.

In the future, the question of where the monks are going can only be posed indirectly. In order not to be meaningless from the outset, it must be reformulated as the question of what becomes of impeded monks; what do "monks" do in a time without cloisters? Where do monastic and world-fleeing impulses find orientation in an era whose self-understanding neither acknowledges a principle desert nor is able to give civil rights to potential ascensionists? To sufficiently answer this, nothing less than a cultural history of modernity would be necessary. Lacking this for the moment, two summarizing theses must suffice, the first with a cultural-diagnostic emphasis, the second with an anthropological emphasis.

The first thesis figures a law of conservation of world-fleeing energies: impulses to flee the world cannot go missing from the world at any time. What is at stake historically is at most the *direction* of the flight. If in a given epoch desert and monastery are blocked off as major highways of the *fuga mundi,* the world-fleeing potential blazes new trails for itself. Hence modernity was possible as a rerouting of world-flight into the world itself *qua* promised, coming, better. Insofar as all modernity has an inherent world-optimizing trait, [111] its structure can be interpreted as that of a generalized flight from the world to the future; this can have either a moderate and melioristic or profusely utopian manifestation. In both cases, world-born concrete negativity is reintroduced into the production of positive world-futures; educated dissatisfaction, says the dialectical materialist Bloch, is the motor of history. If meliorism and utopianism are no longer plausible options in the face of highly reasonable expectations of catastrophe, then the typical European alloy of world-flight and bright progressive dynamics dissolves; it falls into resignation and panic, into realism and apocalypticism, into conservatism and pre-suicidal euphoria.

The second thesis, in contrast, dares to universalize the monastic factor into an anthropological constant. The Hispano-Indian philosopher of religion Raimon Panikkar talks about the "universal archetype" of the monk, which expresses itself from endogenous sources in people of all world regions in a dialectically differentiated but dimensionally identical way. With this monk-archetype hypothesis, Panikkar offers an interpretation for the double predicament of "spirituality" in the twentieth century: on the one hand, he makes understandable why the marginalization of monastic forms of life needn't be synonymous with the expiration of monastic "potential"; at the same time, with his theory of the *anima naturaliter monastica*, he attempts to explain why modern "spirituality" generally considers itself well-advised when it changes course from world-flight to world-celebration. [112] Herein Panikkar meets with a groundswell of new cosmo-theologies in the twentieth century: with Albert Schweitzer's doctrine of the reverence for life, insofar as it proposes to experimentally combine an ethic of neighborly love and a mysticism of world-affirmation; with the cosmophilic system of Teilhard de Chardin, who interprets the trend of the universal process as Christo-morphic evolution; with the neo-Sannyasin concept of the Indian reform-mystic Shree Rajneesh, who repolarized the old Indian idea of the Sannyasins (renunciants or forest saints) into a Dionysian-toned rejection of religious and political miserabilism; with the programs of theologian Hermann Timm, who wants to subject Protestantism as a whole to a recosmization cure; with the nature-religious reformism of the Catholic-semipagan lay theologian Carl Amery, who considers a prophetic deep reformation of nature-ravaging modernity to be the greatest challenge of religion-founding energies of human history up to now. These revisions and redefinitions of basic spiritual concepts all speak to the tendency to reroute world-fleeing energies in a neo-cosmopolitan direction. Of course, Panikkar's theses could only have emerged in an age in which a comparative study of world-flights became possible and necessary. The theses of the "inner monk" and of a monastic dimension of humanity as such are thus particularly suitable [113] as a platform for intermonastic and interreligious communications. I do not know how decidedly non-monastic and non-religious people can be persuaded to join them. The mere fact that persuasion is involved proves that the typicality of this archetype or the universality of this anthropological universal cannot be sufficiently trusted.

Now it becomes apparent that the first reformulation of the question of where the monks can go in modern times was inadequate. Panikkar's generous projection of the "monk" into the archetypical dimension indeed takes into account the modern tendency to think of the world in no other way than affirmatively; however this Catholic-Hindu *entente cordiale* is only possible insofar as it keeps a distance from authentic modernity—that of

Protestant, humanistic and atheistic complexes of money-pantheism, success-saintliness, absolutized communications, experimental existentialism and medial (im)materialism. In view of atheological high modernity, the offer "to find the monk in oneself" does not sound convincing; it lies out of earshot of those who have substantially engaged with the antiplatonic and antimonastic experiment of modernity. If one wishes to render Panikkar's impulse fruitful for the Protestant and atheistic factions of humankind, one would have to once again sublate the monkish archetype itself into a religiously neutral philosophical psychology or acosmology. Thus, it seems more plausible to me to understand the monastic phenomenon as an entirely regional and period metaphor for the greater, still-unconceived problematic of acosmism. [114] But then the question of where the monks are going would have to be reformulated so radically that it would no longer be about monks at all. The question would instead be: how does human acosmicity manifest itself under modern conditions? How do the forces oriented toward resettlement organize themselves in post-metaphysical times? How do modern subjects conduct themselves with their element-changing tendencies, if anachoretic, monastic or psychotheological "paths" no longer stand open? What, in general, will become of the escapist, path-forging impulses of the polyvalent animal?

It bears repeating that an adequate response to these questions would amount to a cultural history of modernity. For the moment, it should suffice to indicate that the unexampled development of western music can only be understood on the basis of the necessity of producing a convincing culture-wide substitute for the lost desert and for the barred monastic refuge. European art music between the seventeenth and early twentieth centuries touches, with its combination of ascesis and metaphysical tension, on the secrets of dyadic extremism formerly accessible only to hermits and mystics—it too had its athletes and its lonely protagonists, it too was oriented toward an external public, which already consisted more of spectators than of listeners. In the last hundred years, music has established itself as a universal transitional thirdness with which the world-age seeks to address its need for world-flight without recourse to the desert. The artificial sonic attack on the exterior world-noises has in this century reached an intensity unprecedented in the entire history of the species. But unlike the desert, which helped free the interior, the mass-medial musicalization of all spaces [115] floods the last breaches of free interiority: the oblivion of being out of every loudspeaker; low-level worldlessness in every household at every time of day. Ever since headphones have existed, the principle of world-shutoff in the modern use of music has taken effect purely at the level of apparatuses. Here a drug-theoretical account of all forms of "light" ambience in modernity suggests itself. There is hardly any phenomenon of contemporary culture in which no traces of quasi-musical world-distancing techniques can be found. The new wave of *cocooning*, the mass-emigration of modern subjects into the unreachable interior of solitudes, trips and symbioses, would be quite impossible without immersion in the tonal menu of sound-systems. World-distance is the lowest common denominator of a poly-escapist society.

The age of metaphysical homelessness (to recall Lukács' formula for modernity) generalizes the habitus of flight. With its progressive constitution the world flees from itself in itself; from each point of the fleeing world, further flights are prepared. The accelerated world of money and of absolutized communication parodies the metaphysical relation to impermanence; it possesses neither an idea of the pleroma of metaphysics nor a conception of positive emptiness. The acosmic needs of people in a monkless time must seek other outlets—routes that, for all their differentiation, have in common that they run perpendicular to the abundance principle of the secular bourgeoisie. The word bourgeoisie here stands for the type of human that seeks wealth not in the expansion of inner space, but in stuffing oneself with content that ensures seamless self-filling.

[116] Flightiness, expanded to an element, makes a compromise between the fluid and the dead. In it move people who recognize themselves neither in the monk nor in the worldling. In a conversation with Boris Groys, the Russian avant-garde artist Ilya Kabakow issued the following statement:

> The willingness to feel out of place is highly developed in me. It was always an especially comforting experience for me to not be anywhere. Whenever I go on a journey, even the foretaste of driving away already makes me happy. This obviously is an infantile trauma expressing the lack of the wish to come to the world. The world in which I was born and the form into which I was born leave me deeply unsatisfied. I don't like my appearance and I don't identify myself with it. I still remember when I saw my profile for the first time in the mirror; I literally moaned in pain: I couldn't believe that that's me. This is the desire to run away from my body, from my things, from my home...

I don't have a home, I always feel that I am in a state of transit. Of such people one often says: they are well nowhere.[17]

Instead of a commentary, I confront this statement with a temporally distant echo that responds to the artist from a nearness, and with a temporally near counterpart that distances itself from it milky-way-wide. In the Manichaean cosmogony that Theodore bar Koni quoted in the seventh century, it is said:

The shining Jesus approached the naïve Adam and awoke him from deathly sleep thereby to redeem him from the many spectres... so it was also with Adam, for the friend found him as he was sunken in deep sleep. He woke him, gave him movement, made him lively and drove the false spirit out of him... Thereafter Adam examined himself and recognized who he was. And he showed to him the fathers of the heights and how his soul was thrown into everything, devoured by those who devour, swallowed by those who swallow...

He erected him and let him eat from the tree of life. Thereafter Adam came to see and wept and cried with a loud voice like a roaring lion. He shook his hair, hit his chest and spoke: "Woe! Woe to him who built my body and to him who bound my soul."[18]

The distant echo resonates in the closing stanzas of Goethe's poem "To the Moon":

>Blessed is he who walks apart,
>Though no hate he bears,
>Holds a friend within his heart;
>And with him he shares
>
>All that steals, by men unguessed,
>Or by men unknown,
>Through the maze of his own breast
>In the night alone.

3

What are drugs for? On the dialectic of world-flight and world-addiction

> Oh who will ever narrate to us the whole history of narcotics! It is almost the history of "education," of our so called "higher" education!
> —Friedrich Nietzsche, *The Gay Science*

1. Cultural history as withdrawal history

[118] Two and a half thousand years ago, the Platonic Socrates introduced a reservation against enthusiasm in philosophical argumentation, the consequences of which are difficult to survey up to the present day. Not every case of overstimulation by so-called divine forces shall henceforth be considered favorable to true insight. Only from rare cases of philosophical mania— the Eros-induced homesickness for reunion with the sphere of ideas—do truth-promoting effects still arise, according to Plato; all other possessions and "influences" are to be discarded as hazings of the soul and its faculty of judgment. Plato's reservation in the division of inspirations became a *de facto* (if not formal) ban on inspiration in Aristotle's school. Philosophy from then on becomes more a science than a study of illumination, more a [119] procession along secure lines of thought than a descent into the beautiful danger of inspiration. To register truth-claims, it no longer suffices for professionals to invoke the god who uses them as a mouthpiece; *veritas in vino* notwithstanding, even a philosopher who carouses has no privileged access to better reasons. Ever since the moment at the ominous symposium when

Socrates dismissed the previous speakers' poetic arguments as mere impulses of inspiration, ecstatic speech has had little credit among philosophers—for even if its themes are lofty, philosophizing is supposed to mean nothing but arguing, and arguing means speaking soberly. The work of the Athenian Academy is founded on the theory-hygienic intent to build a bridge to the perception of ultimate reasons with a dry soul only. Whoever doesn't want to submit to this anti-enthusiastic prohibition should carry on with the traditional medley of intoxication and religion, of hearsay and the blurring of consciousness—the Academy, however, is proud to have freed itself from the moody graces of psychic states of exception; it will cross the country of truth without drugs and other illegal means of transport. Since Aristotle, the honor code of the argumentative community includes the conviction that it is better to err soberly than to have the most extreme insights while drugged.

This flashback may be not entirely useless when it comes to understanding modern Western societies' addiction problems in a historically widened perspective. So too the current wars on drugs, [120] whether therapeutic, religious, political, or legal, deserve to be seen as part of a complex psychohistorical drama. The meaning of these campaigns only becomes clear when one realizes that they are part of a titanic battle between intoxication and sobriety that scans the history of higher cultures for several thousand years. In the struggle for the right amount of sobriety, combined with the right amount of inspiration or "mission,"[1] a depth world war [*Tiefenweltkrieg*] takes place in culture—a war with convoluted fronts and camouflaged alliances on all sides. This dispute between individuals, peoples, and civilizations centers on mitigating the heavy, all-too-heavy conditions of life in so-called advanced civilizations. In these involuntary giant struggles, people have long tried to manipulate the world's ever more excessive weight: by sharing it and carrying it together; by reducing it through the restriction of need; by shifting it onto others; by forgetting it and flying over it in a stupor, not least with help from drugs. No doubt a major portion of humankind has always intuitively understood and practiced the rebellious truth of Fichte's sentence: "for the rational being is not meant to be a load-bearer."[2] Indeed, the will to disburdenment evolved into the backbone of the will to freedom and self-determination. At the same time, another, much larger part of humankind mustered all its reasonableness to patiently bend under the yoke of the world; [121] rationalized and sobered up, man adjusted to interpreting existence as an obedience exercise in the face of the inevitable and unchangeable. One must avoid the error of seeing in these attitudes only an sherpa-metaphysics of the Eastern type; in Western latitudes too, the prevailing notion of the grown-up person contains a strong dose of this obedience-theory; in it, the Stoic heritage survives to this day. Wherever it is still active, the conviction of the basic goodness of the world and thus of the bearableness of the real remains in place. Were it otherwise, then the holders of therapeutic jobs, above all drug counselors, would have to close their offices. For their right to operate these extends only as far as they can credibly act as advocates of a sufficiently sober reality principle in a sufficiently good world. How else would they offer their services against the false ascensions of drugs?

In general, philosophers aren't noted for having much to say on questions of intoxication and drugs. Their reputation is based on their abstinence from life's sweet poisons and on a methodological obstinacy that discards all quick persuasions. Philosophers are commonly and correctly thought of as people who rule out anything that overwhelms reason from outside. If they had something like a professional honor, it would stem from the fact that they form their opinions more laboriously than other people.[3] [122] In a certain sense, philosophizing is nothing other than the process-form of sobriety. In this respect, philosophers can at best qualify as actors in the struggle against psychic emergencies and aberrations of reason, but hardly competent partners for a discussion about the addictive constitution of man.

The philosophic-therapeutic dialogue promises to become more fruitful if one recognizes the equivalent of an intoxication and addiction phenomenon in early philosophical thinking itself. This requires that we no longer banish certain ecstatic and enstatic states known to occur in higher registers of philosophical meditation to the mystical corner, but rather grasp them as the innermost and most typical concern of classical philosophical thinking. If we concede this, Socrates' reserve against enthusiasm appears in a changed light; metaphysics and drug-theory, ontology and endocrinology, light each other up all at once. Epistemology and ecstatics are no longer mutually shielded areas. If we were to admit that the base form of "great" philosophical theory must have originally presented itself as a metaphysical monism, it would follow that the peak of philosophical insight, the *apex theoriae* as ascent into the ineffable One, is not reached without the subject's displacement into an illuminated state of emergency. The "moment of truth" could only occur—in the framework of a monistically interpreted universe—insofar as the subject was prepared to "go to ground" in a vision of unity [*"zu Grunde" zu gehen*]. Without ecstatic rapture, no First Philosophy. [123] A theoretically adequate interpretation of such states, however, remains dependent on a time-shift, and naturally only afterwards finds an articulated verbal form. With it, the sempiternal work of Second Philosophy begins. The latter attempts to lay out in a logically clear way what *in actu* stands beyond speech. From time immemorial, the verbalization of mystical monism was the cliff on which philosophical enthusiasm had to break. What was practiced in the Academy and its successors was therefore always-already Second Philosophy, which talks about the First. When Plato said there used to be real wise men as opposed to today's mere amateurs of wisdom, he was not making aphorisms but blabbing the secret of the profession.[4] He was probably referring to an oral tradition from the times of ecstatic masters, who in old Greece were known as shamans or iatromancers. Philosophy arose when the descendants of magicians immigrated to the polis and had to assimilate to the rules of urban communicability and talkativeness. As ecstasy submitted itself to rhetoric, a civil magic developed, whose students began seemingly completely sober careers as politicians, psychologists, speakers, educators, and jurists. After all, even Plato himself is supposed to have had five or six moments in his life in which he too, the distinguishedly distanced man of letters and logician, found himself not in rumination but in illumination. [124] But whatever it may have been like *in persona* during the peak experiences of the old thought-masters, their discursive work, viewed under such premises, would at first have been nothing more than the retroactive self-capture and sobering up of an initially indefinite epiphany. Having to sober up through its own successful formulations would thus be the immanent fate that philosophy administers to itself in its progress.

This work of sobering up proceeds *grosso modo* in three great phases. In the first, rational ecstasy forms a self-interpretation with help from metaphysics as theological ontology; it hereby develops a routine of great thoughts which reproduce themselves in more or less recognizable forms from Aristotle to Leibniz and Hegel; even in late antiquity, though, the academic skepticism of the elders tended to deplete the power of the great theses; it preferred to float in neutral distance between the schools' positions. In the second phase, further sobered-up reason destroys its metaphysical high-rises and finally converges in a total abstinence from high theses—now it no longer wants to differentiate itself from a clarified everyday thinking. Only thus is it possible that what began with Parmenides ends with Wittgenstein. It seems that philosophical enthusiasm, in its early days, could not appear otherwise than as theology or as a teaching about the First Things. The first discovery of the mind—to borrow Bruno Snell's lovely formula—took place in the language of an epiphanic idealism which was still glad to admit that behind the human word [125] divine irradiations were ultimately at work. A thoroughly sobered-up theory no longer permits such ribaldry. Philosophizing individuals of the present, even if they wanted to express mystical states on their own behalf, would first have to learn to talk soberly about ecstasy, and that means: to advance a biology of extraordinary states in the framework of a general physics of knowledge. Since we live in an epoch of the second discovery of the mind, a speculative endomorphinism would likely be the most appropriate approach to the scientifically-observed psychic states of exception. Eventually, the transmitter-substances that control the states of experienced [*erlebten*] absolute unification would have to be called by their chemical names; furthermore, this appellation would itself have to be identified as an output of the brain or the creative universe or the holographic totality—a demand that would amount to a kind of biochemical Brahmanism.

Now one needn't have a particularly precise insight into the school- and research-business of contemporary philosophy to know that in it there is talk of everything but the endomorphinism of speculation; no doubt it wants to understand something of everything but the production and sublation of the difference between Self and Being through endocrinological or chemo-noetic mechanisms. No age has ever been farther from considering, let alone admitting, that mystical monism is the workload philosophy must shoulder. Rather, contemporary theoreticians are proud to eradicate in themselves even the last traces of ecstasy and its theological reflections. They enjoy [126] helping the spirit of calm sobriety to victory. The entire discipline presents itself today in a perfected and self-conscious non-intoxication—like the thoroughly treated subject of an epoch-spanning withdrawal cure. It has even managed to forget this cure as such, so that it hardly makes sense for people of this guild to talk any more of All-Oneness, epiphany, the self-perception of the divine, and so on from any perspective but a historical one. The profession meets enthusiasm with irony and quotation marks. One can say that a philosopher, almost by definition, is someone who *doesn't* know what high states of contemplation are. The contemporary theory business has lost track of the fact that a deep correspondence was once perceived between elation and self-reference. When Aristotle—really no dreamer among the ancient heads—spoke of a thinking that thinks thinking, there was still at least an echo of a remote peak experience lingering in the air; logic and ecstasy were not yet fully alienated from each other—a common sky, even if it were that of Eleusis and its initiatory drugs, stretched over both poles. Looking back at the enthusiastic factor of the older philosophy, an instructive conclusion can be drawn from the results of the newer. It becomes apparent that even philosophy, understood as a discipline, stays in line psychohistorically speaking, and that it, too, with its means, executes the overall tendency of the civilizing process. Western-style civilization could be interpreted from this perspective as a process of enforcing substitute drugs—while eliminating the awareness that they are substitute drugs. [127] A more advanced society will be all the more helpless at the incursion of "hard" drugs. Perhaps the moment is not far off when the whole history of human culture will be narratable under a substitute-drug-theoretical title: in the beginning was confiscation.

2. Holy drugs

At the outset of any critical reflection on the sources of human drug use, a modern habit of thought must be sacrificed. Historical drug research holds in store the lesson—stunning for contemporary people—that the association of drug and addiction is essentially a modern one. To understand the older reality of drug use, it would be necessary to blow apart the prevailing unholy alliance of drug and addiction and understand them each as fundamentally separate matters. The challenge of this issue for contemporary researchers consists in returning, with the help of historical imagination, to an epoch in which drugs predominantly functioned as vehicles of a ritualized metaphysical border traffic. The ritually-harbored use of drugs belongs, from the perspective of psychohistory, to the lost world-age of Old Mediumism.[5] In the latter, [128] human interiority understands itself, insofar as it is delimited at all, not so much as a self-enclosed and self-legislated soul-sphere, but as a showroom and stage for the incoming, the supervening, the passing-through. Unlike the *Homo clausus* of modern individuality, subjectivity in the age of sacred drugs means an increased availability or accessibility for things not-always-manifest, and yet extremely real, which used to reveal themselves in psychic states of emergency. The human "inside" opens and takes shape to the extent that it is the resonant body and screen for the epiphanies of super- and non-human powers. Their sacred representatives may include substances that in modern pharmacy language are called "drugs." The word *drugs*, however, remains a misnomer as long as we only view them with an interest in their chemical-pharmaceutical and cultural-political identification. In the Old-Mediumistic world order, drugs possess a pharmaco-theological status—they themselves are members, actors, powers in the ordered cosmos into which subjects seek to integrate themselves for the sake of survival. Pharmaceutical helpers are called for especially during times in which individuals feel sick and alienated. People take refuge in them when they become convinced, in their own body and the body politic, [129] that a disorder of global harmony is at hand. The psychotropic substances are therefore not used for personal intoxication, but function as reagents of the holy, as door-openers of the gods. Ernst Jünger formulated a significant aspect of early drug practices when he identified, in the intoxications induced through them, a "triumphal parade of the plant through the psyche."[6] The expression captures well the principle of medial transmissibility that characterized the archaic pre-autonomistic constitution of subjectivity. However, by stressing the word *triumph*, Jünger distorted the essence of the plant's mission; sacred herbs, mushrooms, and extracts have nothing to win nor to lose on the human side; what is at issue is a restoration spell that uses the plant's gift of intoxication in order to restore humanity's participation in the integrity of the world.

The word "integrity" registers something that was as plausible to early man as it is unbelievable to us: a claim to the equivalence of health and holiness [*Heilung und Heiligung*]. Even amid the current renaissance of alternative medicines this correlation remains just as occluded as ever. The altitudes to which the idea of the divine pharmacon reached in olden days and the degree to which healing itself could be considered holy, is testified by a Brahmanic sacrificial song from the *Rig Veda*, one of the oldest collections of Indian sacred hymns:

> I have tasted the sweet drink of life, knowing that it inspires good
> thoughts and joyous expansiveness to the extreme, [130] that
> all the gods and mortals seek it together, calling it honey . . .
> We have drunk the Soma; we have become immortal; we have
> gone to the light; we have found the gods.
> What can hatred and the malice of a mortal do to us now, O
> immortal one? . . .
> For you, Soma, are the guardian of our body; watching over men,
> you have settled down in every limb. . . .
> Weaknesses and diseases have gone; the forces of darkness have
> fled in terror.
> Soma has climbed up in us, expanding. We have reached that
> beginning where men rejuvenate life . . .
> Uniting in agreement with the fathers, O drop of Soma, you have
> extended yourself through sky and earth.
> Let us serve him with an oblation; let us be masters of riches.[7]

Even if we are not initiated into the trade secrets of the Sanskritologists, in a profane reading we can grasp at least *one* point of the holy text: in the logic of this potion-invocation *no* distinction is made between the divine drink and the divine itself—at least not to the degree or with the sharpness that characterizes the Aristotelian distinctions between substance and attribute [131] or essence and effect. Precisely this non-distinction shows how the so-called drugs are included in the sacred sphere without remainder.[8] Therefore, dealing with them can hardly be distinguished from a ritualized traffic with the divine. Furthermore, Indian myth makes no secret of the fact that the god Indra boasted of an enormous consumption of Soma, so that at best it is the god himself, not the Brahmanic small consumers, who seems to be affected by the symptoms of an addiction problem.

What at first glance seems to be a logical problem implies a radical psychological difference between ancient and modern experiences of ecstasy and intoxication. The drink that possesses the quality of immortality shares it with its drinkers, be they gods or humans, by virtue of a magically incorporating participation. Historical fantasy alone probably will not suffice to transfer us into a world in which such a logic obtains; this paleopsychological field must remain closed to contemporary thought insofar as a certain amount of spiritual adventurism doesn't come into play. Not by chance have we found the name of Ernst Jünger among those who have dared to approach the toxicological mysteries of early cultures. I cite from his work on intoxication and drugs a passage in which Jünger, probably on the basis of the research of Germanist Wilhelm Grönbech, attempts to invoke the incantations of a Nordic symposium:

Thus, they sat at their table awaiting the arrival of Wod or Wodan . . .

The drinking horn was still "the heart of the banquet." Like the sword, it was a man's prized possession. Drinking had a purpose more profound than the mere remembrance of the deeds of the fathers and forefathers, even more profound than the evocation of the mythical world. All of these things had to be stripped away, they had to be kept out along with the benevolent and the malevolent, salvation and damnation, as long as the guests sat at the table and drank, as in the heart of a wooden ship, where things become more and more silent and calm, while the internal agitation grows.

Now even the external world becomes mantic, portentous. The noises that come from outside become beckoning, announcing. The ear hears behind the sounds: the barking of dogs, and the calls of birds, acquire an oracular power. Perception is altered; it pierces the walls, including the wall of present reality [*Geschehens*], to penetrate into the distant future. . . . The drinking horn "is passed around the fire"; the men draw power into themselves, but not that other power that bestows the indomitable fury of the berserker. The flame does not burn from the inside out, nor does it enter their swords, nor does it assume a noisy or violent form. It is rather silent and peaceful, but also oppressive. Time stretches out in unbearable ways. This does not mean that its duration is prolonged, but that it spreads and expands until it shatters into pieces. It loses its duration and gains weight. It becomes cutting and pressing, it becomes the time of fate, it becomes the time of the Norns.

This explains the silence that is sometimes interrupted by a sigh, or by a moan. Here, something even stronger than armies and weapons is approaching: it is the breaking of the dawn of active fate. They are birth pains.

[133] They do not end right away. The voices outside weaken and almost fall silent. The fire, around which the drinking horn was passed from hand to hand, burns without flickering, with a peaceful light that lies concealed within the heart of the scorching flame. Now they have entered; each feels it, each knows it, and it hardly matters whether he perceives it in its form or in the radiance they all emanate. Now, time has been abolished.

It still reverberates long afterwards on their faces, hair, weapons and clothing. And also on the eyes that see far into the future.

This explains their bravery. Anyone who has banqueted with them even once retains a sense of gaiety even while the great hall is burning down. It guides you through the flames."[9]

Think what you will about the quality of this prose; at any rate, it is certain that here we have before us an attempt to break through the trivial ontology through which sober worldviews form their dogmatic constitutions. Those lost worlds, in which mysterious arrivals, entrances and passings-through of the depicted kind or other kinds could "occur" at each corner, in every tent, under every magic tree, differ from our contemporary world not least in that they know elaborate drug use but no drug problems. Though the extremest forms of intoxication must have occurred, there is no talk of addiction, as far as we know. To these worlds one could almost apply the rule of thumb: the more profound the drug experience, the more impossible is addiction. [134] What excludes addictive tendencies from the start is the ritual setting of ecstasy and the sacramental definition of the realities opened up through the inebriants. I use the expression sacramental in a strongly magical sense that goes beyond everything that Europeans already understand from their religious everyday experience, even if they are Catholics. Its meaning can only be evoked through a thought experiment. Let's suppose that the consecrated hosts of Catholic ritual were prepared with a drop of Albert Hofmann's famous "problem child" lysergic acid diethylamide: then even the gift of Christian communion would be entitled to be mentioned in the same breath as Soma or peyote. Then there would be Christ-apparitions and Father-visions just as abundant as Eleusinian god-hallucinations. Christendom would then be a synthetic trance-religion like Brazilian Xango or Candomblé, supplemented with the components of Greek theology. With that, however, the experiment would already be over. We now understand that (and why) we cannot ask for more from the key sacrament of old Europe, the communion, than our civilization as a whole is capable of giving. Because it incarnates the worldwide trend toward soberer conditions, the communion is a sacrament of participation without hallucinations. With good reason, then, it offers nutrient-poor Catholic bread for the laypeople and exquisite sacramental wine for the clergy; in both forms, it offers Protestantly pious surrogates; this says enough about the route our civilization has taken *toto genere* in matters of participation in divine substance. [135] Whoever looks closely here won't miss that "occidental rationality" embodies itself exemplarily in a *sacrament of withdrawal*. The theologians had, *nota bene*, already achieved this long before the Enlighteners arrived to completely clear out the ritual. After the victory of Protestant symbol-theoreticians over the Catholic real-presence mystics in the Eucharist debates of the sixteenth century, it became completely clear how the modern soul is driven out of the paradises of ecstatic participation. Calvinistic modernity will only know of the mystery of substitute drugs: the cult of money and of intraworldly success. Whoever cannot attain these substitute drugs is now in fact thrown upon the so-called hard drugs. Not by chance are the United States more troubled by drug problems than any other country in the world. It is the country that lives on substitute drugs more than any other country. Whoever can't drug themselves with money or success simply *must* comfort themselves with "chemical substitutes for grace"—as Aldous Huxley called the "real" drugs. Heroin is the American substitute drug for the substitute drugs success and victory. The divine pharmacon that mediated participation in the immortals' way of being became, in the Protestant world, a narcissistic poison that spoils the soul with mirages of mission and election.

3. The break-in of addiction: On the phenomenology of addictive spirit

After these necessarily very rhapsodic references to the religious and paleopsychological dimensions [136] of drug use, the modern mind is naturally prompted to ask how the connection between drug and addiction, which seems so self-evident to *us*, could have come about. How was it possible that addiction found its way to drugs? In what way did psychotropic substances acquire the reputation of being "drugs" and of being addictive? How could the objectivistic semblance emerge, that there are soul-enslaving addictive substances as such? How could the psychologistic semblance emerge, that there are individuals who are "disposed" to addiction by nature? One cannot expect to find satisfactory answers to these questions here; I doubt that the competences of present-day philosophers and psychohistorians suffice to pose problems of this magnitude with any chance of success. What I will attempt in the following is no more than a provisional sounding of terrain that future research must take up for detailed treatment.

The typical modern association between drugs and addiction could only have arisen, it seems to me, through the interaction of three major events in the history of subjectivity, each taking up a developmental space of several millennia. The scale and incompleteness of these processes is such that we generally cannot gain any distance from them or perspective on them. At the risk of falling prey to excessive speculative diagramming, in the following I would like to name three major subjectivity-historical trends that promise to inform our addiction- and drug-theoretical reflections. [137]

A. The falling silent of the gods

B. The deritualization of the overwhelming

C. The becoming-explicit of the will to nonbeing.

I will try to sketch the relationship of these psychohistorical factors and to indicate their addiction-dynamical implications. It should thereby become clear how the three tendencies merge in a story of individual consciousness stepping out into a neutral, prosaic, overt, and ultimately meaningless world. Jointly would emerge a story about the becoming-untenable [*Haltloswerden*] of subjectivity and the metaphysical homelessness of modernized human beings.

A. The falling silent of the gods—under this title hides probably one of the most important caesuras in the history of consciousness. We generally no longer give a clear account of it just because we ourselves are members of a civilization that has long been shaped by the silence of the gods.[10] Modern men are people who have made themselves safe from revelation—this observation is practically definitional. We consider our homogenous prosaic interpretation of reality and our everyday sober inner states so normal and normative that everything else only registers as mania and nonsense; nothing would be more shocking for us than the intrusion of new revelations from a beyond that wanted to claim official-cultural validity. Through a heavily staggered series of regulations and institutions of a linguistic, psychological, juristic, medicinal, and political nature [138], we have ensured the psychiatrization of the epiphanic short-circuit between God and individual. We narrowly grant that healthy subjects may somehow "believe in God"; we are absolutely sure, however, that only the sick see and hear God or gods. In order to convincingly explain how this anti-epiphanic *status quo* came about, one would have to be able to narrate uninterruptedly the evolution of worldviews and mentality-structures over the last two or three thousand years—a task that seems impossible given the present state of philosophical and historical insights. But however one is seduced into such a great narration—whether one carries on Julian Jaynes' bold speculations about the bicameral mind;[11] whether one is oriented toward Ulrich Sonnemann and Thomas H. Macho's astute attempts to reformulate the philosophy of consciousness in psychoacoustic terms;[12] whether one is inspired by the proposals to transform metaphysics into an anthropological study of metaphors[13]—in each case it must start from the current state of Western consciousness. And the latter is unambiguous in stating that gods are definitively excluded from the set of admissible and possible "contents of experience."[14] [139] We therefore hold it to be self-evident that the divine, if it remains in any way possible to speak of its "existence" at all, is fundamentally incapable of appearing.[15] Accordingly, any claims of a direct epiphany can only be motivated by pathological self-affections of a cognitive apparatus [*Bewußtseinsapparat*] that seduces and abuses itself. Today the desolation of religious mania hangs over direct revelations. These convictions summarize a civilizational process of such great imprinting force, such high coherence and powerful authority that not one person, however dissident, can take the liberty of questioning the necessity of its total course without making self-defeating concessions to irrationalism. Even if, as many believe, something adverse and fatal to the species prevails in this process taken as a whole, we cannot but admit that this is a self-consistent doom. The logic of the evolution of human experience itself sanctions the results of the event, which to this day remain transparent to us. It would thus be impossible for us to wish back an organization of consciousness in which the gods or their delegates go in and out of our interior without preconditions. [140] This impossibility would remain in force even if we could convince ourselves that an increased availability for God or gods meant an immunity against addiction. Even if we wanted to, we could no longer exchange addictive tendencies for divine visitations and private epiphanies. The direction of the civilizing process toward the strengthening of ego-consciousness, the erection of control-subjectivity, and the suppression of mediumistic tendencies remains totally irreversible, aside from subcultural resistances. One of the unsolved riddles of the history of consciousness is surely the question of why the subject becomes more susceptible to being overwhelmed by drugs as its imperviousness to God and gods increases.

    B. When the gods keep quiet, a tendency to decode ecstasy emerges. One should not assume that the use of sacred drugs left the world all of a sudden two or three thousand years ago. However, what has been everywhere observable since then is a trend toward the becoming-unspecific of ecstatic states. Even in ecstasy, people more and more forgot the dialect of their gods; even in the mediums' self-transcendence the gods no longer found their old revelation-security. An author like Plutarch had good reason to bemoan the decay of the oracles. Intoxication and cult split apart. Drugs—now rightly called by that name—are still taken; doors to unwonted inner states are still opened. But informants from a beyond no longer step through them. Now the way lies open to profane and private drug use, and as soon as it is entered, [141] it leads almost irresistibly down into the caves of addiction and drunkenness. Individuals who earlier might have been suited to mediumism are particularly at risk of falling prey to non-informative ecstasies. It will forever be remarkable that it is precisely civilizations with a very ancient and elaborate knowledge of psychotropic substances that, after the collapse of their cultural integrity, ruined themselves with alcoholism in a very short time.

When ecstasy becomes uninformative because the gods are tired of revelation and the figures of intoxication lose the sharpness of their profiles, a blunt and deritualized handling of the mighty substances asserts itself. As soon as the ritual brackets that support the subject's spine in the presence of sacred drugs fall away, the subject finds itself in an unshielded direct relation to what all experience indicates is stronger than the profane self. One of the tragic lessons of the drug is that it forbids the human to build a private relationship with the overwhelming. Under conditions of private consumption, sooner or later every psychotropic substance fulfills the definition of the demonic. In the relationship with the demon, the subject loses its will to the stronger partner. To be sure, any being that does not wish to succumb to prosaic desiccation must consciously relate itself to what it knows to be stronger than itself. The meaning of religious institutions lay not least in the harboring of this connection to a superior power; through ritualized participation and through the codification of relationships of loyalty between gods and mortals, [142] the weaker element was bound to the stronger in a careful and beneficial way. But when the subject decodes its excursions into ecstasy and gets caught in the suction of private and deritualized consumption with its wicked repetition-compulsion, a degenerative tendency breaks through. At times, familial protective spirits still keep their hand extended and retrieve the addict from their chemical worldlessness back into a common sphere; in this connection, the well-known film title "Mothers against the Mafia" names a significant constellation. Wherever the same falls apart, the privatized partaking in the stronger soon turns into a malign overload. The road is clear for acting out tensions from the force fields of primary masochism; the subject becomes dependent on the high of annihilation and on the intoxicating sensation of accelerating combustion. (One could say, after all, that addicts differ from sober people in modern times only in that they have chosen a higher speed of self-destruction.) From then on the subject is trapped insofar as it has become the weaker partner in a relationship consisting of overwhelmings. The subject's legitimate demand to partake in sources of empowerment and elevation leads, in the private consumption of narcotics, to a demonic exchange of places; instead of sucking on the power source, the subject itself becomes the sucked; it empties itself in favor of the overpowering entity by which it previously wished to be filled. This suction-reversal is one of the traits of addiction that most clearly betrays its provenance in an aberrant metaphysics.[16]

[143] Thus it becomes clear that every case of addiction contains a testimony to the difficulties of world-building in modern times. Just where subjects have to settle their bill with the overpowering, modern culture's tendencies toward deritualized ways of life and consumeristic individualism leave open a gateway for all possible addictions. Modern individuals tend to be left alone with everything that is stronger than themselves—at best, they belatedly make alliances with others who are "impacted" in the same way. In the first place they are predestined victims of countless forms of subjective modification and reversal of suction. The Mafia chiefs and the leaders of political sects have grasped this better than the social psychologists and therapists. Just as the psychiatrist Harold Searles once remarked that every crazy person had been driven crazy by someone, analogously one could demonstrate that every fanatic has been fanaticized and every addict has been addicted by someone. At work in every addiction is the motif that the subject has lost sovereignty over what fills it. Over the addict hangs a power that absolutely won't let itself be replaced by anything else: I am your master and your filling—thou shalt have no other filling beside me. [144] The drug-savvy poet Charles Baudelaire one hundred years ago logged the impression "that he was smoked by the pipe"—a sentence that wavers oddly between consent and panic. It sounds both horrified and satisfied, as if Baudelaire could not decide whether self-preservation or self-relinquishment is the greater doom for a civilized person.

C. The emergence of the will to not be—I fear it remains a precarious undertaking to explicitly raise the third of the above-mentioned great subjectivity-historical tendencies. Even for a discipline as ethereal and as well-practiced in negativities as modern philosophy, it is not harmless to talk about things like this, since it evidently involves a forbidden zone of reflection. Furthermore it is always inauspicious to point, as it were with fat positive fingers, at the "dimension" of human existence that "extends" from being into non-being.[17]

According to the language regime of today's prevailing philosophical interpretations of existence, humans are beings of which it is to be said that they are in-the-world. [145] In which sense are we to understand the preposition "in," here? What does the expression "in" mean, when it crops up as part of the great formula being-in-the-world? Are we in the world in the same way we are in this room, which in turn is in this city, which is in this country, which is on this planet, which is in this universe? Obviously we have no trouble localizing ourselves in space and imaginatively thinking ourselves into ever larger containers, into ever larger shells, which enclose and contain us. With this game we remain like the doll inside the doll caught in a spatial classification of our own in successively larger containers. Up to this point, we are all "physicists." But wherein should we place the epitome of all containers, the universe, if not in something that cannot itself be a container: in our representation, our knowledge of it? For where would the universe be, if not *in* us, in our being-there [*Dasein*], which stands ever-open for the rising of the great correlation? From that point on, we go no further as "physicists," and must become inner-world theoreticians—be it as psychologists, epistemologists, or neurocosmologists. As soon as we apply the "in" as an absolute preposition, we become attentive to the abyssal positionality of humankind. If we wish to localize ourselves in an absolute sense, then we find ourselves in the bottomless. We are not in the world like the ring is in the box or like the fly is in the fly bottle; we belong to it like the leap into emptiness or the arrow in the blue[18] or the image in the projector. The "in," employed in an absolute sense, implies an index of movement, which essentially means "into." If it were not unidiomatic, Heidegger would have had to speak not of being-in-the-world [146] but rather being-into-the-world [*In-die-Welt-Hinein-Sein*]. Thus is announced the mode of existence of a being that is in the world to just the degree that it is leaping toward the world—or, falling toward the world, if one prefers this originally gnostic movement-metaphor.

Some years ago I began, on the basis of considerations of this kind, to rework certain impulses of this century's existential philosophy into a sort of philosophical psychology and ontokinetics that I call "analytic of coming-to-the-world."[19] This proceeds from the idea that we must remove the positivistic remainder that adheres to the notion of being-in-the-world. Only then can we adequately understand, without succumbing to the metaphysical addiction to the unmoved, the movedness of the "existing" being in its being-coming, its setting-itself-up and its being-going; as beings of movement, humans are involved in a world-traversing change of element, which implies an exodus just as much as a retreat—with a range of stances and states in between them. Existence is accordingly not only the forward march from a non-existence (or pre-existence) into existence, but also always-already contains in itself a quasi-nirvana-oriented countermovement from existence into non-existence. If one defines the human as a being necessarily involved in going, [147] it also becomes apparent how it always-already revokes and cancels its being-held-in the tension of worldly burdens. In this way we can avoid talking about humans in a language that prejudges them to be settled within an always-positive Being. Existentialism must remain monocular and pathetic as long as it fails to reflect itself in an inexistentialism as its necessary counterpart. Only existentialism and inexistentialism together afford a stereoscopic view of man's ambivalent inhabitation of the world that meets the requirements of a philosophical depth-psychology. The latter acknowledges that not only does the conscious rest upon an unconscious, but also that world-inclined being-there [*Dasein*] is correlated with a world-averse and worldless being-gone [*Fortsein*].

On this basis we can better articulate what addicts' private and uninformative ecstasies are all about. In addiction we are faced with an individualized—that is, split from the complicity [*Mitwissen*] of cultural membership—revolt against the imposition of being-there. The deritualized, private use of drugs allows the subject to so to speak blaze itself a wild trail back into inexistence. Often they expressly believe that they have a right to such excursions, as if thoroughly convinced, in some corner of their consciousness, that they are too sovereign to let themselves be imposed upon by the coarseness of being-there. It's true that nothing grants more superiority than thinking oneself out of the quandary of given conditions; nothing grants more freedom than levitating above the contradiction between will and necessity; hardly anything cheers us up as much as [148] the certainty of being able to escape from enslavement by the drive to self-preservation. It comes as no surprise, I think, that some drug therapists occasionally perceive in their clients a posture that they describe as a coquetry of incurability.[20] Some addicts side with the drugs in order to borrow from them what they can no longer muster by their own power: the power to decide to interrupt the compulsory continuity of a vile reality. In almost all addictions, therefore, a depraved ontological motive plays a role: addiction often signifies a para-metaphysical experiment in global negation, in which all that is the case is bracketed in world-critical intent? Through the alliance with the drug, the subject deprives his existentiality of the power that would hold him in the tension of world-openness—with all the challenges this brings in the form of concerns, struggles, tasks, and social solidarities. Therefore, it would be completely false to see the drug only as a means of escaping the world. No doubt the addict is a deserter in the eyes of society, absent from the reality-troops without leave. More still, the drugged one distances himself from his own self, which by virtue of its existentiality would send him "to the front," into an awake, resilient, responsible, and creative constitution; he wants to avoid the condition in which the appeal of things and of fellow people would keep him awake; he disavows being-there in the watch-room [*Wachraum*] of collective reality. Here one sees that existence is a kind of ontological request, [149] for which there is no enforcement: there is no way to present someone with an arrest warrant that would prove to him that from now on he is obliged to get a hold of himself. In any case the drugs derive their power to overwhelm the psyche not from their chemical effects alone; the compulsion to repeat, which commands the addicted nervous system, can only become overpowering to the degree that the drug makes indispensable an indignation at being. The drug becomes the mistress of the soul only as a private and secret servant of the tendency toward non-existence.

Here we are touching a deep dimension of the history of consciousness, which has largely evaded psychological inquiry. Over the mysteries of inexistentiality lies a spell that petrifies thinking in gestures of helpless positivism. Faced by the Medusa of negativity, even philosophical thought, little different than everyday thinking, grows clammy and stiff. What would be necessary in order to loosen this positivistic block is a Western nirvana concept that opens to us a friendly nothingness. But where can we find approaches to such an idea of inexistentiality?[21] How do we liberate subjects from the stress of permanent existence, and substances from the compulsion of constant presence? Can we detect traces of a nirvanological or inexistential consciousness in the Western tradition?

Historians of ideas will not be able to give sure answers to these questions. At best, one might point to [150] the emergence of the near-Eastern and Mediterranean soteriologies that began revolutionizing mankind's economies of ideas and motivations over two thousand years ago. Without a doubt, the break-in of the idea of salvation into human thinking is one of the most explosive facts in the history of consciousness. Ever since the idea of salvation rose to power in certain traditions, a radical world-critical spark smolders in the world-consciousness of high-cultural peoples. Wherever salvation is taken to be possible and desirable, the thought that all the signs[22] of nature can and must be reversed gains power. The distinction between death and life grows shaky, for this greatest of all subversions teaches that a true death is preferable to a false life. Along with the demand for salvation, the possibility of negating the world enters the world as well—recall that we are dealing here with a holy negation, one that attempts to repel itself from the deception of profane existence. Now the spirit is dizzy in view of the reversibility of all signs—the suspicion that the world as a whole in its status quo is altogether wrong and or upside-down condenses in doctrines of otherworldly true paradises. The redemption-seeking spirit sets out to invalidate "this world" like a false premise. Whoever plays with the fire of salvation is never far from the fantastic temptation to turn his back on the world-edifice and leave it to its ruin—apocalypticism even goes so far as to preach its destruction and, if only it were possible, to set it on fire by one's own hand.

[151] From a psychoanalytic perspective, it is obvious to remark that with the break-in of the Christian and gnostic ideas of liberation, the spirits of primal negation were awakened in the Western psyche. Even if the official Christian piety toward creation toiled over efforts to shelter the goodness of the world from the goodness of its architect against the insurrection of negativity, the awakened primary masochistic and sadistic world-critical forces would never be put to sleep again. The smooth fit of subjects into benevolent totalities is disturbed once and for all. The soul discovers itself

as the discordant factor—as the other in everything and opposite to everything. The greatest psychologists have always had to make concessions to the suggestive wisdoms of dualism. From the gnostic-Manichaean nuclear fission of the Godhead to the Freudian theory of the death drive, the Western tradition has not lacked attempts to metaphysically or meta-psychologically substantialize the great negation of world, body and self.

In our context, what matters is to show that the gnostic movements of late antiquity—combined with tendencies of anachoretic psychology and negative theology—represent the first flareup of a nirvanological impulse on Western soil. Gnostic acosmism—the doctrine of the soul's unbelonging to the world of matter and to the celestial demons—was an effort of the late antique psyche to self-therapeutically detach itself from the powers of "this" grotesque and malignant "world"; it was an attempt, however precarious, [152] to render the pneumata or spirit-souls homeless in the given, in order to open for them a prospect of innermost healing through heavenly self-reintegration. The soul, which now understand itself only as a stray here, passing through and returning home, enjoys from the moment of anamnesis and conversion [Kehre] the certainty that its postexistence will resemble its pre-existence: both signify immersion in a sphere flooded with light and rapture. From the point of view of the phenomenology of religion, a certain affinity between gnosticism and Buddhism is evident.[23] If the gnostic insight deregisters the subject from the cosmos to repatriate it in an original worldlessness, consequently in a being-in-God, this is an unmistakable equivalent of the Buddhist's transition into houselessness. Both are gestures of an ontological resettlement, which is supposed to lead to a kind of world-flight or world-weaning. With the help of the great ascetic negation, the suffering-producing mechanism, the world-addiction, is healed and the greed for worldly power is mitigated. By loosening its world-attachment, the subject holding itself and things as possessions finds its way back into contact with the truths of nomadic life: world-traversing [153] beings travel best with light luggage. As a gnostic free spirit, an Indian sannyasin, a Buddhist monk, or a meditating layperson, the individual is able to liberate him- or herself from obsession with worldly possessions; a metaphorical nomadism dissolves the block of sedentary and world-obsessed ego forms. Buddhist nirvanology and gnostic acosmology produce effects that disarm official realism in an astonishingly analogous way. With gentle rigor, they disengage the subject from the inexorable positivity of being-in-the-world-and-nowhere-else. Thanks to an unprecedented gesture of empathic generosity, the teachings of the Buddha and of the Bright Gnosis offer the dual citizenship of being as well as non-being to the person overburdened and wounded by unbearable realities. They thus unblock the entrance to worldlessness and to inexistentiality; precisely thereby can they contribute to the regeneration of the cosmopolitan capacities of the subject—provided they do not make negativity in turn into an inflexible or "fundamentalist" position.

These are the great events of the history of consciousness, whose scope still exceeds our trivial interpretations of life, world and reality. Even modern philosophers and psychologists are not immune to this triviality, insofar as they are almost without exception addicted to the dogmatism of existentiality. It is true that one expects philosophers to be able to think sympathetically about the darker areas of the *condition humaine*, furthermore, it is considered a professional obligation of psychologists to defend, if necessary, the preconditions of psychic integrity against [154] the sickening norms of official culture. What *de facto* shows up in most cases is a dogmatic existentialism, with which we, in full feeling of our own reality-ability, send the others directly to the front lines of the real, where all experience indicates they are bound to fail. We do this with the good conscience of successful existers, and do it even though we should know that our clients have been less lucky in this than us—why else would they have retreated into their ecstasies and dark rooms? What might they have lost in the niches of addictive and neurotic worldlessness? Why would they have resorted to the psychotic appeal against their unjust pre-condemnation to existence in and endurance in the deadly externality of their worlds?

If we want to go to the height of the aforementioned great consciousness-historical events that have merged into the negative ontologies of Buddhism and gnosticism, it would be important for the philosophical and therapeutic accomplices [*Mitwisser*] of mankind to say goodbye to the dogmatic existentialism that underlies our official ontology, with its creationist positivism and its forced consent to the institution of "reality." The only path that remains open for therapeutic ethics is that of complicity and sympathy with the inexistential tendencies of human life. Along this path insights into our civilization's most hidden addictive dispositions open up.

It would also allow us to understand the explosive development of diffuse and non-narcotic addictions, in which worldly and realist activities take on the function [155] of existence-breakers and ego-extinguishers. Because inexistentialism is ultimately not about fleeing the world but rather about negating egoic tensions, even the most worldly and realistic behavior of humans, namely work, can take on a drug function. The most contemporary form of addiction, workaholism, with its derivatives in entertainment and hobby culture, perfectly illustrates the dynamics of a disheveled and unnoticed inexistentialism. Today, as ever, the subject overloaded by its own existence is less a world fugitive than a world addict—whereby the stuffing of the interior with worldly substances itself possesses a fundamentally negative character. In the outward bustle of activity, the members of the overstrained species steal back into the worldlessness of bustling animals. Christian and Buddhist monastic psychologies were the first to work this out in complete clarity. One suppresses being-in-the-world as well as coming-to-the-world by permanently filling oneself up with "topics," "projects" and *commitments*.[24] What is the point of being there [*Dasein*], once one has discovered the possibility of using the world itself as a means against being in it and being in oneself?

Philosophical therapeutics is a school of being-and-not-being. It faces the task of encountering the unredeemed yearning for redemption and showing the hidden great negation ways out into the free, common, transformable. If the culture as a whole takes up inexistentiality in a theoretically and humanly credible way, individuals might perhaps also be able to resist pharmaceutical escapism more consciously. [156]

4. Of the human potential for withdrawal

After what has been said, it seems to me possible to propose a concept of addiction from the standpoint of a philosophy of religion. Addiction is a decoded, that is, obscured and delinguified desire for liberation from existential compulsion. It is the disaster [*Ernstfall*] of private religion. In its most dangerous variants it stems from a frivolous, that is, private, deritualized, and ignorant handling of potent psychotropic substances. After non-informative ecstasies these leave behind traces demanding repetition in the subjects' pleasure-memories. Formless primal negation plays into the frivolity of experimentation. The beginnings of addiction lie in the subject's venture to form a private relationship with the supervening and overwhelming; it is consumerism in the absolute. *De facto* it is rarely the addictive substance alone that breaks the subject. The great disintegration arises from the interplay of drug ingestions and withdrawal crises. Especially the chronic horror of withdrawal at the peak of a repetitive desire triggers a primary-processual disintegration. It leads to the impossibility of being a person, that is, a being that can affirm its relative emptiness. The course of the process is that of an acute sickness unto death. The sickness wins its enormous power through the synergy of suction-inversion and inexistentialism. Just as Baudelaire knew that he was smoked by his pipe, so too the average drug addict knows that he is taken by his drug. He knows it, because he [157] takes it in order to be taken by it. Seen this way, addiction would be nothing but the obsessive consent to the suction as the will-to-be-taken. In this sense, the advocates of the hard policy and the rude tone are not wrong when they say that one must first of all respect the deliberate self-destroyer in the addict. This means that one must postulate an extraordinary configuration of consciousnesses between the addict and his or her helper; they face each other as subjects who know of each other that [they] can ultimately do nothing for each other. The addict knows that he cannot become unaddicted for the sake of his helper; the helper knows that no amount of maternalizing care will take away the addict's hunger for the overwhelming. Thus the basic situation of addiction therapy is not simply a care agreement between helper and client, but a duel between two consciousnesses that render each other helpless. The helplessness of each toward the other is identical with the power to show to the other his impotence. At some point, however, the helper will make clear to the addict that he can let him go under, just as the seemingly help-seeking addict will, in a moment of truth, make the helper understand that he will hardly ever be able to persuade him to lead a life under the conditions of average sobriety. This diagnosis marks a tragic limit which no therapy can cross. At this border, the spirits separate—some to leave behind the human situation as a whole, others to affirm the uncomfortable humanness of withdrawal. [158]

Tragedy doesn't always have the final word. Even souls stimulated by the great negation know of relenting to reality; they eventually grin and bear it; they practice saying yes to the facts of an adult life after the fact; they consent to their own existence and learn to appreciate the spirit of compromise.

Certainly, existing always means having to accept the disadvantage of having been born. But it also means being able to look for ways to transform this fundamental disadvantage into the advantage of world-discovery. Against the overwhelming power of the worldless, only inspiration by the splendor of the world helps; in this context, Plotinus' polemic against the vulgar gnostics' lostness in dreams is also psychologically clever. For the black forms of world-animus the effective antidote is world-friendship, which advances along the thread of sympathies. Who has come into the world has indicated by this act that he or she wanted to take the chance of trading the drug of perfect nothingness for the substitute drugs of existence. Whoever is "in the world" has *eo ipso* ventured forward into a zone where one has to get along with a little less darkness, a little less tensionlessness, a little less timelessness than in the pre-worldly embryonic state. Thus Dasein always-already implies a thrust into landscapes poorer in ecstasy; it is an expedition into the sober, the neutral. There, the things become clear to us in their being-in-themselves and set their resistance against us. Whoever exists is in a certain way always-already [159] "out there" with the alien, the heavy, the obstinate, the other. For inhabitants of the middle latitudes, the outdoor temperature is typically colder than it was back in the great indoors. The air that we breathe, compared to the comfort of the shared circle of mother and child, means a permanent endorphin-deprivation torture. For the fetus, the motherly medium is, as one now knows, a resonant body that ensures the rhythmic and opioid continuum. But ever since individuals have practiced "existence" [*Dasein*], music and opium have become rare goods. In their place swarm priests, dealers, and therapists, who take excessive fees for suspect services. Are not all of us—we who were reckless enough to come into the open—inmates, fallen out of rhythm and set into withdrawal—but also not entirely hopeless cases, as long as we establish ourselves on the market as middlemen of the substitute drug of the art of living? We spend our days flattening our standard dosage to the lowest tolerable level; which defines what is called reality in our region. It all comes down now to having more worries than liquor, but also not having more liquor than worries; as long as we observe this rule, tragedy keeps its distance. With the distance from extremes granted by welcome sobriety and the will to reality-check, we gain the freedom to participate in the human world. There, abysses know how it is with co-abysses [*Mitabgründe*]. Only from the depth of empathy [*Mitwissen*] do people unite for a common life. One of the signatures of our time is that such alliances are no longer possible without familiarity with the deep world war between cultural and manic systems, [160] and of the risks of technical manipulations of nature. Living in the wake of an almost three-thousand-year history of grand world-negations and in the middle of the hottest phase of constructivistic world-transformations, we are forced to reconceive the stake around which negative and positive ontologies circle. In the human world, what matters, not only for philosophers and therapists, is to prove oneself an accomplice of existence and its opposite; with our kind we share the embarrassment of existing.

4

How was the "death drive" discovered?
Toward a theory of the soul's end goals
with continual references to Socrates,
Jesus, and Freud

> Come, let us talk together
> Those who talk, are not dead
> After all, the flames are already flickering
> Around our plight
> —Gottfried Benn

1. Glad tidings and their price

Who could deny that expressiveness has a demonic side? Who would not know that there are things that absolutely must not be disclosed, if disclosing means telling the truth in a true way? Who would have had so little to say that he would not have had the experience: that there are things that must be voiced only in order to release some of the lethal pressure they possess as silent apprehensions? Who would have ventured out so little in thought that he or she hasn't had the experience: that there are final conclusions which are drawn in order not to be true in the last instance?

The following considerations—midnight exchanges between philosophical and psychological voices—are best read as [162] an introduction to a fringe science [*Grenzwissenschaft*] which today, as in the past, has few teachers and even fewer students. These black reflections roam the uncanny borderland between theory and magic, where talk about life and death can turn into a matter of life and death. Psychiatric and metaphysical interests are hard to distinguish here. Psychoanalysis and fundamental prophetology merge into one and the same discipline; in it, it is a matter of saying precarious truths in such a way that the speaker does not break from what he knows and says. At every step we will have good reason to recall Nietzsche's sentence that we possess art lest we perish of the truth.[1] Art, however, must be supported by a philosophy that knows how to sing in the dark. There is no doubt that we are moving in a terrain staked out by Nietzsche's discoveries concerning the nature and function of "truth": the following explanations of the Freudian hypothesis of the death drive aim to make a small advance in the theory of the awful truth—that is, a critique of those cognitions whose "full possession" would be life-threatening for the subject of knowledge. I note, as a precaution, that this chapter will profit only readers who could imagine enduring a working group with practical exercises in a therapeutic seminar about journeys to hell.

Where sensitive subjects of this kind become a public issue, one must be prepared for scandalous and extravagant theses to infiltrate the bourgeois discussion-sphere. This is what the late-ancient salvation religions [163] and the fierce, unbridled varieties of current depth psychology have in common. They needle the ears of worldlings and conventional believers with new tones and unwelcome speeches. Unacceptable, unheard of, unbearable things enter discussion when the bearers of radical, explosive, dark truths claim a right to be heard. Invariably, someone will experience such newly-spoken sentences from the realm of death and pre-birth as vexing and foolish. The "language of the human race"—to borrow the formula of the language-theologian Eugen Rosenstock-Huessy—seems to be nothing but a history of revolutionary augmentations of the sayable through influxes from the unspeakable, the occult, the latent. All deeper self-experiences arise in conversation with the current of poetic, epistemic and kerygmatic revolutions flooding the generations, through which humanity has come to know, love, and fear itself more fully. Poetry, science, and proclamations of new "freedoms," new truths, and new imperatives, have, as far as written traditions can tell, been introducing good and bad, inspiring and terrifying new-truth into the stream of our familiar retellings for over three millennia. Such new-truth dominates the more recent phase of human history and makes it the force field of good and bad messages; *evangelia* and *dysangelia* share the historical world as the theater of proclaimable news. All history is the history of information wars.

On these questions, Christianity and psychoanalysis lock eyes across an epochal threshold. [164] Two profoundly different ways of bringing good news into the world thus get into a scuffle in a confined space. They see through each other and expose each other—and join forces to cover each other's weaknesses, which no one can know better than the psychoanalyst in relation to the priest and the priest in relation to the psychoanalyst. However joyful or confident the message of either side—redemptive religion or secular soul-healing—may seem, the obverse of its message remains obscure for it—and in each case it is the rival who must perceive it most clearly. Each of these teachings is in fact loaded with a paradoxical antisense that sabotages the cheerfulness of the respective message and binds it to an infinitely bleak, even dysangelic insinuation. The Christian *euangelion* comes forward with the assurance: amid the hopelessness of given circumstances, the true life is nonetheless possible for you in faith, even if only after "this" life; thus, you have reason to feel saved even now, for what awaits you after death casts its light ahead into the present existence. This expectation is vouchsafed by "the logos," the incarnate. Here, of course, the psychoanalytically-trained ear thinks that it can hear whispering behind the exhortation to believe in life a sucking invitation to death. For almost two thousand years, worldlings have complained that Christianity is a grim affair for them just where it appears most rapturous. It charges a depressing fee for its glad tiding—contempt for present joys. But how does psychoanalysis fare with its offerings to the [165] suffering species? Its therapeutic promise introduces a thesis that at first sounds much more moderate. It states: within certain limits, the human psyche is capable of a healing expression of repressed pathogenic secrets—an expression that in the long run enables it to take on even the worst truths and the most mortifying grievances; what can be said no longer needs to be acted out; fatal actions can be replaced by painful confessions. Thus, although this psychotherapeutic does not promise salvation [*Heil*], it does promise the chance of a cure [*Heilung*] through the revitalized word. One need not be a priest to grasp the latently nihilistic, at best stoic tendency of the psychoanalytic theory of ultimate motivations—especially since the older Freud, after the publication of the treatise *Beyond the Pleasure Principle* in 1920, no longer made a secret of his dark theories regarding life's attraction toward the relaxation of death:

> It would be counter to the conservative nature of instinct if the goal of life were a state never hitherto reached. It must rather be an ancient starting point, which the living being left long ago, and to which it harks back again by all the circuitous paths of development. If we may assume as an experience admitting of no exception that everything living dies from causes within itself, and returns to the inorganic, we can only say: *The goal of all life is death*, and, casting back: The inanimate was there before the animate.'" (*Beyond the Pleasure Principle*, V)

With this, the prospective healing power of expressing pathogenic secrets is compromised from the ground up. Somewhere along the line of sounding latent impulses, [166] psychoanalytic talk reaches the limit where it can only disclose its medical helplessness. For what would the disabled life have to say at the end of its confused search for itself and for happiness, except the confession that mocks any hope of healing: that in its most basic instinct, it wants only to be saved from itself in order to return to the nirvana of the minerals?[2]

Thus Christianity and psychoanalysis, ideal-typically contrasted, seem to relate to each other like two rival cure systems with at least as much in common that they buy their successes with potentially absurd and life-threatening side effects.[3] The Christian cure relies on the healing power of belief in the utterly improbable—it mobilizes a hopeful thinking-oneself-out-of-this-life into a higher, later, true one—and risks missing the fight for the chances of the present life; the analytic cure, conversely, bets everything on the healing power of speaking bitter truths—to the point of making explicit the unspeakable drive-tendency that strives for "death" as the most thorough cure. [167]

Which of the two contenders in the titanic battle over the interpretation of mankind's basic strivings has picked the better approach? Is human life, in its ultimate motivational structure, a however-misguided quest for postmortem transfiguration of the self "with God"—as Christian anthropology would have it? Or is life—as taught by the deepened metapsychology of the elderly Freud—a detour function of the death drive, which, on its long march through the interim destinations of self-preservation and genital pleasure, never loses sight of the end goal: expiration in inorganic no-longer-having-to-feel?—It seems advisable to me to postpone our verdict on these questions until a wide-ranging reflection has enabled us to gauge the anthropological and philosophical dimensions of the controversy around what Freud identified—or should one say proclaimed?—as the death drive.

2. Socratic memorabilia—or, The culture of the metaphysical death-appetite

"Death drive"—it sounds so strange. Are we dealing here with a conceptual monster, which names something that otherwise wouldn't exist? Doesn't the expression patently belong to the autosuggestive mirages by which psychological thought fools itself about what it thinks it "substantively" has in mind? Did Freud, with his notorious coinage, "grasp" a nexus of strivings inherent in the laws of the psyche—or did he simply invent a name [168] which attaches itself to various phenomena without sufficient ground in the nature of things? In his excursions into the catacombs beyond the pleasure principle, did the great psychologist simply hoodwink himself and seduce his pupils into submission to his masterly self-deception? Or did the old gentleman know what he was talking about, and was this ostensibly speculative movement of life—weary of the compulsion to be—toward its own end actually a distinct personal experience and present evidence to him? Did Freud invent the "death drive" and pseudo-conceptually fix the fiction—or did he therein discover and accurately conceive a real tendency of psychic life?

In the following, I will plead for the discovery hypothesis, but with the qualification that it is not a question of an original discovery, but of a rediscovery, in which modern psychology adopted known pieces of classical metaphysics under biological pseudonyms. So if I want to characterize Freud's late teachings as those of a discoverer and psychological realist, a touch of irony cannot be avoided. For as far as Freud proved himself a positivist [*Realwissenschaftler*] about the soul, he would emerge as an imitator of classical philosophy—without being fully conscious of this role himself, of course.[4] He translated open secrets of metaphysical and religious tradition into a secular and scientific language—and thereby pulled off the feat of not immediately getting caught in the act of metaphysics. [169] It can easily appear here as if I wanted to say that the soul-researcher must—in order to remain a realist—occasionally switch disciplines, even against his will, inasmuch as it is a structural property of the factical region called soul to produce those phenomena which in the following I wish to call the metaphysical death-appetites. Am I hereby bringing the old *anima naturaliter metaphysica* back into play? Am I offering a new version of the doctrine of mankind's constitutive need for metaphysics? One will see in a moment that things won't turn out so badly; for even if "souls" are typically living opinions on the riddles of the end, not all statements are metaphysical, nor are all metaphysical statements marked by an appetite for death.

The reader will have noticed: replacing the phrase "death drive" with the expression "death-appetite" is not without a critical point. Discussions of a psychic pull toward death should stay as close as possible to the realm of conscious intentions, so as to prevent the seduction of thought by profound drive-suggestions. At this stage of reflection, one mustn't give too much credit to the misleading psychoanalytic-mythological way of talking about Thanatos as a primal tendency of sentient life. If we demand that a psychic intention present itself also as a consciously experienceable *appetitus*, we impede the Brahmanic abuse of psychoanalytic depth interpretation. For who is unfamiliar with the psychologizing form of intellectual dishonesty that knows how to be right ad infinitum as long as [170] its puts into play ultradeep motivations working behind the subject's back? If we speak of appetites instead of drives, we apply the principle of speaking publicly only of the conscious self-representations of the *"Triebgründe"* in experienced inclinations.

To speak of appetites means keeping in mind the individual who experiences them. But how could we track down authors and voices who bear witness to the strangest of all desires? Where did traces of an explicit appetite for one's own death first appear on the stage of our culture? When and where do people begin to openly set off—and if not set off, then thoughtfully consider—the disadvantages of being born against the advantages of not-yet-or-no-longer-needing-to-live? I formulate so circuitously in order to keep in mind as best I can the leading question: what was Freud, in his dark metapsychology, the discoverer of, if he discovered anything at all? The purpose here cannot be to reel off a history of manifold misgivings about existence as they have unfolded since the days of Job and Buddha in the East as well as in the West. It would be all too captious an undertaking to trace the procession of noble and suspect life-deniers across three millennia, including all the hidden front men and sheer suicides.

In order not to have to become unduly epic in such a strange investigation, I want to fix our gaze on an exemplary incident, of which one could rightly say that it represents the primal scene of "occidental" philosophy. Of course, we are talking about [171] the legendary proceedings surrounding the death of Socrates, which, according to tradition, took place in the year 399 before the zero year of the Christian calendar. It is to be credited to Plato's poetic genius that European philosophy possesses, from the moment of its authentic origin, an image, or rather a scene, whose luminosity and proclamatory power rivals in every respect the Passion narratives of the Christian gospels. It can be said that the way of life of ancient philosophy is divided into two epochs—before and after the cup of hemlock—and that the heroic age of philosophical thought couldn't have broken forth prior to the death of Socrates. Only then does a new messianism of intelligence unfold and the inspiring gospel of truth seeking spread throughout the Mediterranean with newly won irresistibility. From the moment when the sage, increasingly paralyzed by poison, hides his head under a cloth in order to endure the convulsions of the last breaths without eyewitnesses, all at once the preconditions for a new kind of proclamation of the "truth" about the pursuit of wisdom are fulfilled. To go by the impression of the Platonic texts, at the sight of the Socratic mastery of death, the psyche of his greatest disciple ignites with a proclaimable conviction of far-reaching energy—one would have to call it apostolic, if the expression were not Christianly occupied. Only the testimony of this philosophical departure from the world gives the disciple the authority to establish himself as the master's successor. As confidant, witness, and proclaimer of the masterly death, the disciple Plato reserves [172] the right to found, under Socrates' name, a new, truth-seeking life-form.

On this view, the dialogues *Phaedo* and *Crito*, together with the *Apology*, comprise an eminent group not only in the Corpus Platonicum; they can be considered the initiatory texts of philosophy par excellence. What we call "truth" has taken on a new manifestation ever since that event in the Athenian prison cell 2,400 years ago. Since then, it authenticates itself in the power of the philosophizing subject to give a superior form to its own end. Nowhere does Socrates' daimonion betray itself more clearly than in the staging of his departure; in refusing to save himself despite the obvious misjudgment of his judges, he at last fully grows into the Delphic prophecy that had called him the wisest man of his time. Thus he creates the conditions for memories of him to become the New Testament of wisdom; his death pantomime makes possible the master-text of the disciple Plato. In his silent departure from the world stage lies the key to the worldwide promulgation of his doctrine. What ever since then has been called philosophy goes back to the latent message of the Socratic death scene and its explicit Platonic editorial. According to this, philosopher is whoever has tried so hard to increase his death force that he can take over his own end as an act of will. The idea of the wise man merges with the concept of the man who practices the cessation of life as art. Wherever something of the *ars moriendi* of the post-Socratic millennium could survive in memory into modern times, [173] the Socratic gospel according to Plato has remained active. At the center of it we find a disclosure, concealed by the philosopher's vita: there is a wisdom that has full authority to break with a life that cannot rightly be continued.

Is philosophy, then, essentially a euthanatology—a doctrine of beautiful and skillful and evidential death? If we could answer this question in the affirmative, even with reservations—and the case of Socrates suggests the affirmative—we would have fortified the hypothesis of the death-appetite with an outstanding example. In order to convince, however, we lack the most important piece. We would have it in our hands if for Socrates himself death had meant more than the opportunity to exhibit an extraordinary degree of manly courage and civic honor; conclusive alone would be statements by the master indicating that he felt not only pleasure in provocation but also a taste for the thought of death as such. And of just this the Platonic text offers the hyperexplicit example. If one may ascribe testimonial value to the twists of the *Phaedo*, then the name of Socrates would have to appear in the annals of psychology—as that of the man who discovered the metaphysical appetite for death and elevated it to a doctrine of the noblest risk for the highest good:

> I want to make my argument before you, my judges, as to why I think that a man who has truly spent his life in philosophy is probably right to be of good [174] cheer in the face of death and to be very hopeful that after death he will attain the greatest blessings yonder. I will try to tell you, Simmias and Cebes, how this may be so.
>
> I am afraid that other people do not realize that the one aim of those who practice philosophy in the proper manner is to practice for dying and death. Now if this is true, it would be strange indeed if they were eager for this all their lives and then resent it when what they have wanted and practiced for a long time comes upon them. (*Phaedo*, 63e–64a)[5]

Clearly, the philosopher proclaims death a positive condition of access to a way of being of higher insight. From then on, being dead stands for the most fascinating of the metaphysical ideas—it represents the phantasm of an intelligence that, as a pure, soulful being-for-itself, would be relieved from compulsory service to the body and to the world of sensations and cares. The discovery of a desirable being dead is tied to the emergence in the philosophical meditation and discussion processes of a clear and irresistible image of an acosmic inner sphere in which the soul would possess itself as pure life and unobstructed view of God-near ideas.

One has never paid sufficient attention to the fact that the roots of psychology are to be sought in an acosmology. The authoritative statements about what the soul actually is have since then been gathered along a *via negativa*, by thinking away and erasing sensual world-traces from the soul. Soul is being minus participation in the hindering cosmos.[6] [175] The Platonic doctrine of the desirable, beautiful death is thus based on a radical purification fantasy; this spells out the final consequences of the soul's desire for itself. Because no soul in the world can already be sufficiently itself, its desire to possess itself in complete purity must extend toward extreme matter- and cosmos-critical solutions. Half a millennium later, this move toward pneumatic extremism would break forth aggressively in the world-hostile gnoses of late antiquity and early Christianity. But great philosophical psychology was already from the start a wager on the expendability of the world. No argument can seem too forcible in lifting obstacles that stand in the way of the soul's love for its highest possibilities; this highest would be total immersion in the unperturbed, pain-, substance-, and world-free inner sphere of godliness. In it the soul celebrates its assignation with its primordial ground.

Plato's successes with posterity prove that he succeeded in digging a symbolic streambed for philosophical madness. Thanks to Plato, Europe possessed an epoch-spanning standard language for the soul's tendency to break away from the physical world. Until Nietzsche's intervention, Platonism represented the possibility of articulating the dream of the infinite life of the soul as a rational and noble appetite for death. [176] No less than the modern destruction of the idea of a self-subsistent soul was necessary before Nietzsche could express his devastating suspicion: that Socratism as a whole was an attack by the inhibited life against itself. Since then, a suspicion—which understands itself as an unmasking—of illness arises against all Platonizing metaphysics. Modern physiologism, whether psychoanalytically oriented or not, sets itself the task of healing the body of its possession by a soul that indulges in the hysterical conceit of being able to surpass it and survive without it. But in all attempts to interpret the physical, psychical, and spiritual existence of mankind in an exclusively naturalistic perspective, the embarrassment arises as to how the emergence of life-weary and extra-worldly tendencies can be derived from the life process itself. Freud's pseudobiological "death drive" is an ominous monument to this embarrassment. It is a reminder of the cost of thinking the soul, with its obscure, exuberant, and body-fleeing tendencies, as a bodily effect. No longer is the body (*soma*) a tomb (*sema*) for the soul, as in Plato's school, but rather the "soul," unable to distinguish itself from the body, manifests itself, when eavesdropped in its "ultimate truth," as nothing but a suicidal homesickness for peace in the inorganic. [177]

3. *Moriamur igitur*: Toward a critique of the soul's ultimate intentions

> Mors illi Venus est, sola est in morte voluptas.
> —Lactantius, *De ave phoenice*

The preceding reflections should have made this much clear: translating Freud's death-drive hypothesis investigation of articulated traces of conscious death-appetites brings us immediately into the center of classical metaphysics. Who expected to strike upon solid psychobiological laws instead finds himself in the midst of the beautiful risks of manic hopes for life after death. This change of subject from psychological biology to metaphysics has an instructive side; it makes clear what kind of effort is needed to speak in a modern scientific and secular language about possible terminal goals of the psyche—always assuming that such final ends or ultimate aims do not operate as arbitrarily acquired and learned tendencies but assert themselves as endogenous intention-tensions [*Zielspannungen*] born from the nature of the psychic itself. Accordingly, an experienced appetite for death is not likely to be just a symptom of fatigue; human avowals of a wish to end the world and life mustn't, if they are to fulfill the qualities Freud intended, emerge merely in consequence of the depletion of life-force and the ability to suffer.[7] For [178] the "death drive" to live up to its name, it would have to be based on an active endogenous end-intentionality of the psyche itself. Such an intentionality is difficult to establish at the biological level. The *bios* knows little of an end projected as an inner goal; as far as it is understood in the circumference of pure vitality, life, whether human, animal, or vegetable, as far as we can know, has no sense for ultimate ends. Even where living beings surrender to their end, there is little room for the imputation of death drives in the Freudian sense.

It is different with the phenomenon of the psychic itself, which is posited for itself. We have just indicated how Platonism documents the splitting off of an inner sphere from the bodily world. When I say "documented," I mean to indicate that Platonic thought also rides on an older and more powerful wave that leads to the formation of an inwardness that can be posited for itself. The enormous long-distance effects of Platonism spring not least from a demonism of explicitness; once articulated and conceptualized, the tendency to posit an autonomous inner being becomes generally copyable and capable of extreme augmentations in the copies. With the emergence of a language of the soul, animation itself starts to gallop; contrary to what the moderns think, it is psychology that first brings the psyche to flower.[8] [179] In this sphere-for-itself—to call it soul is actually too familiar or folkloric now—extreme sorts of intentions and intention-tensions can form. Within the sphere-for-itself, imaginary activities are launched, hasting toward perfect, ultimate, godly targets. In this sense, the psyche is nothing other than the organ of overhaste and perfectionism, or better, of perfectivism. Wherever the soul—this eschatological projector—is given room for its consummation thoughts, it settles more and more into a self-conscious remoteness from the world, even severance from the world, and subordinates all outside resistances to an intra-psychic logic of perfection. It does not strive for the end because it wants to die but wants to die if necessary in order to reach its target. Thus, the soul becomes the factory and theater of target setting and with typical recklessness goes all out in running ahead to the last, best, highest. If, therefore, one may speak at all of a death drive of the soul, it is only because the highest-strung subjects tend to fall victim to the confusability of goals and endings. The perfectivist death-appetite can thus be interpreted as the effect of a category mistake in eschatology; this results from the conflation of the real end and the imaginary consumption. It is one of the ironies of eschatology that finite minds can make mistakes right up to the last things. Maybe eschatology then would just be the science of final errors? As a doctrine of last things, it has from the beginning risked being the school of the last fallacies. [180]

Now a few words on Christology are in order, and I will be brief. From the point of view of religious studies, Jesus—a man who was possibly called Yeshua ben Pantera and to whom the Greeks, translating the Jewish title *Messiah*, gave the glorious name Christ, the salved—embodies the historical type of the savior; from the dogmatic point of view, Christ is not a titular epithet to the first name Jesus but a statement of essence about the man who ipso facto was and remains the savior. But what does the title mean? In the present context it suffices to summarize the subtleties of general soteriology in one sentence: saviors are mediators, gate openers, forders toward a good end. In the ecology of spirit, savior figures emerge when the members of evolutionarily more riskful cultures who have embarked on the adventure of the soul have gotten into mass existential and psychological crises. Such a crisis results when numerous individuals, in view of their certain death, are seized with restlessness as to whether their end will be good or evil. The crisis progresses to the extent that people evidently know or feel that they are living morally and physically worse than is right.[9] In this respect, the idea of redemption is itself the "shadow" of a world history of despair. The hair-raising, threatening Jesuanic speeches in Matthew 24, Mark 13, and Luke 21 bear witness to the rising tide of panic; [181] saviors deal, in themselves and in others, with people up to their necks in water. Here, nothing helps but the total mobilization of emergency consciousness. The star of salvation must always outshine a counter-truth that has empirical priority and whose quintessence is called despair. Its light must shine stronger than the prior profane evidence that men, insofar as they live in times of adversity, accumulate more and more reasons for despair; hell is just a mythical name for the real pain archive of individuals and peoples. Glad tidings, launched and authenticated by saviors, believe themselves able to counterevidently sublate the precipitation of worldly experiences in the psyche—and indeed in such a way that the saving light presents itself as ontologically earlier. Against the obvious and gruesomely coherent despair that sees everything running out to a bad end, religions of salvation would liberate a deep-eyesight, which sees something "totally different"; these other eyes are supposed to open—or reopen—themselves to the overwhelming evidence of our older and deeper reasons for salvation. "The" savior is the one who succeeds in uprooting me from my experience; he decouples me from my coherent despair. If I have a savior, then I have met a "god-man" or a "messenger" who confutes my realism and turns me on to a new approach to life; this would stand henceforth under a star that can no longer sink. In view of the savior, I would know of no other end for myself than a good one.

One may well say that the [182] orientation toward the good, the highest, the best ending, brought about by Greek metaphysics and the Christian religion of salvation, has grown over the course of two and a half thousand years into the *idée fixe* of Western or even monotheistic humankind as a whole. Western culture is the march forth from one termination project to another. For this epoch, the sentence *anima naturaliter eschatologica* almost becomes true. "Mankind," represented by its plenipotentiaries in the monotheistic West, forms itself into the enterprise of history insofar as its pilot groups have set out under the spell of overhaste toward the good end. For the authentically history-making faction of mankind, historicity means offensive happy-endism.[10] What we call "history" is initially nothing more than the projection of their psychofinalism into the time of political movements. Christianity as a historical religion draws a major part of its strength from the ability to mobilize in individuals and peoples the notion of being involved with matchless seriousness in dramas of consummation and ultimate battles; the life of the soul is thus always-already an endgame for a good ending in God—or in his substitutes.

Christian-type soteriology as mass movement, as state cult, as imperial, and as finally "world religion" implies a paradox that has its price. Black books of church history have tried to give an idea of the horrific costs of mass Christianization. The propagation of the Christian phenomenon has from the beginning manifested the explosive effects of perfectivistic impatience with all that is called world. [183] The monotheistic alloy of holiness and cruelty proves irresistibly superior to the loose formations of polytheistic soul culture. Undeniably, "after Christ," openly death-craving tendencies come more and more into view on the open stage—this finding speaks from most of the ancient third-party testimonies about the protagonists of the new religion.[11] It concerns not only the apostles and their successors in the arenas but also the founder of the movement himself. After the voluntary—some say even wanton—death of the young man who had dared to say, "I am it," an attitude flourishes that consciously accepts early death as the price of fulfillment. The early Christians are surrounded by a suspicious, even sinister atmosphere in which confessional courage is sometimes hard to distinguish from a lasciviousness toward death. For Suetonius, the Christians are psychopathic assassins against life—which seems to justify their shocking labeling as "enemies of the human race"; hence, he lists their execution among the good deeds of Emperor Nero. Indeed, not a few of the early Christian "death-heroes"[12]—as Hölderlin called the followers of the "death-lust" god Christ—could be said to have been in a strange hurry to die. In this respect, they too—together with their master [184]—come into question as discoverers and witnesses of the "death drive" under investigation here. But it is precisely in them that it becomes clear how Freud's misunderstanding of the drive missed the essence of psychoperfectivistic endeavors. An attraction to a mineral nirvana can play no role in the self-conscious appetite for the afterlife of these supposed returners to God. For them, the will to the end is a vital, albeit dangerously obsessive will to ascend to a state in which bliss and eternity would become one. Anyone who believes in a "resurrection" in this sense follows an idea of life that cannot be stopped in its ascent even by death. There is no room here for a regressive movement into indolence and eternal night. The finalism and perfectivism of the soul shows, however, what price had to be paid for the self-positing of the inside. There is an unmistakable tendency for the disinhibited interiors to regard "external things" as means or indifferences—a perennial motif of "dangerous thinking." But any psychologist who reacts directly to this with the imputation of a "death drive" betrays only that he underestimates the metaphysical peak tensions of the soul's desire for consummation—either because he doesn't find them in himself or, if he does, fights them as an unwelcome and dangerous tendency. Consequently, a psychological head of this type will translate the phenomena of psychotheological perfectivism down into the seemingly manageable [*überschaubaren*] "bioenergetic" relationships of drives, tensions, and discharges. It is worth considering further how this ambivalence could arise [185] in the interpretation of "homecoming" to the ultimate and highest. For the question remains open: how is it possible that secular psychologists understand as regression to minerals and mothers what for the metaphysical spirit promises the ascension to a father-shaped God?

One thing is certain: the great metaphysical and mystical thinkers of the Occidental tradition—insofar as they do not belong to the materialistic minority—leave no doubt that, for the spirit or soul of man, the way to the end is a way up. They consider lost any life that does not work to end itself on a climactic peak.[13] Under the pressure of their teachings the idea of perfection becomes so overpowering that beside it the worry about the end of life recedes. How far this can go is shown by the doctrines of metempsychosis; they conceive the final destination with such exaggeration that death becomes something incidental, through which the soul, always gazing forward and upward, has to pass repeatedly.

It is characteristic of perfectivism that death, even if there were only one, is conceived as something that belongs more to the can than to the must. This trait was noticeable already in Plato's proclamation of the wisdom of his teacher. The Christologists had to [186] exaggerate it to the extreme; the god-man, they say, can experience everything in the flesh, except necessity, which is completely alien to him. Thus, Anselm of Canterbury emphasizes that Christ took death upon himself absolutely voluntarily ("sponte mortuus"; *Cur Deus homo* 1.9) and according to his own ability ("moriatur ex sua potestate"; 2.11). Insofar as the divine nature was an a priori accomplished fact in Christ, for him dying was a pure ability. Because nothing could be added to his mode of being as *deus verus*, death for him meant a condescension to the necessities of animals and sinners. But to Christ's followers, inasmuch as they were invested in a radical *imitatio*, the god-man nature presented itself as a task still to be completed; for those who first had to verify themselves as "sons of the highest," it was a matter of continuously dying up toward perfection. No ladder could be too steep and no mortification too cruel for those who were serious about this self-project toward God. If you have the nerve for it, you can persuade yourself of this by means of monk-psychological literature, not least the treatise on the Ladder of Paradise penned by the greatest of all psychologists of torture and transfiguration: John Climacus. Not much is missing for one to be able to speak of the birth of the Christian concentration camp from the spirit of theurgy. Also the vita of the enlightened clubber Shenoute of Atripe, a Coptic abbot from the fifth century, belongs in the annals of consummation terror. The disciples of these early extremists were, according to Hugo Ball's fine expression, true "athletes of despair"; they threw themselves into God's detention cell so that in the race against death they would have done full penance before the physical end. [187] To this day, anyone who wants to know what Christian perfectivism was all about—long before psychoanalysis included perfectionism in its catalog of symptoms—can do no better than to study the phenomenon from its theological extremes and anachoretic escalations. These show how the Neoplatonic ladder and step model of theosis, or becoming-God, connects to the Christian scale of cleansing humiliations and self-annihilations. If Freud's "antithetical meaning of the primal word" ever had full meaning, it is here, where up and down become identical in a progressive terror of transfiguration. The passion for perfection in God is an affliction that fevers toward the outermost ability.

Up to the High Middle Ages, and far beyond, the mental and kinetic image of life on the ladder to the highest retains its power; Bonaventure (d. 1274) still interprets the world as a whole as a stairway ascending to God—*rerum universitas sit scala ad ascendum in Deum* (*Itinerarium mentis in Deum*, ch. I.2). Ascending the ladder is synonymous with *perfectio evangelica*. Here, however, moral and psychic perfectivism move into ontological and cosmological dimensions. For the general of the Franciscan Order, the soul's path to God is a seven-step path (1) from contemplation of God's traces in the physical world, (2) through reflection on the delight of perceiving things and the mystery of numbers, (3) to contemplation of the soul in itself as the natural *imago Dei*. From there (4) ignites a [188] Christological reflection on the soul as the organ for experiencing the gracious restoration of the image of god. Then (5) God is conceived in his first name, which becomes evident to us from above: Being. Of it, our intellect grasps that it is *simplicissimum*, *actualissimum*, and *perfectissimum*. After that, (6) the spirit climbs the step of insight into the second name of the Godhead, as far as this gives itself to be understood in the idea of the good. With that, the human mind has completed its hexaemeron. Yet above everything rises the step of the seventh day; (7) in it the activity of mind comes to a complete rest as the mind "goes over" [*hinübergeht*] to God without remainder. This transire provides the password to perfectivistic death; not for nothing does Bonaventure speak of an *excessus mentalis et mysticus*. The great transit (*transitus*; Itinerarium VII.2) leads the soul through the Red Sea, out of Egypt—and all matter and mothers are Egyptian in this regard—until it rests at last beside Christ in the tomb. With the sublimest extremism, Bonaventure finally divulges the grand formulas of all Christianized death-appetites: "Who loves this death is able to see God, for it is indubitably true: 'No man shall see me and live.' Let us therefore die and enter into the dark" (*Quam mortem qui diligit videre potest Deum, quia indubitanter verum est: Non videbit me homo et vivet (Ex. 33.20).—Moriamur igitur et ingrediamur in caliginem*"; *Itinerarium* VII.6). Knowing these extreme twists of soul-travel literature, who can doubt that death, as interpreted by monotheistic mysticism, is the origin and goal of the idea of progress and perfection? [189] Six hundred fifty years after Bonaventure's oath of disclosure, Freud's last insights still speak in a perfectivistic dialect, recognizable through all modernizations and phonetic changes; only that now, after the "death of God," the psyche seems to be condemned to desiring an end for the sake of the end. But don't we know by now that "death," in metaphysical as in post-metaphysical time, functions as a metaphor for completion and a formula for final destinations? Does not the secular soul too wish to someday be able to say, like Hercules at the end of his series of deeds against death and gravity, "It is finished"? For post-Christian souls, it will then be only one step from the *perfectum est* to the *perfectus sum*. Accomplishments are the ultimate adult secrets.

Despite these proofs of "progressive" soul-perfecting works, a persistent psychologist will not let himself be so easily talked out of his suspicion of regression vis-à-vis all efforts at elevation and ascension. In fact, this suspicion finds a strong basis in the fact that all self-perfecters, God seekers, and ascensionists—in Neoplatonism, in Christianity, in Islam, and in the Indian systems—characterize themselves as beings who have nothing else in mind than to return whence they came. According to classical teachings, completion and homecoming are only two names for one and the same thing. If so, this would fulfill the diagnosis of a "regression tendency"—except for a strange and highly dissonant detail, which deserves to be stressed; it is striking that the secular psychologists localize the point of homecoming in a rather spiritlessly interpreted below [*Unteren*] [190]—whereby for them all earlier stages of psychical and biological evolution come into consideration, from early childhood and fetal conditions down to the indolent peace of dead matter. In contrast, the metaphysicians and soul travelers to perfection derive themselves from an unspeakably high homeland; to reenter or return to it is a task that, according to them, could be mastered only by the accumulated forces of the most spiritual and most mature life. If it is not possible to resolve this contradiction between the psychological and metaphysical interpretation of the return, then one must declare all attempts at a theory of ultimate psychic motivations, whether they are called drives or goals, to have failed. But a final word on this remains to be spoken—and perhaps it will always be too early for such a word, as long as there are people who notice that "soul" means that which is not absorbed in the external.

4. Uterodicy as Teaching of Last Things

> The gods have not revealed everything to men from the beginning, but in the course of time they seek and find better things.
> —Xenophanes, *Fragment 31*

The diagnosis is now clear: the dispute over the death "drive" mirrors the extremes of the interpretation of who or what "really" is the womb out of which human subjects come. Without uterodicy, thoughts about the *conditio humana* remain flat—for [191] humans are the beings who come from within. Only a critique of wombs can give insight about what returning really means. Regarding this question, two basic positions must be distinguished. First, the womb is the tomb: whoever assumes this interprets the thought of a will to return into the originary chamber as a malign regression. If the equation of womb and tomb grounds considerations of the end goals of psychic life, one must expose the will to womb as a masked death wish; in general to envision or to eye at the womb as a goal would then mean accepting death as a project—a situation understandable as the matrix of perversion. Only on this line do the Freudian sentences about the death drive make sense; for as far as psychoanalysis remains a psychology of exodus, it must reject every tendency to return—into the tender mother and into comfortable Egypt—as a betrayal of the promises of world-openness. Thus, Thomas Mann rightfully calls the fascination about death to which artists and neurotics commit themselves in the bourgeois era a wantonness. Its protagonists succumb to the temptation to put what should lie behind consciousness as supporting pastness in front of itself as a goal and space of fascination. In contrast, psychoanalysis and philosophy of the Western type would have to define themselves as schools of defascination.[14]

Second, the womb is pre-existential perfection in God: whoever accepts this sentence immediately leaves the [192] zone in which the word womb implies psycho-matriarchal regression. Every advance in the effort for self-perfection, however extreme, circuitous, and outlandish, could then be interpreted as part of an ascent to the lost height. The thought of the father's womb, even if it thinks in backward steps, gives the idea of homecoming a potentially progressive meaning. If the light is the womb of all evolution—we can also say: if everything "originates" in the logos, from the pleroma, from the patromorphic fullness of spirit—then homesickness for it would perhaps be nothing but the cunning of a reason that can never be sufficiently in the clear [im Freien].

What is regression and what is progression can thus no longer be decided by psychological means alone. The suspicion of regression against all psychic life, left to its natural gradient, proves itself to be a cryptotheological figure of thought. It implies a critique of the tendencies of the soul that do not want to undergo the hardships of the long march into the future and instead dream of the death-comforts of Egypt. Womb-critique means critique of paganism; that in turn means critique of life in intoxication, obsession, and addiction. Moses and Freud present themselves as guides through the ego-building desert; they both try to escort their people or clients to a Canaan for grown-ups. Their refusal of soul-death in Egyptian comfort is a monotheistic, or more precisely a Deuteronomistic banishing spell against false gods: against incest-prone, pampering, narcoticizing wombs that keep the subject from moving through the Red Sea into the clear [ins Freie]. If something of Freud's metapsychological speculations should persist in the future, [193] then probably only in such a way that the developable aspects of the death drive-hypothesis, made impossible on the whole, are sublated into an uterodicy.

That the "critique of the womb" must become a fundamental discipline of philosophical psychology is also evident from the fact that classical metaphysics *and* modern psychology recognize the uterine *numinosum* as a radiator of the most powerful psychic magnetism. Wherever this magnetism is operative, the sentence applies: the wherefrom is the whereto. As a self-posited being-inside, the soul is nothing but the power to run in the largest possible circuit, which would be a circuit under the condition that no finite power can have already run through it completely. "God," then, is only a name for the circuit which the extremist yearning intends to run through. "I love him who desires the impossible?" Where do I want to go? To where I come from. Where do I come from? Out of a womb. Out of which womb?

Division of spirits—division of wombs. Now follow stories of gardens and gods, of seas and heavens; [194] so too there hover cities in the light and palaces under water—from there must be explained the dowries of innermost self-consciousness that glitter beneath everyday concerns. Womb becomes a thought-image that evokes the "god from beneath": from the goddess and the earth; later he turns into the uranic, when the godly is interpreted as distant from the earth and as ruling from above. Since the heavens became womb, they can anchor the just, as Catholics have learned to sing. From an intellectual-historical perspective, it makes good sense that it was theologians who illuminated the enigma of a being *in gremio* of fatherly nature with fantastic explicitness, even before psychoanalysts, gynecologists, and perinatalists entered the field to disenchant the matter. From a philosophical as well as a psychological perspective, "womb" is the ontic region that has the power to endow further beings of similar or "iconic" nature and to give the endowed, inspired, or spawned life the idea of bliss-bestowing highest good. The philosophical teachings of remembrance as well as the religious teachings of iconicity represent interpretations of this riddle of dowries.

From a psychological perspective, the wombly power of orientation can easily be understood as a zone and condition. Regardless of whether the *in gremio* is conceived psychologically as being-in-the-mother or imagined metaphysically as a pre-existence near God—in either case it is linked to the being-in-itself in the womb insofar as no traces of catastrophe intervene, to belief in the pre-objective hovering in the optimum. Hovering names a mode of selfhood that is given before the possibility of contact with anything. Hovering is dissolution in an ur-something that [195] mediates between formlessness and form. Who wishes to learn something about being-from-the-womb must, as it were, learn to speak the language of water—but even more the language of heaven, which has become the most alien to modern subjects of sobriety. *Le grand Bleu* is also a title for something that shines beyond all mothers and oceans. Uterodicy spells out the beatitude to which the fish and birds would testify if they could talk. These beatitudes, elusive as they may be, hover in human consciousnesses since ancient times as final fascinations. A language of hovering that valued both poles would have to sound like the confession of sea and sky.[15]

I claim that uranophatic and oceanophatic speeches can reveal the secrets of self-experience of the self-positing interior. Perhaps this must be expressed this bizarrely, for in both cases we are dealing with speeches that do not belong to everyday language. One who speaks urano- or oceanophatically speaks not *about* sea or sky, nor *of* both, but *from* the wet element and *from* the empyrean, and in fact in such a way that the power of the womb in which he is dissolved is not diminished by its protrusion and articulation. The Christological example [196] demonstrates this most clearly. Typologically speaking, Jesus is the original image of the subject that crosses out every belonging to a motherly womb. His sense of mission springs from the most extreme daring to legitimize himself entirely by the dowry of the ontological force of a fatherly, uranic womb. The radiance of the words of Jesus spread by the canonical gospels originate not least from the fact that they transmit the clearest uranophatic sentences of the preceding millennia. Their gnostic variations make this even clearer. They speak as though heaven could say "I." In Jesus' speeches, heaven is not the topic but the subject; the sentences of the god-man are substantially heavenly, heaven-soluble, heaven-housed "expressions." Even when they go out to profane ears, these sentences do not cease to testify to their womb's mode of being: psycho-uranic immensity; to it belongs the euphoria of authority. In more recent times, no one has captured this more deeply than Nietzsche; for not only did he rightly interpret the Jesuanic semantics of the "Father"—"the feeling of a general transfiguration of all things," "the feeling of eternity, of consummation"—he also, as a kind of twin and accomplice of heaven, produced the most sublime uranophatic text since late antiquity in the canto "Before Sunrise" from the third part of *Thus Spoke Zarathustra*.[16] He who is in heaven [197] knows what it means to speak from there. Inasmuch as heaven possesses womb-power, it also transfers its productivity to its offspring. From this masculine-toned womb-abundance consciousness, the logos-metaphysics of the Gospel of John can be comprehended in all its millennia-piercing suggestiveness. The certainty of the fatherly womb seems to be the energetic secret of those who are able to combine inner repose with a prophetic demeanor in the world; they are the authentic existentialists—individuals who understand being outside from deep inside.

Moving on to the oceanic side of womb hermeneutics, it is important to remember the motif of heavenly spaciousness while floating in and out of the womb. Without explicitly broadening the horizon to the heavenly, the return of the psychic to the maritime interior would have to immediately deteriorate into gynecological platitudes. Amniotic fluid games as a substitute for metaphysics?—psychoanalysts seem mostly satisfied with this. Perhaps no psychology is free from the temptation of confusing heaven and cavern. The evidences are suggestive, however. From an individual-biographical as well as a species-historical perspective, the archaic equation of mother's womb and ocean—*mater* and *mare*—is so well grounded that any further word on the topic would be superfluous, if the state of discussion were commonly known. From Thales to Ferenczi and Rank, all the most famous theorists of origination have everything emerge from the water; [198] they understand the oceanic element on the basis of its encompassing and sheltering as well as its springlike and productive features (I remark in passing that Heidegger's meditation on the *Ge-birge* analyzes the features of the motherly ocean in terms of the dry earthly element).

What is strange about the mode of being of water-born life-forms of the human type is that in their early history they had to suffer a more or less catastrophic transition from the wet to the dry and from water to air. In view of this transition the thesis can be maintained, that there can be no science of man without a theory of element-change. As far as humans are element-changers in their deep structure, their being-in-the-world contains an insurmountable ambiguity. Element-change—the basic form of drama—implies memory as the continuum in which links from the earlier to the later and back must be carried out. If on the way to land the maritime continuum is destroyed, element-pathological deformations develop in man—hybrids of all kinds, will-o'-the-wisps, water-spirits, air-dwellers, beings desiccated, shriveled, turned to stone. Perhaps all psychopathology must begin with an elemental pathology. Humans are beings that err elementally. Indeed, what appears to them as orientation in the world is often only the certainty of being in the wrong place, the wrong element. Thus, whereto?

The pull backward from the dry, solid-grounded to the oceanic-liquid mode of being is a basic motif of life's inexistential tendencies; one who seeks the ocean intends to inwardly sublate the external. [199] If we wanted to keep tracking down a psychic striving suspected of being a death "drive," we would do well to look more closely at this pull toward the inner sea, this tendency to retract existence into inexistence. To find representatives of this tendency, one need not seek in remote places; phenomena belonging to the forms of addiction have evolved *en masse* following the modern recession of explicit metaphysical perfectionism and have moved to the foreground of cultural stages. And as always, its purest forms are found at the extremes. It is the subscribers to hard drugs, lustful suicides, who exhibit most sharply the tendency to short-circuit their life cycle; instead of exodus tensions, they are interested in the shortest way to world-annihilation. There is a criminal side to their inexistentialism, insofar as they use the drug as the megabomb against their inner representations of all that is the case; addiction generates only collapsing world-relations—it follows a scorched-reality policy. From the subjects' point of view, attacks on everything that forces itself on them as reality are acts of self-defense.

This distinguishes the druggies from the mystics, with whom they are neighbors in all other things. Mystically gifted individuals do not feel the need to fight back reality as they perceive it; they feel grounded in themselves. Even under great stress they are as unresisting as "water amid water," to speak with Georges Bataille. They are so embedded in becoming that it does not [200] occur to them to change the course of things with wishes and avoidances. To that extent the thesis is correct, that mysticism is the most intense form of "realism." Mystics decompose the institution of reality to such a degree that nothing remains of the established world but an all-encompassing *fluidum* that, like film, possesses a wondrous homogeneous superficiality. Mysticism is the mode of being of the psyche in its fetal condition. In its tendencylessness, it is neither existential nor inexistential. Its condition is dark insofar as it knows nothing of any object or goal and bright insofar as it does not avoid its own clarity. He who is in it drowns in air and breathes underwater; what speaks from him is the ocean endowed with words. When he is silent, it is the sea that stays present without thesis. *O mort, où est ton appetit?*

5. Crito's Plea

With his death-drive hypothesis, the late Freud was engaged in a style of speculation that until then had remained, for better or worse, the domain of philosophers. At the same time, he touched on questions of salvation and healing that hitherto found responses more often in the teachings of leaders of men and founders of religions than among physicians. So it's no wonder that behind the psychologist the shadows of Socrates and Plato, of Jesus and

Bonaventure, are visible. It seems as if, given that it is a matter of first and last things, the great spirits remain among their own kind.

[201] But could it not be that, in searching for the discoverer of the death drive, we have been following a false lead up to now? Might it have been baseless prejudice to seek the phenomenon in its heroic, self-conscious, and explicit testimonies? Is it possible that the original discoverer of the psyche's terminal pull was someone who didn't understand the discovery himself? Perhaps in order to become the discoverer of the X in question, a subject can in no way feel affinity or familiarity with it. Is it a foregone conclusion that the death "drive" or appetite for one's own end is something that must be understood or felt? Might not astonishment and alienation be the only attitude in which the X can be discovered? In this case the discoverer of the death drive would be one who remains unmoved by the temptation of understanding.

My candidate is a figure who plays a semi-laughable, semi-poignant role in the Platonic account of the death of Socrates. Crito, Socrates' friend in the last hour, appears in Plato's report as a figure who stands in the center of the margin—the margin of the death-stage, as a privileged witness and helper, in the center of ridicule about his incorrigible childlike worldliness—a position as thankless as it is thought provoking. In a specific sense, it could be said that Crito, the worried friend who must endure the master's final pedantries and ironies, was the discoverer and provocateur of the "death drive" phenomenon. It's him in front of whom the X [202] confessed for the first time. His standing by at what he cannot grasp results in a self-representation of the Socratic death-indulgence without which we would know even less of the dark subject than is the case. Here I do not want to talk about the fatal short dialogue that Plato named after Crito; it offers the uneasy scenario of how a friend must bear with a friend who is talking him into the ground. The clues about Crito that should interest us here stem from the final chapter of the *Phaedo*, in which Plato narrated the death of Socrates with the highest expenditure of literary and metaphysical transfiguring artistry. Shortly before the conclusion of this sublimest dialogue, Crito appears as a reluctant observer of alienating tendencies—for a fleeting moment underestimated by the history of philosophy. For Crito is not only the old friend of Socrates and the disciple who has most persistently advised him to flee; he is also the one who took care of him in the most insistent or friendly—one could also say the naïvest—way in the hours before the cup of hemlock. In asking how one should bury him, Crito elicits Socrates' last humoristic retort: "so then I have talked in vain to this man," says the master, "for he still mistakes me for my corpse, which will soon be lounging here." A little later Socrates demands that the potion be mixed and delivered:

> Yet, said Crito, the sun is still upon the hill-tops, [203] and I know that many a one has taken the draught late, and after the announcement has been made to him, he has eaten and drunk, and enjoyed the society of his beloved; do not hurry—there is time enough.
>
> Socrates said: Yes, Crito, and they of whom you speak are right in so acting, for they think that they will be gainers by the delay; but I am right in not following their example, for I do not think that I should gain anything by drinking the poison a little later; I should only be ridiculous in my own eyes for sparing and saving a life which is already forfeit. Please then to do as I say, and not to refuse me.
>
> Crito made a sign to the slave who was standing by. And he went out, and having been absent for some time, returned with the jailer carrying the cup of poison. Socrates said: You, my good friend, who are experienced in these matters, shall give me directions how I am to proceed.

It is Crito's obscure glory to have not let himself become an accomplice in what begins to show itself in the death-keen Socrates. To the last moment he defends the non-beyond against the master's transitional tendency; only when, at last, he feels the superior power of that wherein Socrates will be proved right does he sink into a silence of which no one knows whether it was shameful, resigned, [204] or confused. I want to assume that, whatever its tone may have been, it was a silence that concealed a germ of dissent. For a man who still reminds a *moriturus* among men of the pleasures of love and food will in the last instance calmly accept everything but the abandonment of the good things of life; and this also not or especially not from a mouth who sees nothing good here any longer, and is in a hurry to put the full stop at the end of the story. Thus, one may presume that the discovery of the X remained hidden in a sentence that Crito kept to himself in consideration of his friend's rush to end things. He looks with the eyes of a worldling at that which wants to remain right until the end—at this formidable, energetic peace of mind, which can be employed as a collaborator in what brings about the end. Crito says nothing more—but he sees something that Socrates does not see; he feels the presence of a contrary principle that transcends him and his friend. Without further argument he faces a power that intends to shape life into a self-contained form—is it pride that wants to forestall an existence of dishonor and decrepitude? Is it an ambition to transform one's own life wholly into the statue on whose pedestal stands the Delphic predicate of "most wise"? Or does a breeze of what truth itself is—a *numinosum* that needs the state of emergency to become present—waft through Socrates' remaining right unto death? No doubt Crito gets a dark inkling of what it means to have a teacher before him—for what is a teacher but a man who [205] turns even his last breath into an argument and his last hour into a piece of evidence? The teacher of all teachers is giving his last lecture—that is what Crito cannot grasp that evening in the Athenian jailhouse—he, the bad student to the end. Crito becomes witness of how the extinguishing life transitions into a didactic beyond, into an infinite speech, where it becomes a legend that can no longer die. He who knows how to say only ordinary things experiences at the death of Socrates something of the power of another language. For what Socrates now intends to say challenges truth and death at the same time. Crito experiences that there is something in the world that is as strong as death and that speaks of transformation and transition. Muzzled by Socrates' and Plato's combined ironies, he has had to keep this experience to himself—a humiliated worldling among deep souls. He remains at the margin of the sublime scene as the sensual man among initiates who, like intimate friends of death, luxuriate in proofs of immortality [*Unsterblichkeitsbeweisen*]. Plato left poor Crito behind in the run-up to the manic mysteries while putting himself in the master-soul's ascent to heaven. Crito, who sees "only the external," feels obscurely the presence of the ungrasped—excluded as he is from the communion of the consenting. In this way he gets the unsought opportunity to notice, undazed by suction and sultriness, what others leave aside as inessential. Is it not time to speak of Crito the discoverer?

The *X* that appears to Crito's consciousness has no name, but it has an indicator—haste. "So don't rush, there's still time," Crito says to [206] the master at the critical moment; the master rejects the plea that he stay a little longer; instead, Socrates takes a minute to distinguish one last time his mode of being, that of the wise, from that of the profane and sensual. The existence of the master, it becomes clear, is pure time of teaching—time to talk, time to prove, time to clarify great things in the light of the ever-awake logos. Insofar as what is called life manifests itself in that which the living take time for, Socrates has time only for that which, for him, is life: teaching. But his teaching requires a proof that ceasing to be in the body is possible and necessary. What is ceaseless in him, the life that is a teaching, in this case must engage in the cessation of life for the sake of the teaching. Thus, the master's life culminates in the syllogism "the best life is teaching; I teach by dying; therefore, I live in accordance with the best if I die." This conclusion moves through Socrates' last hours like one of the flashes that are said to stem from the spirit; it motivates the haste that alienates the uncomprehending Crito. Crito sees well that he sees something; but he cannot know what he has in front of his eyes. For him, as for the others, it remains obscure why Socrates must teach, hasten, die.

Only after more than two thousand years, at a new turning point in the history of spirit, did the opportunity arise to strengthen Crito's standpoint against Plato's. In holding Platonizing metaphysics in suspicion of illness, Nietzsche also identified the archphilosopher Socrates as a pathological case. Whether he was right or wrong about that shall not be discussed here. I see Nietzsche's strength [207] in the fact that he freed Crito's intimated position from its world-childlike naïveté and built it up to a metaphysical perspective dignified in its own right. He argues as if wishing to give Crito's plea—"so do not rush, there is still some time"—the rank of a principle. He hears "life itself" speaking from Crito's mouth, just as from Socrates' mouth he thinks he hears a morbidity calling itself wisdom. For Nietzsche, life as such seems to be the epitome of Critonism; by its very nature it raises a never-ending demand for time for the good things of the world, and cunningly seeks abridgements of the evils. This is what deep midnight knows in Zarathustra's roundelay. So what suffering is can be understood only from its tendency to cessation, pleasure only from its will to duration. Wherever a whiff of the will to cease comes into play, there, according to Nietzsche, would be reason to suspect a source of illness; where, in contrast, the prolongation of the game can be desired, there the lines of success of the good life lead into the serialization called eternity. Life is the dream that can wish for continuation, and it is the wishing power itself that knows how to look for ever-new ways into abiding and continuing. The opposite of the dream is not awakening, but death. Thus Nietzsche can express his agreement with it,

that among all these dreamers, I, too, who "know," am dancing my dance; that the knower is a means for prolonging the earthly dance and thus belongs to the masters of ceremony of existence [208]; and that the sublime consistency and interrelatedness of all knowledge perhaps is and will be the highest means to preserve the universality of dreaming and the mutual comprehension of all dreamers and thus also *the continuation of the dream*. (*The Gay Science* §54)

Continuation of the dream here means continuation of world and life. The time in which this life wants to live eternally is not the dead eternity of metaphysics but the infinite line of serial self-affirmations of life through countless turns of pain to pleasure. For Nietzsche, the seriousness of life consists in the continuous test of the power to affirm. Those hasting toward the end lose this self-invigoration of life, which produces its own eternity. The prolonging form of time that produces its own future *usque ad infinitum* then turns into the short-cutting form of time. Short-cutters are people who are in a hurry. They would like to have finally finished with the bad that is present and the worst that is to come. Who could deny that short-cutters and tailgaters have managed to organize themselves as the most effective psychopolitical *pressure group*[17] for the past two thousand years?

Why do you seek good days here on earth where they are not to be found? What do you want? Perhaps that years and years will come, and that the end of these years will not? Your striving is absurd; you want to wander, but you do not want to arrive! (Augustine, *Sermon* 108)

[209] Nietzsche's metaphysics of the self-affirmation of pleasure is formulated in direct opposition to the official apparatuses of life-weariness—theology and church—even in the microstructure of his argumentation. Thereby he discovers, with a rage that resembles despair, that in the Christian speed-pilgrims and the ideologues of passing beyond, suffering itself became inspired—as if woe had discovered a trick whereby it no longer had to say, "Stop, cease," but rather, "Wait a while, I will be back soon, I just need a break before continuing the misery." For Nietzsche, Christianity was the ingenious psychopolitical invention necessary to make misery reach old age. Where Christian miserabilism came to power, there began essential, history-making history, and where the same took root, a subtle perversion of pleasure into pain asserted itself until woe could no longer say go and pleasure could no longer say stay. Historicity, in the sense of the Christian pursuit of ending, is therefore based on the confusion of the temporal meaning of pleasure and pain; it produces the exodus into the world of mixed feelings that for us is part of being an adult. What shall now last; what

shall cease? This Christianity is the metaphysics of rhythmically-challenged life. The manic overhaste of the unhappy prevails over the pulse of the old nature. When Nietzsche absolutized Crito's "Don't rush, there is still time" and understood life as the time that pleasure gives itself, he outlined a post-Christian age in which the neurotic historicity of the previous type would be overcome. World-time "after history" would be a time without the primacy of haste and without the surplus of human pains [210] of yesterday. What model of world and time would today be more relevant and simultaneously vain than this one?

Even after Nietzsche's intervention, the X that Crito had in front of his eyes remains enigmatic. Death "drive"—a variety of impatience? Or rather the afterglow of individuals' and peoples' old pain, which defers its wish for cessation in order to take revenge on everything? Perhaps a positive theory of haste could deter the suspected death "drive" of individuals like Socrates of Jesus at the last minute? Have we already sufficiently conceptualized the haste of the great teachers by tracing it back to the "woe implores: go"? Doesn't the X in the philosopher's haste to die also point to the fact that certain overbright people already grasped thousands of years ago the vocation of confronting their fellow humans as guardians, teachers, and alarm-sounders, of clarifying to them the new kind of seriousness concerning the search for truth in the self-disbanding world? As teachers, they live as if they perceived a fundamental right to unsettle their still narrow-minded contemporaries; they radiate the evidence that in the future men will have too much to see for there to be time to lose. They do not accept that their contemporaries just want to live as before and not much better, much brighter, much more open to the drama of collective prudence. Figures like Socrates and Jesus embody the avant-garde of a species intelligence that doesn't settle for the self-destructive half-prudence of most.

What Crito experiences in Socrates' haste is the seriousness of a doctrine that answers to the coercion to learn in just a few years what [211] must be known in order for souls and communities not to meet a bad end. Philosophy as a simultaneous study of politics and of the soul only exists since singular individuals have developed a sense of how hard it is to be prudent in the increasingly dynamic world at large. Since Socrates, philosophy has been a search for wisdom as the art of steering souls and states through the storm in spite of surging risks. It is a school of awakening on a planet increasingly sunken in anesthesia—an obstetrics for the prudence that is equipped to deal with life on a larger scale. Such prudence is not megalomanic as the recklessness that meddles in everything, but megalopathic as the responsibility that keeps itself ready for long cosmopolitan workdays. This pedagogy for existence in enormous worlds is serious because it must determine, in the briefness of time, what is necessary for cities and empires: hence the antinarcotic choice of the serious doctrines.

How serious this urge to learn how to live had to become in finite time was shown not least in the historical compromise between Greek philosophy and Christianity. The function of revelation religion in semi-enlightened great societies can be interpreted not least as a means of acceleration; faith in the truths of revelation was, in the past two millennia, the organ of a reasonable overhaste that was supposed to help searching souls orient themselves already toward what they couldn't yet possess by their own insight. Faith gave countless people the courage to accept from the great teachers that for which the light of their own intelligence wasn't yet sufficiently bright.

[212] Perhaps one must live shortly before the year 2000 after Christ to understand, without any esotericism and metaphysics, the connection between time scarcity and learning about life and death. Do not animal species and forests die today as if they wanted to say something thereby? Though not willingly, they die too early. Their "teaching" too seeks insightful interpreters. It is still unclear what conclusions those who remain should draw from the premature death of teachers and other living beings. In the age of globalization, the remaining time of the human world becomes ever scarcer; a study of life-forms for the interior and exterior affairs of the planetary complex becomes ever more urgent. What gives us pause for thought today is not an ominous death drive innate to life itself; what alarms us is the urgent seriousness of the adventure of intelligence through the species as a whole.

5

Is the world negatable? On Indian spirit and Occidental gnosis

> The absence of pain means the presence of world. The presence of pain means the absence of world. By way of these equations, pain becomes power.
> —Elaine Scarry, *The Body in Pain*

It is one of the confidences of the philosophical profession that where ultimate knowledge is spoken of in positive tones, madness is often not far off. In the draw toward the greatest thoughts of metaphysics and in the pull of the psychiatrically relevant ego-death, the same magnetism, the same attraction of an extraordinary and eccentric pole is assumed to be at work. The well-known kinship of mysticism and madness reminds us that height and depth are equivalents in psychic space and that the thrust upward is hard to distinguish from the pull downward.

On the way to its present state, professionally conducted philosophy has withdrawn more and more from this magnetic pole of high-deep "problems"—for reasons that, I concede, it itself must consider good ones; for a long time it has been behaving as if direct reference to the so-called absolute were no longer appropriate for Protestant, bourgeois, reality-calibrated people. [214] For them, the monsters of enthusiasm belong to the past. In the end, all that remained of the mystical ungrounds were psychiatric grimaces. After its last manic culmination in German idealism, the ancient doctrine of worldly and godly wisdom seems to have finally disciplined itself pragmatically—it has turned into a historicizing and systematizing research enterprise that has dismissed truth seeking like an infantile disorder of mankind. Wherever research has become an institution, the climate is determined by the stoic maturity postulated by Max Weber; manias have been reduced to the format of ambitions; the pull upward no longer means transcendence but success through maximum performance. To the extent that modern thought places itself under the sign of method and science, it has learned to turn off its exuberant, manic engine; it is now more interested in transparency and self-control than in the melting of thinkers into ineffable final unities. Nothing is more important to cool-headed intellectuality than dissociating from the danger of great thoughts; where the latter still venture out today, they seem archaic, their thinkers naïve.

On its long and circuitous passage into sobriety, modern philosophizing benefits from a historically unprecedented process: the transformation of metaphysics into metapsychology and depth psychology, which has been underway for about two hundred years. These young disciplines cast a lateral glance, as it were, at the play of philosophical reflection and ask for the psychological diagnosis [215] of those subjects who still sign up as volunteers for metaphysics. Philosophers in the old sense have become even rarer than genuine hysterics. The modern world at large has defeated smallpox and metaphysics. Only in exceptional cases does an author become notable as a patient of great ideas. Nothing characterizes the current situation of metaphysical thought better than the diagnosis that the contagious effect of classical sentences has been largely eliminated among intellectual populations; it seems that collective immune systems are now almost completely resistant to metaphysics.[1]

There are strong intellectual-historical and civilizational reasons for this general recession of metaphysical consciousness, of which only the decisive one is to be mentioned here. With the emergence of depth-psychological ways of thinking, interested parties have at their disposal a second tongue in which to rearticulate the passion of being-in-the-world whose initial high-cultural formulation took shape as metaphysics and religious thought. In this second tongue—sharpened especially by Nietzsche—an aggressive resistance to the entire Platonic and "ontotheological" complex takes place. In it, some analysts today speak bluntly of the pathologies of metaphysical thought and of the malignity of philosophical thought processes, which not infrequently systematically derange their subject. Novalis' remark, as brilliant as it is dangerous: [216] "The authentic philosophical act is suicide; this is the real beginning of all philosophy, this is where all aspirations of the philosophical apostle lead, and this act alone meets every condition and characteristic of the transcendent act. Further elaboration of this highly interesting thought"—may make clear how the *furor metaphysicus* recently knocked once more at the doors of modernity. Quite obviously, this iridescent sentence is still formulated entirely in the first, the metaphysical tongue—the "further elaboration" of the aphorism, however, the early deceased author owed to posterity. I am convinced that a proper elaboration of the thought would have been possible in any case only in the second tongue, which explores psychogenetically, on anti- and post-metaphysical paths, the connection between the sickness of living and the sickness of thinking. The pathophilosophical fragments of Novalis prove that he, for his part, was already underway to modernity. The resolute speakers of the second, let us say psychoanalytic and anthropological, language will one day claim to have illuminated the connection between truth and successful life more deeply than the ailing metaphysicians from Parmenides to Schopenhauer could have dreamed of. What in the first language claimed to be truth itself, the second revalues as a true symptom of the false, inhibited, injured life.

In these sensitive transitional processes, the Orientalist disciplines of the West play both an important and a strange role. They enjoy the privilege of being able to handle with official documents [217] the still-hot manic tradition—the term *manic* being understood here in line with Plato's doctrine of mania in the *Phaedrus*. It is true that the working climate of academic Indology, Sinology, and Orientalism is as cool as one expects of philologically oriented disciplines, but the most important materials of these studies themselves by no means belong only to obsolete cultures and extinct cults. For a cross-check, it suffices to take a sidelong glance at our Latinists and Hellenists, who keep alive the aghast memory of dead gods in the midst of a world that has other concerns. On the other hand, whoever has encountered Indian sadhus or Vedantists, whoever has been exposed to the teachings of a Sufi master or Tibetan lama, will know that at the end of the twentieth century, in some centers of the world, doctrines and practices live on which plunge their clients into incandescent metaphysics. There are still schools—partly concealed, partly public—of the great teachings that attempt to lay hold of the subject as a whole in order to uproot it from its previous life—hardly different from the Pythagorean, Neoplatonic, and Gnostic schools of our own hemisphere during their most self-confident times. At their peak, the Western metaphysical teachings too were not "theory" in the modern sense but, at least according to their own self-understanding, disciplines of the true life under the guidance of a new striving to true speech. In the old *bios theoretikos*, it was not texts and propositional systems that centered the endeavors; what mobilized all forces was far rather the prospect of a transformation of the thinker himself in the light of [218] the equation of truth and the goodness of life. Whoever considers the knowledge of such possibilities—apart from hasty psychologizing—to be an existential and intellectual privilege, can only be jealous of his Indological and Sinological colleagues. In them, metaphysical enthusiasm found a serious refuge after its exodus from Western academia. Orientalists are at least philological confidantes of the extinguished metaphysical élan of foreign cultures; they function, whether they like it or not, as vicars of enlightenments that have been consummated in faraway parts of the world and, if one believes the testimony of the adepts, haven't ceased to be consummated. They are the bookkeepers of ecstasies of which extraordinary individuals in Syria, Persia, India, China, and Japan left textual traces—traces that confront us, for the most part, as documents of the alien. Löwith's ironic remark about Heidegger as a "thinker in destitute times" is even more valid with regard to the scientific trustees of the East. For even if as employees of Western universities and research institutes they practice a rather prosaic profession, this doesn't change the fact that for them the theorem about non-duality is part of everyday philological life; they can casually cite the thesis that nescience, *avidya*, is the stuff of which reality is made. They handle the "great sayings" of the East by profession, just as trusty bank employees go back and forth with gold bars in the security cellars under Zurich's Bahnhofstrasse. Unlike their colleagues from the faculty of philosophy, the Orientalists are hardly obliged to supersede the old sentences in the history of ideas. [219] For Eastern systems it is hard to see the need for modernization. They breathe the spirit of a timelessness that seems to be exempt from being perceived as medieval. In the West, not even Catholic heads enjoy such an exemption. Instead, non-Orientalist non-metaphysics of our latitudes see themselves sentenced for a hundred years to explain the state of the world by means of sociology, systemics, semiotics, and psychoanalytic theories of psychosis—and the more successful they are, the sadder their science becomes.

In the following, I wish to try to partake a little in the privileges of an acute metaphysically oriented orientalism. I attempt to sketch in a few pages a bilingual explanation of the metaphysical embarrassment that, so it seems to us, first revealed itself in its abyssal character to Indian and Mediterranean peoples. Thousands of years ago this embarrassment manifested itself in the royal therapeutics of the Vedanta and old Buddhism—similar to the monisms and mysticisms of the old West. I would like, however, to insist that the *difficulté d'être* is articulated in a completely new way under modern conditions, namely, in the anti-metaphysical effort to master reality technically and psychoanalytically. The bilingual character of the following essay—metaphysically interested and at the same time psychologically oriented—proves that the struggle for [220] reality stays open to reality—especially in a phase of Western culture in which our pride about the superior sobriety of our definition of reality proves more and more to be unsubstantiated.

1. Fingertip thoughts

I begin my investigation with a dualistic thesis, the perspective of which belongs to historical anthropology and the tonality of which belongs to the second tongue: relatively recently—that is, more than three thousand or at most four thousand years ago— "the human" became the metaphysical or metacosmic life-form due to a development whereby he experienced himself as the animal that does not fit in. The element of old metaphysics—put modernly, its nutritive solution, its lifeworld—is a flood wave of existential dissonance that swells up heavily in historical time. Metaphysics—especially in Egypt, India, Persia, and Greece—is the language of a new engagement vis a vis the ever more powerful breaking and disorganizing aspect of life. The world hurts—there must be reasons for this; as soon as one knows them, one is able to sing it into order. Ever since states have existed, humans have had in view novel forms of collapse and qualities of fragility. The former is no longer the good old Paleolithic death; the latter are no longer the great rhythms of natural coming and going. Looking at the cultures of the axial age, one is forced to postulate a deep structural transformation in the experience of negativity. In the high cultures of the Near East, India and the [221] eastern Mediterranean, one can perceive a radical revolution of the old conception of life and death, motion and rest, transience and permanence, that hasn't been completed to the present day. For the first time, a reaction against world and life emerges in the world-age of the state, of writing, of majesties, of fatherly laws and of master narratives; it articulates itself in the metaphysical or metacosmic revolution of consciousness. Metaphysics of this type is an ecstatic and ascetic revolt against banality, everyday violence, chronic suffering, frightful dissonance; the great systems are music therapies for the cosmos and its awakened inhabitants. But both ecstasy and ascesis as medium and goal of metaphysical work on the self would be impossible without the increased gaping of the original discord between the individual and the surrounding world, which, we have just claimed, stands at the beginning of the high-cultural self-discovery of mankind as the *animal metaphysicum*.

Metaphysical asceticism is basically only the conscious working out of this discorrelation. It amplifies the rift between the individual and his former life and increasingly draws him into a realm in which he becomes for himself the entirely other, the actual, that which truly is. This most actual otherness is the ecstasy to which all metaphysics of East and West lead before their decadence and decline from ascesis to chatter [*Gerede*] as to their sole cause. In ecstasy they have their foundational peak. Truth, therefore, does not appear so much in sentences and their concatenations; *a fortiori* it is not merely a property of utterances; no one finds their way to it [222] by following sentence rows "to the end," however well connected they are. Truth in the sense of classical unity-metaphysics is much more the result of an ascetic mutation of the subject who searches for it. It appears as the fusion experience that takes the thinker "to itself" at the end of a series of exercises. Her evidence is more epiphanic than argumentative, her brightness falls rather onto the thinker himself than onto some "mundane" matter of fact.

Thus, at the beginning of the rise of metaphysical disciplines there is an ascetic revolt against triviality and a secession of the newly-illuminated from old collective opinion. What high-cultural metaphysics is and wants is better characterized by a monastic-mystical need than by the will for knowledge. Therefore, the break-in of monkish and ascetic ideals into the motivational economy of high cultures is a major soul- and idea-historical event that we will learn to appreciate only if we experiment with untimely ways of thinking and feeling. Modern thought has no understanding of its metaphysical prehistory anymore, because it itself stemmed from laical, anti-monastic and anti-ascetic impulses. It is hard to understand how ascetic techniques could once have carried the whole weight of that anti-trivial revolution by which the first metaphysicians ejected themselves from their environments and their own former lives. The profound codependency of metaphysics and asceticism determines the tenor of metaphysics as the first language of world-passion. This is a singular invitation to the work on the state in [223] which seekers become worthy of the self-evidence of the absolute.

One must, however, pass into the second, modern language of existential interpretation to disclose what it *means* that becoming worthy of the *apex theoriae*, the "apex of contemplation," is almost always tied to the precondition of leading a life diametrically opposed to the ordinary. Every aspirant is required to relate in spirit to a sphere totally unlike the ordinary world. From now on, part of the essence of truth is that it does *not* appear to worldlings. That is why metaphysics, as a breakthrough to the "deep structure," always requires a renunciation of life, accompanied by a renunciation of the world. Its dignity, its persuasive power, its aura of secrecy, accrue from this excessive ability to renounce. Its magic is the ability to reverse the portents of nature; metaphysics can negate what everyday thinking affirms and affirm what it negates.[2] Did not Empedocles define the world as "the unknown country in which death and rage and countless other evils dwell"? Could not Plato say, with Euripides, that this life is only death, whereas death opens access to the true life? For these grand masters of reversal, we men of the world, we once born, we lovers of the body, are nothing other than corpses buried in these bodies. Our ill-advised affection for the transient disqualifies us for the new seeing in the eternal light. Where these reversals form milieus, there emerge force fields in which a darker consensus against the superficial, [224] the illusory, the generally agreeable comes to power—herein the Western tradition proceeds from the Pythagoreans, who saw through the world to its numerical ground, to the Adorno disciples, who detected in all that is the case the demonic judgment of the capitalist principle of identity.

Against the violence of metaphysically driven reversal, critical cosmophilic thought must one day, however late, defend itself. In the second language, the proud metaphysical talk of world-renunciation is translated into the expression escapism [*Weltflucht*]—in the sense of desertion from reality, evasion of the facts of life, vulnerability to the temptations of the so-called death drive. Since Nietzsche, we have become used to holding all Platonizing metaphysics under suspicion of escapism—this later becomes a psychoanalytic suspicion of defense—a suspicion that occasionally sharpens into the diagnosis of insane denial of reality. Whoever thinks metaphysically is also already—in the sense of the second language—in need of metaphysics. Only inverted life can have an interest in seeking in thought the power to reverse all natural signs [*Vorzeichen*].

Of course, it remains to be considered whether we, as speakers of this second tongue, know what we are saying when we speak of metaphysics as symptom. What does "having a need for metaphysics" mean from an anthropological and psychoanalytic perspective? What does it mean except that we are sure of the possibility of deriving thought from biological conditions? What gives us this certainty, though? Above, we have indicated how the birth of the *animal metaphysicum* resulted two or three millennia ago from a real-historical schism [225]—an increasing gaping of the discord between individual and world, and a crescendo of existential dissonance.[3] These base truths of historical anthropology translate the first theorem of Buddhism into cultural-historical diction. All life is suffering—*sarvam dukha*—this is a sentence that, when spoken with the full seriousness of the first language, definitively articulated an entire sense of the world, a synopsis of the injured life and the impatience of the desire for liberation. In the second language, we measure the seriousness of the situation precisely when we attribute the dark sentence itself to a world situation in which it could have been uttered with surrounding evidence. From a spiritual- and idea-historical perspective, the *sarvam dukha*, "all is suffering," is the equivalent of a disaster declaration. From it follows that everything that is to be said about the world, life, and being, must bring about the decision to disable the world, life, and being through salutary negations. Thus the metaphysical priority of the No and the motivational primacy of the idea of redemption are established for the first time. Life in "reality" appears from then on as the totality of errors due for a clearing-up [*Aufklärung*]. Reality is henceforth the epitome of that in which inner and outer have come apart. As soon as there appears an outside that is different from the undamaged inside, there is for the metaphysician no more happiness and no more truth to be found out there. [226]

Perhaps it is no coincidence that it was one of the completers of Western metaphysics, Hegel, who with his phrase "unhappy consciousness" created the formula with which modernity could begin its revolt against the metaphysically fixed split between true and real life. Only for the partisans of this revolt, that is, for the carriers of an essential modernity, does it make sense to engage in the development of a second language for the interpretation of being-in-the-world. All truth of the second language flows from the fundamental engagement against the acknowledgment and perpetuation of unhappy consciousness. Therefore, the thought of the modern age must stand by the immodest thesis that it understands the unhappy consciousness better—and cures it more successfully—than the latter understands and cures itself. Such an avowal presupposes that we distrust the exuberant sentences of the ancient sages about their ineffable ultimate beatitude—even that we reject beatitude itself and, in a symptomatological attitude, keep it away from us like an inverted disease state. The risk of this turn is undoubtedly high—might we not thereby gamble away the highest good from the outset? The anti-metaphysical democratic hedonism of modern times wagers that its work for average happiness is superior to the pursuit of excessive enlightenments. In turn, enlightenment-free modernity commits itself to producing enough happiness to justify existence without transfiguration. Who could deny that here the titanic battle over the interpretation of "truth" shines through the everydayness of modern cultural studies? [227]

After all, one of the advantages of the second language is that, in it, certain points of the first can be brought out more clearly than in the first itself. This is especially true when it comes to understanding the irruption of negations into early metaphysical thinking. These great negations, without which the first revolt against triviality would have remained logically destitute, imply a gesture that is one of the most inconspicuous and at the same time most significant things humans do with speech. They point with their finger at the noted object—in the literal as well as metaphorical sense—and thus indicate that they are talking about something physically and temporally present. Classical metaphysics entails—I would like to say *always* entails—such an imperceptible and consequential act of pointing. This gesture is accompanied by a glance which, with wonder, surprise and horror, becomes aware of existing in the great circle of things. Precisely because a world-distancing ascesis has already radicalized the subject; precisely because a rage against its own body has already largely delivered it from the metabolic compulsions of physical and social life; precisely because a stubborn yearning for liberation has already carried the soul of the ascetic up into high zones of interiority and worldless purity—precisely for that reason are individuals of early metaphysical epochs able to set the world over and against themselves and reflect upon it, even while they also exist within it. This being-over-and-against, this transcendental distance and advantage over all that is the case, is already assumed as soon as the first metaphysical speech act takes place. It is above all those who have gone missing from the world who begin to define [228] what the world is as a whole. To be able to specify the world in its basic features, one must have already experienced the possibility of negating it—or perhaps we should say, of losing it or distancing oneself from it. Whoever speaks of the world as a whole is returning to it out of the artificial nighttime of meditation, or rediscovering its obstinate appearance and endurance following the soul's voyage to heaven. It is always still there—this balloon of beingness in general, this massif of sensual appearances, this ball of Being, which contains and is all things. Thus, the great world-predications of metaphysics, all the sublime fundamental sayings, all the sentences that start with "The world is all that . . ." or "All life is. . . ," are accompanied by an imperceptible wave of the hand, a subtle *mudra,* a finger that points with highest delicacy and utmost gravity to the world, as if the speaker were facing it like a distance mountain range, a mysterious constellation, a fatal archive. In this gesture, ascesis becomes theory, contemplation becomes a speech act. Its grammatical traces are demonstrative pronouns in the absolute application: "this is," *tat, tode ti*; "this world," "this life," "this body." Which reminds us that metaphysics, even before it becomes narratological or eschatological, is primarily deictic, ostensive, demonstrative, indicating the block of the world and pointing up at its transcendence. The god of philosophers incarnates himself in the fingertip that points to the impossible whole named "world," as if it were something present before us; at once fatal and imperceptible, this gesture evokes the panel painting of totality, comprising figure and ground in one. [229] What the pointer knows is in any case the direction in which he has to point: that is what's actually "there." At that which is "there," one may point: as at a "world-region," a region called world. Raphael's *The School of Athens* illustrated such a sublime finger pointer in the divine Plato, who, with the *Timaeus* in one hand, advances through the center of the hall; the thinker lifts his free hand toward the sky and points with his finger at all that is the case "up there." His point is the uranic world, of which "our" world represents a clouded downward projection. Plato's fingertip moves quasi-critically from below to above, from here to there—like the gesture of a man who was undoubtedly "there" himself at some time or another, albeit now he has rejoined us here below in the half-dark region of mortals—presumably to execute the office of transition assistance.

The Raphaelian reference represents a rather harmless case of idea-heavenly romanticism—a breath of metacosmic nostalgia envelops Plato's gesture. Not so with the darker successors of this philosophical psychocosmonaut. The finger-pointing of many later gnostics—all the way up to Heidegger—distinguishes itself from that of the Raphaelian Plato through the radical risk taken by those who point to the world from the opposite direction. With demonstrative pronouns and thin fingers they point directly to our world, to "this" given and present world, as if they had pulled off the ecstatic stunt of completely dislocating themselves and remaining in "this world" only in appearance or errantly-provisionally. [230] Classical examples of such ecstasies, pointing to the world with the finger, are offered by certain great aphorisms from the Gospel of John—in the first place the enabling word of the Christian age which read: "In the world (this world) you are anxious/fearful, but I have overcome the world (this world)" (16.33). From then on, the factual world is dismissed like a demonic past and distanced like the sum of all revocable errors. Also in Philo of Alexandria we find formulations like this, that according to our intelligible soul we are strangers in "this world," who sojourn in it like migrants in a foreign city (*peregrini*) until they have fulfilled their measure of lifetime and wander back to their great Wherefrom. Such words displace the speaker and localize him in a zone that Wittgenstein in the *Tractatus* called the "border of the world." From the border one can point to the land, the continent of being as if to a strange land, a distant continent. By pointing, the pointer actualizes his *borderline* nature. The metaphysician is not a patriot of being; he may have settled down quite well "here"—or as the Christians say "down here"; still he must admit that he, in Fichte's formulation, "no longer has any heart at all for the transitory," winged as he is by candidacy for citizenship beyond the border.

The Indian counterpart to the gnostic-tinted demonstrative acts of John and Philo is the *tat tvam asi* from the *Chandogya Upanishad*, which, in its conspicuous abundance, corresponds like a negative to the Western fingers indicating the visible, all too visible:

"Bring me a fruit from the fig-tree."—"Here it is, sir."—"Split it."—"I've split it, sir."—"What do you see inside?"—"Very tiny seeds, sir."—"Split one of them, my dear!"—"Sir, I've split it, sir."—"What do you see inside?"—"Nothing at all, sir.". . . "Believe me, my dear: What this tininess is, that is the Self of the universe. That is the Truth. That is the (individual) Self. That thou art, Śhvetaketu."

The absolute indication that emerges from the most significant of the Vedic "great words" (*mahavakya*) aims not at the developed totality of the world, not at the mountain range of things and laws in their positive presence and their phenomenal recalcitrance, but rather at a seminal nothingness, which in its nonappearance shelters all world-seeds and world-grounds. The Brahmanic genius interprets the whole world with a finger pointing to a nonappearance. The All, the existent, is expounded from the vanishing, from the nothing. The speaker, of course, could not have uttered his mystical *tat*, his "that" or "this here," if he lacked the grounds to assert that he himself speaks out of this nothingness, as one pervaded by it, as its brain and its voice. In breaking the original muteness of this nothingness, the speaker repeats the swelling of Brahman, who flows from nothingness into being as a stream of self-realizations. The indication of the simultaneously seminal and uterine ur-nothingness presupposes that the thinker is finished with the phenomenal world [232] and has experienced its downgoing into the final nothingness, which brings about death with open eyes, the entry into nonduality, *nirvikalpa-samadhi*. The enlightened Brahman's finger points to the second nothingness, in which the world has perished and continues to perish, through the world to the first nothingness from which the world arose and continues to arise.

That pointing to the world is simultaneously the basic gesture of metaphysics *and* of what transcends it is shown by Heidegger's attempt to locate his new beginning of thought in the inceptual space where the opening of the "world there" is considered as such. For that something is there: in this we experience, before any conceptual coding, the touch of the foundational enigma. Even before the finger is lifted to indicate the whole, it has dawned on the more contemplative thinking that it is displaced into the adventurous heart of a context that philosophers and profane alike call "world." Heidegger's beginning with existence as "being-there" ("Dasein") aims to juxtapose the conspicuousness of the world in general with its specificity, its knownness, its familiarity. For the analyst of Dasein, thinking means pointing to the world as all that of which it is conspicuous that it is the case. In this way, pointing gains a primacy over touching and grasping that is both alienating and inspiring for theoreticians as well as practitioners. Even the organ of the practice, the human hand, is placed by Heidegger into the service of wonder, in that it does not manipulate and grasp the known and unknown, but only points to the luminous enigma as a whole.

With these remarks, fleeting as they must remain here, we have reached the point at which our introductory reflections can be broken off. We have touched on the center of metaphysical magic—on our part indicating rather than carrying out—and for a few moments have joined voices with the first language of the interpretation of world- and selfhood; this happened in a citing or best reciting manner, yet in such a way that the thesis became clear: everything depends on meeting the old thoughts in the innermost circumference of their strength. One must have at least faintly surmised wherein lay the irresistibility of the great metaphysical formulas felt over thousands of years by countless individuals, the basis of their logical power, their psychagogic spell, their sublime terror. Only then does the task of doing justice to the truth and untruth of these formulas in the second language become apparent. In the following I shall try to draw a few lines of a preliminary sketch of a great project: to sublate the metaphysical "life-form" into postmetaphysical life games—following insight into its ascetic, ecstatic, apocalyptic and suicidal dimensions.

2. "In this life." Critical theory of birth

If Spinoza's proposition that every determination (*determinatio*) is a negation (*negatio*) applies also on the level of the greatest or the all-encompassing, which is called world, then determining the world means at the same time saying what it is not. If the world is everything that is the case, then I must be able to indicate that from which everything differs and against which the whole stands out. [234] No world-determination without world-negation. As a rule, metaphysical finger-pointing goes together with speech acts that possess the character of world-determinations, of cosmodicies or ontologies. The gestural deixis, the pointing to all that is the case, corresponds to a logical agglomeration of the universe into one sentence, or better, a gathering of all particles into one circumference, into one continuum, into one togetherness. By virtue of such world-determining gatherings, the word world can become a token of philosophical, political and religious language games. These seem to permit talking with a knowing attitude about *what* the world is as such, in essence, in principle and at ground. In such determining speeches, the existing world becomes the figure on a ground of non-being, the appearance on a ground of non-appearance. Even more, it becomes—to say it more correctly—the "figure as such" on a "ground as such," the "originated as such" from an "origin as such." One could plainly define metaphysics in its discursive part as the play of thought with totality as figure.[4] Such thinking expresses in positive, distinct strokes what all that is, is all about—whereby the definite article is immediately added to "all that is": "the all," in which the demonstrative pronoun, the world-determining and world-negating index finger is already waiting. I say totality or world [235] or universe, and already my imagining mind draws the largest, the "all" encompassing circle on the blackboard of consciousness; I think "the all," and already know at least two things, namely that it is *not* its parts and is *not* nothingness, insofar as the parts ought to be contained in the all and insofar as nothingness provides the thematic (as in India) or unthematic (as in Greece) ground of the whole [*des Ganzen*]. As long as we remain in the non-ecstatic sphere of representation, the duality of figure and ground cannot be eliminated. The world to which I point and the world that I determine are imagined worlds in the literal sense, worlds before eyes, before me in representational space, total gatherings and general assemblies of beings in the single, homogeneous, coherent, sharp-edged, and utterly abstract image.

Is that terribly boring? I admit, these considerations seem to lead away from the task formulated above. It is not evident how to felicitously rework the initial metaphysical fingertip-thoughts from an anthropological and depth-psychological point of view. But I maintain: it suffices to rotate the subject a little to see how a field opens up in which metaphysics and psychoanalysis will speak bilingually and with a high degree of univocity about "the same." "The same" appears in two fundamentally different projections which nevertheless can no longer be separated without endangering the continuum of human learning processes. This "same," which can be expressed only multilingually, shows itself when one observes how humans of different cultures [236] and ages relate the metaphysical question of the whence, the from-what and the whither, to themselves, to their own lives, and, in modern terms, "confront" themselves with the fact of their being born, with all its consequences. From the question concerning one's own being-born emerges the at first astonishing coincidence of metaphysics and psychoanalysis, of originary meditations and autobiography, of ontological contemplation and self-exploration—although it would perhaps be more appropriate to speak of cooperation instead of coincidence. Both disciplines function as schools of memory; both take up arms against pathogenic forgetfulness; both confront passionate resistances to deep recollection. Both move along the thread of self-attention into ever more elemental layers of the half-forgotten. Both wield the axiom that the "real self" loses nothing forever.

I maintain that metaphysical finger-pointing at all that is the case and psychoanalytic listening to that which speaks itself in me amount to the same thing—provided we now properly understand all that is the case as all that is there and conceive that which speaks itself in us as the trace of the trouble of coming-to-the-world. Psychoanalysis listens to the inhibited world-language within me, while metaphysics points uninhibitedly to "all that there" in which Dasein is immersed.

The individual's getting caught in the flood, their immersion in the coming experience, their exodus into all that will befall them, is colloquially called being born. There would be nothing more to say about this if we, as born anti-metaphysicians and [237] anti-psychoanalysands, took the stance that there is nothing more to know about it. We live, indeed, in a world dominated by the illusion that being born is a triviality that can be left to itself in the deepest implicitness, the mutest self-evidence, until the day of the opposite, which has always been thought about more deeply. Indeed, since the beginnings of polis-metaphysics humans have been called mortals—and during the Christian age, an urgent memento mori hangs over every human life. Thus, it seems that for the majority of the tradition the thesis holds true: death means thinking. Does the concept of spirit not point to something that comes to us from the dead and their dominion? If one goes even further back than the metaphysics of the realm of the dead, it becomes clear that in truth it is birth that is "called" thinking. Hitherto metaphysical discourses of birth served to divert attention from consideration of the deadly implications of one's own being born; instead, they pointed pathetically to a mode of being or a condition in which birth, as the beginning of the movement toward death, would be rescinded. Births are whims of the absolute, which whiles away eternity with the infinite comedy of individuations. But individuation in the strictest sense—the result of passage through the birth canal—is regretted, doubted and devalued by metaphysical thought to the point of mystical negation of every semblance of isolation, separation, difference. Thus one must speak of a forgetfulness of birth[5] in high-cultural and imperial metaphysics—[238] they want to fundamentally revise the formation of the self in the perinatal canal and do not shy away from theses that to profane ears must seem like excesses of denialist intensity, not to mention madness. Every Indologist hears the Vedic hymns in which the unborn, deathless, formless, blissful-omnipotent ground of the world says "I" and celebrates itself in the mouth of the Brahmanic reciters. Every Orientalist knows the languages of manic jubilation in which never-born souls celebrate their freedom from all that is heavy world.

The specifically psychoanalytic engagement in these questions begins where the metaphysical talk of births, and the jubilatory denial thereof, fall silent. Only then can the autobiographical enigma unfold, that the memory of one's own birth always-already appears to us as an "impossibility." The word *memory* is not unambiguous here, since the place where such a memory could appear displays nothing to the subject but a comprehensive I-know-not. This not-knowing is of an intimate kind: it is my darkness, the darkness that makes me possible. Only I myself come into question as the owner of this not knowing, this not remembering; only I live in the core shadow of this traceless forgetting, only I benefit from the expulsion from my symbolic memory of my departure into the outside. Only I can feel as though I had entered my own life only later, and learned to recognize myself as myself through subsequent training. [239] My non-remembrance of my birth is—much more than the Heideggerian running ahead into one's own death—my existential signature. I know, by not remembering it at all, that I stand in the shadow of an unknowing that belongs only to me; I know that I do not know what leads to me like one who was there. If I feel comfortable in my skin, then perhaps this not-knowing is to be read as an assertion: my well-being indicates that on my way to myself, nothing happened that constituted a reason for me to remember it. The personal forgetfulness of birth in the vast majority of people would then be nothing more than a trace of their relatively lucky beginning; inability to remember would simply mean: not having anything to remember; our forgetting would be the white page of the life- and world-chronicle. Having nothing, nothing yet, to remember would mean having experienced nothing, nothing yet, that is insurmountably awful.

Whether something awful stands at the beginning or not: birth-amnesia is always to be understood as the metaphysical signature of human existence. Indeed, forgetting the event, even and especially if it was as traumatic as hell, protects the front border of one's own life from the dangers of awareness. This is a non-trivial fact in the highest degree. Since we do not have the beginning of our world-time, i.e. neither conception nor birth, stored in our memory-reservoir, at our egoic and willful disposal, we are protected from having to see ourselves from the outside as beings that pass through a relatively defined timespan and disappear. If we had been witnesses of our own birth, then—overwhelmed by the [240] unforgettableness of the event—from second to second we would have the feeling of being in the world as in a cell on death row. Only because our memory is dark toward the rear, only because we have appeared virtually out of nothingness can we, in spite of the narrow passage and vague guesses about the finitude of the remaining time, experience normal seconds, which is to say moments that are not measured and so flow like a living stream. Non-memory is the dowry of a fairy who wipes from our forehead like a meaningless nightmare the original event: the departure into the world in which clocks run down, and the imprint of the trace of death. Without the help of amnesia, we would immediately be metaphysicians on our own behalf; we would have to point to our life and continuously utter the fatal demonstrative: "this life." If forgetfulness of the initial caesura does not help maintain the original levity, my life becomes "this life," this piece of panicky finitude, this laborious melancholic and greedy processing of life-contents in time. Who could deny that this corresponds to the existential mood of the severest mental disorders?

Now it becomes clear why a broadly conceived psychoanalysis—or better, a historical anthropology—can occasionally understand metaphysics better than metaphysics itself. For one of the most characteristic features of the revolt by the spirit—as shown—is the fatal dictum "this life." Hardly any metaphysician had omitted this finger-pointing of the living to itself as mortal. One says "this life" insofar as it is possible and necessary to decisively determine life as measured, self-contained, [241] hopelessly finite existence in time, and to place it as such upon a background that reveals it as a figure of miniature wholeness. When I say "this life" and mean thereby the content of my lifetime, I point with the metaphysical index finger to the microcosmos that I am. I speak of myself as if I already no longer belonged to myself. Just as the metaphysician's indicative clause "this world" in a certain sense excludes him from the same, so too my pointing to "this life" takes me out of my existence; that is micro-metaphysics in action. In humor and in cynicism it happens that I drop "this life" completely into "this world"—I take myself as restlessly finite and incorrigibly empirical and reveal myself as a special case of all that is the case.[6]

Through the indexing of my case [*Fall*], the world becomes the content of case histories; every thinking self holds a hearing of its case; self-psychology, understood thus, is only possible as metaphysical casuistry. However, one who recognizes or senses "this life" as limited and lost in advance can no longer be absorbed in the rush of life like the unmarked world-children who are immortal thanks to their forgetfulness of limitation. Those who are metaphysically marked must set out to discover another immortality—an immortality more heavenly, more unborn than that of ordinary mortals who are not overly concerned about life and death. Metaphysics as conquest of deathlessness by those marked by death inaugurates the adventure of radical negativity increase.

[242] I would now like briefly to suggest how Indian thought and the gnosticism of late-antique Mediterranean cultures have their common foundation in the act of demonstrating "this world"—if it isn't too odd to speak of a gesture as a foundation. At the core of both worlds we find a casuistic metaphysics which lays out the existence of "this life" in "this world" in the frame of an absolute case history [*Fallgeschichte*]. Only because metaphysics is casuistry both in India and in gnosticism are Indian and gnostic thought able to link self- and world-consciousness in the deepest way; for both, each individual life can mean a theater of god or an eye of the absolute. Insofar as it is a world-eye, spark of light, pneuma, purusha (witness-self) or Atman, each subject can achieve a panoramic view of its own coming-to-the-world and being-in-the-world—be it as god-immanent catastrophe or as metaphysical dance-theater of cruelty. But here as there, even in enlightenment the ultimate reason for the fall into "this world," "this life," remains obscure. In

every case, what steps into the light is the that and the how of the fall into individuality, or rather the punctual spinning-onward of the karmic thread. In view of this glaring consciousness of each single life as a case history of the absolute, casuistic metaphysics deserve to be recognized as the first critical theories of birth. Whoever makes a sufficiently radical account of an individual's coming-to-the-world reaches the point at which the case history is to be referred to as the history of being. [243]

3. Toward a hermeneutics of getting-into. On Indian and gnostic doctrines of entanglement and liberation

Our fingertip-ontology now leads to the critical point: with the finger pointing at the world, the emergency case of being-in-the-world has occurred. How do I myself come to be a case of conscious life in the midst of all that is the case? Out of the abundance of cases, one has led to me—the *casus* doesn't only make me laugh. Now casuistic metaphysics is also narrative metaphysics—and theory of drama. What it deals with is the universal case history of which biographies are particular copies; narrative metaphysics, as casuistic, produces necessarily grand birth-narrations for ontological and soteriological purposes; it says wherein the truth- or untruth-value of "this world" consists; it says, furthermore, how it was I who turned up in this world; and it says, finally, how this case of having gotten into the world can be dissolved. Since narrative metaphysics doesn't tell fairy tales but wants to present real cases [*Kasus*]—histories of Dasein's emergency case—the closures of the case histories are unsecured. In all eschatologies qua doctrines of the end of history, the happy ending remains to the final moment more a promise than a matter of fact, more a guiding image than a saving possession; the menacing possibility that everything comes to a standstill in a final image of horror is just as powerful as the urge to design the end as the absolute peak. [244] Thus a theory of right cessation is essential to narrative metaphysics. In right cessation lies the idea of a good negation of the world. Of course, from a logical point of view the world can neither be thought away nor negated, since it always remains the premise of all exercises of negation and thinking-away; but from the perspective of a casuistic metaphysics, a total negation becomes possible if the world-case is terminable simultaneous with the final annulment of my own case. The world then becomes all that is dispensed with by one who has reached the end of their own case. In this sense, the key religious and metaphysical ideas of the Indian as well as the gnostic tradition: *moksha*, liberation, *theosis*, return to the pleroma, can be understood as metaphors for an amicable end of the world.

Thought in terms of the second language, of course, the wisdoms of casuistic metaphysics too remain subject to a principled suspicion of escapism. Even if no masterful subjectivity is erected, as in the *Gestell-* and substance-metaphysics criticized by Heidegger, the gnostic and Indian histories of falls into the absolute still have an edifying sense—and it will forever be difficult to prove that they are not formulated within the cyclone of manic reality-denial. No doubt the world-traversals of casuistic and nomadic metaphysics are in many respects superior to the world-fixations of empirical settlement-metaphysics; but even a thinking that understands the world from the event of our passing through it and not from a stock of principles is [245] obviously metaphysically motivated to the core—and wants to be.

To grasp the advantages of casuistic interpretations of being, one must perceive in the Indian and gnostic case histories of the absolute more than just their mythological facades. The gnostic stories about the fall of the first man into the dark depth, the Brahmanic and Buddhistic tales of the transmigration of souls, appear hopelessly naïve only to a superficial hearing. On the contrary, they use the narrative means of their time to conquer the space of problems from which modern subjects cannot remove themselves without betraying themselves—by flight into anesthetized life or into machine-thinking. In this space of problems, the living wakefully and skeptically look back upon the birth-giving, the procreative, the life-bearing powers. Such sights remain effortlessly open to modern thought—and psychology as the therapeutic historicizing of one's own life must, if it reaches deep enough, lead as inexorably into the center of this space as the ancient meditation which understood "this life" as the consequence of natal heavenly or karmic premises. When it comes to unfolding a true language for the embarrassment of being-in-the-world, modern depth-psychological idioms and traditional casuistic metaphysics are equally suitable and/or equally unsuitable. As hermeneutics of getting into worlds of suffering, they offer two variants of birth theory. Both are critical insofar as the remembrance of the event always serves the purpose of radically revising its meaning. If our life is obscure, [246] it is always also because we have taken from the event that led to it a fundamental distortion, an impulse to errancy, into failure, into misjudgment. The hermeneutics of having-gotten-into becomes—beyond metaphysics and non-metaphysics—the basic task of all thought that works through the consequences of a not entirely felicitous, perhaps even inevitably flawed having-been-born.[7] The problem-space of which we are speaking turns out to be as great as the evidence of the equation of birth and failed birth. In order to conceive it, we would have to revolutionize our field of vision and gain the expansiveness of sight according to which all casuistic metaphysics, all salvation religions, and all (non-mechanistic) psychotherapies are nothing but answers to the same postnatal discomforts. A theory of birth is a critical one if it brightens the obscure and obscured side of the event. Only in a casuistic metaphysics could the thought gain strength that the world as a whole is something properly met by negation and renunciation. The hermeneutics of being-born-into imply that the titanic battle over the meaning of being is directly linked to the revision of the meaning of being-born. Birth-consciousness peaks in a general critique of wombs. Why are they still fertile; what crawls out of them so persistently; wherein consists the secret of the great reproduction? What keeps the wheel of reincarnation turning? Why can't we remain in the pleroma and persevere in prenatality? Why does something happen at all and not nothing?

An early document of the consciousness of the inevitability of such questions, coming from our own cultural circle, appears in the Valentinian formula of baptism, which sketches the complete program of gnosis as a hermeneutics of having-gotten-into; Clement of Alexandria translated the text of the formula as follows in his excerpts from the writings of the gnostic theologian Theodotus:

Thus, until the baptism they say that fate is in effect, thereafter the astrologers no longer speak truth. Not only the bad liberates us, but the gnosis as well: Who were we? What have we become? Wherein have we been thrown? What are we hasting toward? From what are we liberated? What is birth? What is rebirth?

The couplets of images "before baptism" and "after baptism," birth and rebirth, "thrown" and "liberated," draw a schematic picture of existence as world-traversing movement ahead downward and back upward. *Katabasis* and *anabasis, kathodos* and *anodos,* fall and rise, hell ride into the foreign dominated by forgetfulness and heavenly ascent into the remembered home: these are the ontokinetic universals of the gnostic type of casuistic metaphysics. With the double movement of *descensus* into the world and *ascensus* out of it is tied to a radical conversion of the meaning of truth. So long as the fall from the hyperheaven through the spheres of planet-demons down to "this world" continues and no reversal can be expected, the astrologers speak truth insofar as the fates of individuals can be derived from the demonic radiations and fatal dowries [248] of the world-rulers. On the way down, the soul has become charged with the properties of the traversed spheres; no wonder, then, that they, upon reaching the ground of this earth, surrounded by equally evil-burdened and self-forgetful co-exiles, become the plaything of astral charges. After the demonization of the seventh heaven—the characteristic reinterpretation of height by gnostic acosmism—the soul in *descensus* must receive an abrasion from the spheres that contain the preconditions for all misfortune. In this dark astrology it is understood that the planetary spirits have nothing but vices to give to the falling passersby—different than in the bright or at least ambivalent astrologers in which the planets fix the parameters of each individual life in the form of impediments *and* alleviations, vices *and* virtues, inhibitions *and* blessings. For the gnosis, the stars are exclusively the ministers of evil. From Saturn the soul took on its sad dullness, from Mars its irascibility, from Venus its voluptuous desires, from Mercury its greed for riches, from Jupiter its imperiousness. But if the gnostic revolution has occurred, then the astrologers can no longer speak the truth, because the preconditions for the astral corruption of the soul no longer apply. With the ascent back into the hyperuranic abundance, the soul as homecoming, has relinquished all acquired properties. Consequently, one has to imagine the gnosis in its ritual part as a comprehensive exercise in the restitution of properties. The hermetic tractus *Poimandres* ("the shepherd of men") provides a clear model for the sublation [249] of the power of destiny, which is individually consummated through gnosis, through memory, through ascension and world-expropriation. Thus, another type of truth is put into effect, a truth that refers only to the *soul without properties*. For it, the truth of the ascension yields a world-revolutionary meaning:

The adept speaks: "You have taught me all that I wanted, Nous; but tell me yet how the ascension occurs." To this Poimandres replies: "First, in dissolving the body, you give over the body to transformation, and the figure that you had disappears, and you give over the character to the demon as inoperative.... And he then goes up through the spheres, to the first circle he gives the capacity for waxing or waning, to the second the evil assaults, the cunning, inoperable, to the third the fraud of lust, inoperable, to the fourth the ostentation of command, now useless, to the fifth the godless audacity and the overhaste of insolence, to the sixth the evil drive for riches, inoperable, and to the seventh the lurking lie. And then, stripped of all effects of the spheres, he comes into the nature of eightness by his own power and praises the Father in company with those who are there ... Then they go in order up to the Father, transform into forces, and as forces they will be in God. That is the good end of those who have received knowledge, to become God."

The heavenly journey of the soul—centerpiece of gnostic individual-eschatology—closes the hermeneutic circle [250] that was set in motion by the question concerning the conditions of one's own birth-fall. Because the ascent is only the reverse image of the descent, the interpretation of getting-into in this case history of the absolute depends on the truth about the total movement being articulated from a standpoint beyond the errant life. From this ground the gnosis drills out divine messengers, mouthpieces of the absolute, which make an evangelic breach in the world of the lower, self-sufficient realisms. Through this breach, buoyant souls can escape in the future. In buoyancy, potential gnostics recognize their light ancestry. Actually the gnostic world-doctors or logotherapists are nothing but metaphysical flight-helpers for people from yonder, for cosmic wall-jumpers. Of course these therapies are successful only when they manage to satisfy their patients with the "good end" in God, so much that they are no longer motivated to ask why the passage through the cosmic loop was necessary.

While the individuations of souls in gnosticism present themselves almost without exception as case histories of light, the figures of "this life" in ancient Indian literature are often case histories of fire; indeed, "this world" itself is only the epitome of all that is a "fall" of fire:

> 5.4.1. Truly, Gautama, this world is a fire. Its firewood is the sun; its smoke the sun's rays; its flame the day; its coals the moon; its sparks the stars.
>
> 2. Into this fire the celestials pour their faith [251] as sacrificial offering. From this libation arises King Soma (the drink of the gods).
>
> 5.5.1. Truly, Gautama, the thundershower is a fire. Its firewood is the forest; its smoke the clouds; its flame the shivering lightning; its coals the falling lightning; its sparks the hail.
>
> 2. Into this fire the celestials pour King Soma as sacrificial

offering. From this libation arises the monsoon rain.

5.6.1. Truly, Gautama, the earth is a fire. Its firewood is the year; its smoke, space; its flame the night; its coals the cardinal points; its sparks the half-cardinal points.

2. Into this fire the celestials pour the monsoon rain as sacrificial offering. From this libation arises nutrition.

5.7.1. Truly, Gautama, man is a fire. His firewood is language, his smoke breath, his frame the tongue, his coals the eye, his sparks the ear.

2. Into this fire the celestials pour nutrition as sacrificial offering. From this libation arises the sperm.

5.8.1. Truly, Gautama, woman is a fire. Her firewood is the womb; her smoke her inviting speech; her flame the vulva; her coals what man inserts; her sparks pleasure.

2. Into this fire the celestials pour the semen as sacrificial offering. From this libation arises the embryo.

5.9.1. ... After this embryo, enveloped by the egg-skin, has lain inside for ten months—or as long as always –, he is born [252]

2. After he is born, he lives as long as his lifetime lasts. Then, when he dies, is dismissed from here, he is taken to the fire from which he came, from which he tends to arise. (*Chandogya Upanishad*, 5.4.1–5.9.2)

The sacramental cycle from the fire through the series of forms up to man and back into the fire seems to sovereignly ignore the question concerning the meaning of the soul's getting-into the world. For Brahmanic sacramentalism there is still no "problem" of existence. The world is a wheel that turns in the continual metamorphosis of fire (for other traditions, water is considered the basic material and identity-principle of all arisings); man is welded to his revolutions without difference. Only with the semen's choice of womb is a moral factor mixed into the morally indifferent turning; by virtue of the general causality of reprisal, of *karma,* the semen of those who have virtuously returned to the fire find in the new rotation a favorable womb. Insofar as all life is contained in the metamorphoses of Brahmanic fire, a hermeneutic of getting-in cannot yet really come into question; souls are not to be thought as enterings but only as always already moved in the cycle. Nevertheless, the inequality of individual fates raises the question of rightness or justice in the entry of the semen into the womb. These questions are answered by the karma-formula; everyone gets into what they deserve:

Those who live in a pleasant way—for them there is hope of landing in a pleasant [253] womb: the womb (the woman) of a Brahman, or the womb of a kṣatriya (prince), of the womb of a vaiśya (merchant, farmer).—But those who live in an evil-smelling way—for them there is hope of landing in an evil-smelling womb: the womb of a dog, or the womb of a boar, or the womb of an untouchable. (*Chandogya Upanishad*, 5.10.7–8)

Thus the choice of womb becomes a martial-law tribunal of souls about themselves. Each of them gives to itself exactly that life that it is able to, in accordance with its degree of perfection. But above this cruel and sublime spectacle of the long march through the wombs levitates the Brahmanic motto for salvation or liberation, *moksha*. It is bound up with the hope that at last there will be a womb that is the final one. Who after countless lives in progressive transfiguration would know to choose such a one, would never return; "adorned with Brahmanic adornment, recognizing the Brahman," the non-returner "enters into the Brahman" (*Kausitaki Upanishad*, 1.4). In the negation of return, the negation of world and life as a whole already casts its shadow over the jubilant positivism of old Indian mysticism.

How it became possible for negation to grow into a worldly power reveals itself in India since the fifth century BC with the advent of Buddhism. In it, the critique of wombs passes into a radical stage. Buddhism intensified the awareness of the calamity of having-gotten-into to the limits [254] of bearability—this is its intellectual-historical signature. Its hermeneutic of births pushes forward to the point that the break with the womb principle becomes due. Here the renunciation of women's wombs—in the first place, that of one's own mother—is generalized to the renunciation of the suffering-producing rotation of the world-wheel as such. The Buddhist teaching is nothing other than the gospel of the evitability of wombs. Herewith it also executes the dark tendencies of the *Upanishads*. The motif of liberation becomes powerful to such a degree that even the strongest proofs of Brahmanic philosophy—such as the deep identity of Atman and Brahman—are swept away like irritating accessories. Here Brahmanism, as doctrine of the fertility of the absolute, meets its most implacable opponent. In the concepts of Brahman and Atman the Buddhist analyses still smell the principles of ensnarement. The Brahmanic metaphysic appears from the perspective of the radical will to liberation, as an enormous system of indolence; the Brahmans themselves, even where they submit to ascesis, are sheer collaborators of reincarnation. What they take as Atman is only a final mask of the womb-principle, that is, a form of attachment that leads to rebirth. Since Buddhism has studied everything that fosters tendencies toward wombs with crushing vigilance, it possesses the most profoundly elaborated hermeneutic of having-gotten-into. For it, it is evident that there exists no compelling reason why "this life" should not be the last; but if "this life" is potentially my last, then every womb could potentially be a final one. In place of the long march through the chain of rebirths, [255] the possibility looms of sealing that womb, from which one's own life came, behind oneself as the final one; what Buddha starts to spread like a gospel is the news of the discovery of a shortcut to liberation.

The key to this lies in the complete penetration of the process that conditions the revolutions of *samsara*. As in gnosis, so too in Buddhist liberation doctrine, the precise understanding of having-gotten-into is immediately significant for healing. Precision can be claimed by any understanding that knows how to go through the entire causal sequence that leads to birth seamlessly and with perfect explicitness. This is precisely what is accomplished in the doctrine of the causal nexus, the *paticcasamuppada*, which strings the entire emergence of suffering on a twelve-linked chain of tightly coupled conditions. Between the ur-link of nescience, *avijja*, and the ultimate link of sufferings, *dukka*—which encompasses age, death, pain, lamentation, suffering, sorrow, and despair—the ten mutually conditioning intermediate links follow each other in indissoluble compulsory consecution. From nescience emerge the figurative impulses of the will; from the impulses of will, cognition; from cognition emerges name and figure (*namarupa*), that is, the real world of appearance and the worldly personality; from name and figure emerge the six domains, the senses and thought; from the six domains emerge haptics; from haptics, the emotions; from the emotions, greed and thirst; from and thirst emerge grasping; from grasping, becoming; from becoming, birth; from birth, the entire drove of sufferings, death and the endless continuation of the process.

[256] In this chain, three links are especially conspicuous insofar as they represent the strategic points for the intervention of the great therapeutics. In the first place, the beginning itself, nescience, deserves the highest attention; if the first condition of the entire sequence were to be suspended in its emergence, the sickness of becoming would be cured as a whole. The

annihilation of nescience encapsulates the essence of the work of liberation. In this sense, Buddhism is from the ground up a gnoseotherapy, which wipes out the passions of nescience through knowledge. The second access point for the redemptive cure lies in the eighth link, thirst or greed, *tanhā*. Just as a fire in which no new combustibles are thrown burns down by itself and goes out, so too, according to the noble doctrine, thirst ceases as soon as it is no longer tantalized by ever-new emotions. Finally, the fourth link, *nama-rupa,* name and figure, personality, plays an outstanding role in the dissolution of the chain of emergence. The Buddha, in his explanation of the causal sequence to his favorite disciple, says the following about the initial nidation of name and figure:

> If cognition, Ananda, were not sunken into the mother's womb, then could name and figure form in the mother's womb?—No, master.—And if cognition, ananda, were to leave its place again after having sunken into the mother's womb, would name and figure then be present in the birth of this life?—No, master.—And if cognition, Ananda, were lost among boys and girls during their childhood, would name and figure then [257] attain growth, extension, and prosperity?—No, master. (*Mahanidanasutta des Dighanikaya,* XV.21)

I tend to read this passage as the key to the praxis of non-representational meditation or deep contemplation: if the hermeneutic of having-gotten-into is supposed to encompass coming-to-oneself in "this life," under this name, in this form, with this ego, then it must dive back before the emergence of the ego kernel. Non-representational meditation would then be the preparatory exercise for the dissolution of even the first traces of personality. Meditation climbs back into the fetal cave, which lies before all that will be called world and self; there it neutralizes with its attention the earliest inscriptions of ego-forming experience.

4. Acosmism

If extended psychoanalysis and historical anthropology want to tell us in non-metaphysical language how we came to be what we are, both must endeavor to translate the ancient wisdom-doctrines into a modern diction. Translating here means claiming to express the content of an idea more truly in terms other than its own. With the emergence of the second tongue in the modern human sciences looms the seldom explicitly formulated task of exfoliating, so to speak, the old metaphysical texts in order to purify their core of [258] psychoanalytic-anthropological truth. In the present case, this would mean that the truth of gnosis could not be expressed in gnostic terms alone; the same would be true for Buddhism, Brahmanism, and so forth. If one pushed the collision of the two languages to the limit, then from the basic premises of modernity it would have to be demanded that the gnostic submit to an extended psychoanalysis *as* gnostic, the Buddhist *as* Buddhist, the Vedantin *as* Vedantin, if these do not wish to let be said *about* them what they cannot or will not know about themselves. The assumption, of course, is that it is necessary for a self-respecting psychoanalysis to read even gnosis and Indian metaphysics symptomatologically. Because questions of truth are at stake, in the deployment of the second language as the world-language of the passion of existence, tolerance for older versions of language can by no means be presupposed. Non-metaphysics can only distinguish itself as a new world-language by declaring war on the old languages of local metaphysics. This is the strategic meaning of the modern psychiatrization of metaphysics and religion. The case histories of the absolute must become—during the attack phase of the second language—cases of metaphysically coded compensatory psychosis. Speakers of the second language set the clinic against spiritual practice; they arrange earthly therapies for celestial evasions. Perhaps still too cavalierly they risk offering nothing but salvos of hard diagnosis, especially to the most severe cases. From the perspective of the spiritual patients, [259] the situation is, unsurprisingly, reversed; for them, suffering from the world has been compounded by suffering from the doctors' ignorance. The anti-metaphysical doctors appear in turn as symptomatic carriers of nescience, as worldlings blinded by their thirst, as agents of drives (*psychikoi*), as bags of dust. Because they are committed to affirming and carrying on, they can know nothing of the truths that stem from negation and cessation.

If a future intellectual historian were to look back at our time from a distance of thousands of years to identify the most significant event of this epoch, he would probably point to the duel between the old metaphysical and new post-metaphysical languages, and indicate how the future of "this world" was prepared therein. The epochal fertility of this duel of languages derives from the necessity that within it the second language learns from the first how to utter the passion of existence for a future eon. Whoever thinks that the unfoldings of psychology and anthropology will mean in the future what the high religions meant in the past, must today be a second to metaphysics; only in struggling with the strengths of metaphysical tradition can the second language become rich enough to be convincing as the world-language of a psychological-anthropological ecumene.

The second tongue will become rich—in the sense of a world-openness that needn't fear early onset exhaustion—at the moment when it has translated into itself, without intolerable damage, the fundamental words of the old casuistic metaphysics: enlightenment, salvation, liberation. [260] Even if such translations haven't quite succeeded anywhere yet, one can state the direction in which the most promising attempts point: the enlightenment complex can be translated into a theory of worldlessness or acosmism; the salvation complex can be translated into a theory of cessation; the liberation complex can be translated into a theory of creativity.

This list represents three levels of increasing obviousness. Every modern person is more or less blindly convinced that the metaphysical concept of liberation is well sublated in the ostensibly non-metaphysical modern notion of creativity. Creativity means for us the freedom to pursue happiness in novelty and artificiality. The triumphal parade of the creativity principle in contemporary culture demonstrates how forcefully the old metaphysical stream of language has dug itself a new bed. This foundational word of modernity articulates the imitation of the Creator by individuals who define themselves by the fact that it is too late for them to believe in gods. In their partisanship for the improbability of the artwork, non-metaphysical modernity carries on the revolt against triviality by other means. It seeks liberation from facticity through creative metamorphoses.

More difficult are the translation problems that arise from the second fundamental word of the metaphysical-religious world-age, salvation. It may no longer seem clear to most interested parties why the issue of salvation can only be sublated in a theory of cessation. In general, modernity has [261] thrown itself upon therapeutic strategies to cope with the evils referred to by the old yearning for salvation. If one looks closer, it appears that reform-politic, technic and clinic—the modern campaigns against said evils—are grounded in an implicit theory of cessation. Without such a theory there could be no reform-praxis, since the latter is possible only on the basis of a belief that evils are alleviated, while the good tends to longevity. On the border between metaphysical and post-metaphysical languages, Nietzsche, in Zarathustra's roundelay sharply differentiated between the will to cease and the will to eternity. Ever since, modernity is rather embarrassed when it comes to speaking of the ceaseless and the ceasing beyond mere therapy jargon. Salvation is the relief that sets in when one has at one's disposal a technique for getting out of vicious circles.

Most difficult, no doubt, is the translation of enlightenment from the metaphysical into the post-metaphysical tongue—if this is not an entirely absurd enterprise. As things stand, the mere thought of it is a nuisance for metaphysics and a folly for post-metaphysics. Additionally, the cultures still remain strictly divided on this question. He to whom something like enlightenment seems possible lives, at least according to the inner calendar, mostly in an early world-age. Moderns have stricken the term from their vocabulary without regret—for them, enlightenment is neither a possible reality nor a possible value. Under these conditions, one can hardly speak of a translation problem. [262] Why create new expressions when the expressed itself has already been annulled? Only at the outer edge of the modern universe can enlightenment-type states be neurologically and psychiatrically characterized—for example as white psychoses or as animistic variants of megalomania. On the progressive wing of depth-psychology, the light-mystical elements of enlightenment are interpreted with reenactments of birth out of the theatrical memory of the body; their blessed and ecstatic attributes make sense in the framework of a phenomenology of endomorphinism. Even the most liberal interpretations of the enlightenment phenomenon thereby remain reductionistic; they too let the undercutting of the phenomenon pass as its translation.

Here it can be shown especially clearly what it means to second metaphysics for non-metaphysics' sake. The gnostic and mystic subtradition of the West as well as the Brahmanic and Buddhist mainstreams of the East have created enlightenment cultures of such power that in the long run they could not be hushed out of the world. As soon as the translation problem becomes acute, it must be shown that the still metaphysically conceived enlightenment complex can be reproduced only in a post-metaphysical theory of acosmism, worldlessness or deworlding. One must be prepared that the enlightenment phenomenon turns out to be something that metaphysics itself does not absorb. Enlightenments had metaphysics-speaking worlds as stages for their first shows, but they do not depend on those stages for all time. The discovery of the world in the age of metaphysics [263] was always-already accompanied by the discovery of worldlessness. The exodus of man into the world has always implied a hunch that the wherefrom of world-entry is itself not world. Precisely the gnostic and Indian type of casuistic metaphysics that recognized every human life as a case history of the absolute conceived the entire world-incident as negatable, by means partially naïve, partially subtle. They taught that the case of the world can be closed altogether through enlightenment—not in the sense of profane death, but that within the subject the process of polarization between ego and world-objects ceases. This is how enlightenment leads to deworlding; it also leads beyond all positive doctrines of being, to the extent that the level of fingertip thinking is transcended. When the ego-world polarity comes to an end, then the duality of pointer and pointed-at can no longer exist. Therefore the position of the enlightened is in no way above the world; worldlessness is only there in the world itself.

The East and the West have coined great names for the way of being of highest worldlessness. From the point of view of worldlessness research the expressions moksha and nirvana are precise equivalents of the gnostic pleroma, that supernal heaven of virtual fullness, untouched by the crudeness of realizations. To reunite with the pleroma during one's lifetime is the goal of gnostic ascent; the mission of entering nirvana even in "this life" hovers over the Buddhist retreat. Both movements, ascent and retreat, do not reach a good cessation, [264] the doctrines teach with great severity, so long as even a whiff of addictive or escapist energy is active in them. Escapism [*Weltflucht*] and enlightenment-addiction are thoroughly worldly conditions, motivated by case-historical experiences. These motivations must be burned down or neutralized before a non-escapist and unaddicted condition of sublime worldlessness can enter. That is why classical Buddhism teaches the unity of samsara and nirvana (wheel of birth and unbornness, rotation and rest), and why an unhindered gnosis at its peak can teach the unity of pleroma and *kenoma* (fullness and emptiness, elevation and abasement). Enlightenment, according to such traditions, happens exactly on the hovering point between "freedom from" and "freedom to"—beyond appetite and avoidance. It is the end of the reality-based psyche and the beginning of the soul without qualities. The illuminated peak form of acosmism is stillness in the eye of the world-cyclone. A preview of the splendor of a possible non-metaphysical language of negation glimmers when it makes its first attempt to translate the old keyword *enlightenment*; with ontological precision and not unpoetically the Austrian philosopher Thomas H. Macho recently captured the state of evasionless freedom in a persuasive formula: world-open worldlessness [*weltoffene Weltlosigkeit*].[8]

What is striking about this formulation is that it does not reserve itself for extreme cases. In fact, a theory of acosmism must interest itself not just in maximum liminal values but also and especially in average values—the lower limit included. A [265] psychoanalytic-anthropological discussion of worldless states will emphasize precisely the acosmism of everyday life; this also brings into view the worldlessness of idiots. For the assumption that "man" qua existence is from the ground up "in the world" can no longer be maintained unconditionally even in a Heideggerian perspective. Rather, he is always-already primarily the one who is away. "The human is the away," Heidegger himself will say in the revision of his initial formulation.[9] The phenomenology of being-away in the sense of vulgar worldlessness encompasses all stages of relief, of distraction and intentional oblivion. Sleep and swoon, daydream and nightdream, ecstasy and drugging, inattention and absentmindedness, self-petrifaction and specialization—these are only the most obvious manifestations of the principle of acosmicity in its average forms. On the pathological wing of the phenomenon row, madness and imbecility line up—both attitudes in which the subject plays dead to the impositions of cosmopolitanism [*Weltoffenheit*].

If it is admitted that a theory of acosmism is the necessary complement to any psychology, then the old talk of enlightenment loses much of its alienness for members of the modern world. Enlightened worldlessness is distinguished from the vulgar only by its claim to full wakefulness and by its unshielded openness to compassion for all that it encounters. In profane sleep and its half-awake diurnal equivalent, [266] this readiness for all encounters is clouded; the dreamer experiences only a stump of the world in the interior of an averted, unlistening and defensive "subjectivity." Vulgar worldlessness, under other names, has long been a theme of every psychology that is not oblivious to the fact that all souls practice in their own way the art of being in and simultaneously not being in the world. This is better understood now that modern neurophysiology has elaborated the selective and defensive character of our basic epistemic-biological equipment. It now becomes comprehensible why Dasein is the exception. Permanently "being there" in the sense of chronic awakeness to the onslaught of alarming information would mean permanent torture; medieval fantasies of hell emblematize the notion of being exposed to an ever-present pain without recourse to nonbeing; such fantasies play out the dark side of the idea of eternity as uninterrupted presence. Thus, the psychoanalytic theory of defense mechanisms must be understood as a special case of the general phenomenology of worldlessness and its breach by the rising real.

The world is not always the case; what is the case is not always the world. Still, for every difficult case, the world is all that really shouldn't be the case.

6

What does it mean to take oneself over?
Experiment in affirmation

1. The Kantian notion of maturity, understood as
retroactive consent to one's own existence

[267] Whoever knows even a little about the two disciplines that inquire about the human being in the modern era—about the venerable old one, philosophy, and the dubious new one, psychology—will be aware that there is little good to report about the relationship between the two. The current business of philosophy is the way it is because the "love of wisdom" has declared bankruptcy as psychology; contemporary psychology is the way it is because it had to file for bankruptcy as philosophy. Institutionalized philosophy has never been able to make sense of the fact that individuals actually exist—if existence means the clearing of singularities [*Einmaligen*] that lies out of range for conceptual representation. Psychology, for its part, has never found a clear enough connection to the fact that individuals think, and that thinking is not only a function of the psyche but also the theater in which the world makes its appearance. Thus, the philosophers grasp the human fact too indirectly, the psychologists too meagerly—as if they were both uneasy toward their object. Anyone who wants to learn how to elaborately talk past man can [268] do no better than to become a player in the contemporary philosophical enterprise; anyone interested in routinely gliding over the ontological seriousness of human cognitive potentials will find contentment splashing in the shallows of institutionalized exact psychologies. If one were

authorized to infer from the current state of the human sciences the nature of their object, one would have to define man as the being who avoids himself as long as it is somehow possible.

If we want to step back from this result to a point where the game still seemed promising, we find ourselves in the late eighteenth century, when the amazing story of mankind's evasive behavior toward mankind "begins." It may seem strange that the discussion should turn to Immanuel Kant—an author mostly known to the public only by his intimidating outer aspect as the author of the critiques of reason. His major works are correctly regarded as milestones on philosophy's path to unpopularity; after Kant, philosophical thought climbs like never before into the exclusivity of professionalized argument-games; only after the *Critique of Pure Reason* is it true that popular interest in philosophical theses must always be based on misunderstandings. Nevertheless, a brief review of Kant is in order when it comes to determining the moment when the concerns of philosophy coincided with those of psychology for the last time. It is the moment when Kant the skeptical psychologist and connoisseur of human nature owes Kant the teacher of reason an answer to the question of [269] how the potential subject of reason, man, is to be brought to reason *de facto* and with existential consequence. One may claim that this question is directly responsible for the emergence of anthropology and indirectly causes the development of modern psychotherapeutics. The anthropologists of the dawning bourgeois age recognize in man the being that does not satisfy or only imperfectly satisfies its idea as *animal rationale*. The modernly conceived difference between the idea and the reality of man[1] provokes many authors, not least Kant, to excel in the dual role of subject and object of a new kind of reflection on "the human." The fruitful embarrassment of the human condition will now become the impetus of a critical self-assessment that characterizes the human as a transitional subject: if humans were already completely rational, then they, like angels, would only need to practice mathematics, music, ontology, and color theory in order to fully realize themselves. If, in contrast, they were completely irrational, then a kind of human zoology would be in order—if there were a genus above the human which, for reasons unknown, wanted to occupy itself with these strange erectile creatures. But since humans are beings in transition and in twilight—that is, historical animals—what suits them best is, according to enlightened conviction, an anthropology from a pragmatic point of view. A theory of man becomes pragmatic as soon as it shows that [270] he is already free enough to become freer, already rational enough to become more rational. Reason takes time—in this formula one could sum up the modern experiments in the optimization of human reasoning powers. Thus the modern conception of man inevitably includes a didactic part, which establishes educational processes for individuals, and a historical-philosophical part, which designs educational processes for peoples and societies, indeed for the species as a whole. The age of evolutionary and curricular thought begins. Complementary to the Enlightenment's didactic and historical-philosophical programs, from the late eighteenth century onward emerge psychotherapeutics devoted to correcting disturbed educational processes.[2] In the framework of an enlightenment anthropology, therapy can mean nothing other than reeducation of malformed souls under more favorable conditions; through an encouragement at once medicinal and political, it gives individuals the "courage to exist." It is in the nature of things that, over time, efforts to make people more reasonable and active have had to limit themselves more and more to the individual. Thus, modern psychotherapy has achieved extraordinary things in its attempts to renormalize individuals. Conversely, in the realm of political therapeutics, a worldwide reticence that can easily be mistaken for resignation has prevailed since the *terreur* of the French Revolution, and even more so since the debacle of the [271] communist system-cures. In the case of traumatically damaged and miseducated individuals, contemporary psychotherapy can rightly expect to make a difference. But at the moment no one seriously considers himself responsible for the healing of traumatized peoples and for the civilizing repetition of failed social formations. I say this on the assumption that Gandhi's generous folk-therapeutic experiment has failed and that, for the time being, the prerequisites for the successful repetition of large-scale constitutional acts remain unclear.

For Kant, as for the Enlightenment tradition as a whole, educational processes are successful when they are used as paths to maturity [*Mündigkeit*]. This means more than being of age, legal competence, and eligibility to vote. In the Kantian sense, a mature person is one who knows how to use their mind "without guidance from another," above all in matters of religion. The formula expresses an independence-pathos of a special type. The mature spirit is expected to arrive in an original way at the same conclusions all mature and reasonable beings have reached before it. The originality of reason is that it overcomes the originality of idiocy. Maturity is deidiotization. Those who become mature can be trusted to speak for themselves and still utter only generally applaudable things. The consummate mark of moral maturity would be that under all conceivable conditions I want only what I also should want according to the known moral law. If my want always [272] corresponded to my ought, then, according to the idealistic tradition, I would have to have fully emancipated myself from my inner instinctive nature, insofar as it operates as the source of passions or interests that render me immature. But how might I achieve that without mortifying myself in the manner of ancient ascetics or medieval monks? How else than over my empirical corpse can I help the moral demands of "pure reason" within me to triumph? Is the difference between citizens and anchorites, fought for by the Reformation, only an apparent one? If one takes the demands of moral idealism at their word, then the history of post-Kantian reasoners becomes a bourgeois appendix to the history of the saints. No one who has explored the terrain will deny that the phenomenology of resolute moral and logical idealisms presents a sample catalog of high-minded self-tortures. Should the enlightened theory of maturity be quietly added to it? Here, however—where the reasoning of modern people becomes aware of their unfitness for sainthood—Kant the connoisseur of man and world comes into creative conflict with the formulator of the categorical imperative. He knows too well that it would be overreaching to want to impose an infinite ought directly on the finite subject. That may have worked in the middle ages—the golden age of unhappy consciousness—but it no longer works in the century of bourgeois man. Anthropology is not dealing with a race of heroes and holy men but with [273] a crowd of bourgeois individuals of middling morality. Precisely because the content of moral demands is more important to Kant than anything else, he cleaves to the insight that they cannot be enforced with superego-terror, let alone with monkish threats. But how to bring the poor sensuous ego nearer to its superegoic callings? Faced with this question, Kant becomes an anthropologist of the first hour. The anthropologist is the administrator of the task of mediating between the realistic and the idealistic factions in the inner forum of modern subjects. Thus the philosophical anthropologist goes to work as an honest broker between the empirical human being and the citizen of the intelligible world—one could also say, as the liaison officer between the animal interested in sensation and the subject of the categorical imperative. For the last time, philosophy becomes psychologically fascinating—for in his empirical-transcendental back-and-forth, Kant the anthropologist employs a cunning whose profundity commands admiration even from the depth-psychologists of our century. Namely: if people are not yet capable of wanting what they should from an early age, according to Kant they must nevertheless be treated from the start as if they were already capable of wanting what they should. Kant did not have to wait for one of his epigones to invent the philosophy of as if. He himself knew that the fiction of freedom is capable of bringing us closer to real freedom, just as the fiction of maturity prepares us for actual maturity. Were it otherwise, no civic education would be possible.[3] [274] Rigorism and fictionalism still live under the same roof. The thinker is aware that people can only be seduced to become human by treating them, from the first moments of their existence, as human beings in the noble sense of the genus title. The philosopher is a Prussian Pygmalion who addresses humanity in the most courteous tone, as if it were not a depraved, war-torn agglomerate of evil-eyed egoists, but always already a society of mature cosmopolitans: *My Fair Lady*, Königsberg edition. Professor Kant and Professor Higgins share the ambition to make unabashed human raw material presentable in society. Thus the scene is set for the comedy of humanity—the maturity training may begin. The only way to make a society lady think you're one yourself is to perfectly act like one. Imposture obliges. It is no different with the gents—it applies to good men, mature philosophers, empathic therapists and godly pastors without exception, to all, therefore, who never quite reach the height of their roles if they don't make a little more of themselves than is in them.

A mature person, we said, is one who is able to speak for him or herself. But because people start infantile, that is, non-speaking, for a long time their maturity can only be assumed as a future chance [275]. From a psychological point of view, the date of maturation cannot be fixed in advance, and it is not certain that there will be such a date in the life of every individual. In this respect, civil society's rules of legal age merely provide a form whose content remains open. If individuals want to transition from mere being-there or objective presence to mature existence in Kant's sense, they must become the directors of their lives and give their existence a kind of constitution. This means that, in an act of subsequent consent, they would have to approve their parents' caprice in letting their intercourse lead to a procreation. Lucidly and tactfully Kant indicates the basic contradiction of the human condition: that people must be expected to become mature and free, despite having had no vote in the most important question of their life: whether they wanted to come into being at all.

I am now able to clarify the assertion that in Kant the concerns of philosophy and psychology merged with strict consistency for the last time. If it is true that humans are thrown into life "without being asked," then they can either never become mature at all—since a retroactive hearing on the procreation question is impossible—or at the moment when the individual retroactively affirms the patronizing appointment to life by his or her progenitors and consents to all the consequences of their sexual self-indulgence.[4] The date of maturity [276] would therefore be the day on which the subject, in full awareness of the costs and risks of life, including the certainty of death, decides to retroactively grant procuration to its parents for the coitus that led to this life.[5] This may sound bizarre, but it is only an exaggeration of the well-accepted notion that people can become mature and take responsibility for their own lives. This means that maturity exists only together with a positive theory of finitude: we will die; do we therefore not want to live? The idea of a retroactive authorization of progenitors, as extravagant as it seems, draws the consequences of the principle that mature life must take itself into its own competence in all respects. The enlightenment idea of adulthood conceals the metaphysical question of whether humans will ever be able to fully retroactively appropriate the overwhelming event of their own production or "creation." If appropriation is possible, then the life of the individual must contain a moment of perfect balance between self-assertion and gratitude.[6] If it is impossible, then Dostoevsky's underground man had the last word when he defined man as "the ungrateful biped." [277]

2. Being-there and being-away in primal scenes

It is an absolute certainty that I am, that I know this, and that I love it.
—St. Augustine, *City of God* XI.26

One recognizes that indiscretion is not an exclusive right of id-psychologists. A rigorous ego-philosophy takes things just as far. On the line of philosophical questioning too, one comes to the threshold of the parental bedroom—only that now an ontological palpitation is superimposed on the psychosexual one. For the Kantian child, this threshold concerns being or non-being, whereas the Freudian child is concerned only with being there or not being there. I think that an exchange of indiscretions might entangle the mutually estranged disciplines of philosophy and psychology in a new kind of cooperation.

Whichever the scene in which the subject apprehends itself, in each case it could begin its self-apprehension with the sentence: "I am there." These three words are unsurpassable in their triviality but from a psychological and philosophical perspective they carry a number of nontrivial primal-scenic charges. In a Freudian sense, the infantile "I am there" vis-à-vis the parents' coitus signifies that the subject is about to get caught in the ego-forming position of the excluded third—from which position, in the "normal case," the psychosexual life-program is formed to usurp one of the two primary positions at any price. Being there on the stage of triadic envy—wrongly called "the primal scene"[7]—implies the desire to remove the barrier that blocks access to the desired object. The psychosexual subject would thus be "there" to the degree that it is able to succeed the father or the mother in the "fulfilling" role. In the attempt to fall into the role, however, such serious complications often arise that many individuals take recourse in a desexualized lifestyle or degenitalized sexual style, that is, in being away [*Fortsein*] from the stage of "full" erotic tension.[8]

In Melanie Klein's view, the early infantile "I am there" signifies: knowing that one is delivered over to the sovereign motherly power over absence or presence, at whose discretion I may be torn up or made whole again. Being there now means entering a stage on which I develop a *modus vivendi* within the primal conflict between envy and gratitude. On this stage, I am he who is torn to pieces and gathers himself back up into a complete self-image. Being "there" here means exposing oneself to the dramas of dependence on others. A vacillation between devotion and the frenzy of independence indicates how high the stakes are. The subject finds itself in the position where the fervor of connection and the passion for separation are both in a state of emergency: if Dasein comes to terms with its possession by the second [279] as the big Other, then the decision arises as to whether the subject becomes a grateful or an ungrateful biped. Because being obliged to such great replies triggers tendencies to negate the question as such, an intense pull toward being-away is at play on this stage as well. Its goal is to become unassailable by intimacy. For more than two millennia, the high cultures of East and West have handed down philosophical and moral teachings that aim to make the subject independent of the felicity and misery of dyadic passions. They arrange the flight from excessive proximity into so-called autonomy. No wonder that individualism, autonomism, and asceticism can still draw from the ancient reservoirs today. Here, good is what leads away from "love," and wise is what distances us from the other without whom we think we cannot live. Awayness from the Kleinian scene implies provisional ingratitude as indecisiveness toward the (in)evitable Other.

Finally, in the Heideggerian sense, the sentence "I am there" signifies the ontological primal scene of waking finite life. It witnesses a thought that is coextensive with an event. It is the sentence that opens and bears witness to a destiny. "I am there" marks a catastrophe report from Being, in which the report and the catastrophe are one. In every present "there" [*Da*] ticks quietly and uncannily the time bomb of the question of being. Spoken without addenda, the *Da* tears open the scene into which I know I am absolutely exposed, "set out." Through this absolute "out" I am thrown into the world, among the things, [280] and condemned to freedom. On this deepest level of primal-scenic consciousness, I befall myself as a trace of exposure to a "world." The situation corresponds to the context-free question: where am I? Against this question the everyday understanding with its vulgar conception of space can only bang its head—for it may be prepared for anything, but not the problem of absolute localization. It doesn't want to know that being-in-the-world means something radically other than residing in a large container. If I am "there" in a whole, it is because I have fallen [*zugefallen*] to myself in consequence of a birth. But if I am an absolute accident [*Zufall*] to myself, then the space in which I encounter myself is an outside, an uncontainer, an openness, an extrauterine scene. Consequently, being in the world first of all means only as much as being—with things, with people—outside and under the pressure of facticity. Amid the inventory of facts, human Dasein experiences itself as not a thing, as a pure absurdity [*Unding*]. It falls to it to have to be an existing self that cannot grasp itself in the mirror of external things. In "authentic" Dasein, it would completely become the resolute "fall"—an animated groundlessness, willing to endure in the uncomfortable ecstasy. This is what is defended against by the primary tendency toward being-away or being-gone, in which Dasein dwells "proximally and for the most part." Heidegger's saying, "Man is the *away*"—the away!—means that subjects can initially be nothing other than compulsive deserters into external business.

Now it is a matter of gauging the distance between the simple existential assertion and the subject's commentary on it. If the assertion [281] is simply "I am there"—at most "I find myself there," or "Dasein is"—then the subject's comment would have to be, in the most favorable case, "I approve of my being there," and in a less favorable but still felicitous variant, "I take responsibility for everything that follows from my being there"—or even, in a lyrical or religious turn, "I am grateful for myself." No doubt there are certain mentalities—which in passing one could dub "world-infantile"—for which it is out of the question to let a significant difference arise between the basic assertion and the commentary. Consciousness of Dasein and affirmation of Dasein lie so close together that the problems discussed in the following must seem unreal. It is the wickedness of lucky people never to know what the less lucky ones are talking about. In the ideal case of happy positivism, the subject experiences itself as the best of all possible egos in the best of all possible worlds. Such contentment seems, if not to sublate the difference between world and self, to prevent it from becoming conspicuous. The human has remained a good animal or a blessed idiot spared from the force of the negative.

No effort is needed in order to defend the thesis that the majority of people feel less happy in historical times. The silent majorities of all ages live in the consensus of average unhappiness. Their life-feelings and self-consciousness are colored by the knowledge that the transition from the "I am there" to the affirmation thereof will not come without a cost. Perhaps the high religions of the past millennia were basically just collective fortifications of the endangered affirmational capacity of those who belong to chronically hard times. Such individuals certainly form the psychosocial bulk of modern societies, and I don't think I am exaggerating when I claim that they make up the clientele of psychological and philosophical services in the present-day therapeutic and counseling establishment. From a philosophical perspective, one could call this eternal majority, in homage to Heidegger, the *Sorgen-Kinder* ("problem children"); from a psychological perspective, as just said, the clients; and from a sociological perspective, most likely: the stressed class.

At the edge of this main field of stressed and self-preoccupied people stands an extreme minority of rebellious, despairing, disintegrated subjects, who could be characterized as problem children of the second degree. These are individuals who will not succeed in transitioning from the existential sentence to a positive commentary, not even with great effort—perhaps because their capacity for exertion is damaged, or because a continual overload has corrupted their forces of affirmation and replaced them with a renunciatory tendency. For these people, such dark clouds hang over the sentence "I am there" that the obligation to proceed to positive addenda can only seem like an excessive demand. Under these conditions, approving of one's thereness amounts to affirming a catastrophe. From such existential positions, a transition into the affirmative can only be carried out cynically. In fact, dark modernity articulates a cynicism that proceeds from the existential sentence to the heroic stance of "I take over the calamity of my being," or the hysterical disclosure "I celebrate the catastrophe that I am." It seems to me that it is just such affirmations of despair that accompany modern philosophy on its way from Kant to Schopenhauer and Nietzsche, Heidegger, Bataille, Foucault. With the emergence of the gay science a mad laughter breaks free—the laughter of subjects who are there no differently than meteors on eccentric trajectories. It would also not be difficult to show that affirmations of plight have gained in incisiveness along the path of modern depth-psychology from Mesmer and Puységur to Charcot and Freud, up to Lacan, Deleuze, Guattari, and Laing. The problem of transitioning from the simple to the confirmed existential statement has been acutely radicalized in the two centuries after Kant and the French Revolution. The sentence "I am there"—whether uttered explicitly or covertly—takes on a threatening tone. Ever more often it appears independently of confirmative addenda. Sartre, in a still scholastically controlled turn, will teach that existence precedes essence. Wherever this conception of the naked, empty, meaning-evacuated thereness works itself up and becomes articulate, the domesticating moral controls of the Kantian wholesome-bourgeois age disintegrate. The isolated being-in-the-world goes wild and performs its wildness—existence and morality split apart, goodwill appears to the wild self as an insipid mask, a nauseating preciousness. Through the mouths of numberless individuals, the There declares: I am no man, I am dynamite; I am no citizen, I am trash; I am no subject, I am desiring machine; I have no companions, I am a meteor.

[284] A neo-pagan pride in despair finds its words and mocks the consolations of the metaphysical tradition.

It seems plausible to me to see in the excessive discourses of the modern expression-sphere more than a long-term trend toward the psychotization of the zeitgeist; they also manifest an experiment in providing contemporary people with a deepened therapeutic approach. Unlimited articulation releases historically untested possibilities of transaction [*Erledigung*]. In fact, modern psychotherapies, in their perspective on extreme disorders of the self-affirmational capacity, are seized by the tendency to position the concept of healing, under non-religious conditions, at a depth that would otherwise correspond only to salvation religions. Functionally speaking, such religions represent nothing but authoritarian solutions to the problem of retroactively affirming existence. They proffer consolation-formulas that show the inconsolable life paths to self-acceptance; inconsolability means that a subject cannot possibly transition by its own strength from the depressive insight "I am there" to the avowal "I deem my existence good." Old-style salvation religions could field strong consolatory formulas because they could bring into play helpers from the absolute—whether in priestly-sacramental or in mediumistic, prophetic and angelistic forms. If a modern therapeutic wishes to become a healing art in the ambitious sense, it must repeat this stunt by secular and non-authoritarian means. Thus falls to it a task that, if taken up, will necessarily overwhelm it. This reveals the antinomy of every secular psychotherapeutic: if it takes up the task without further ado, it promises more than it can keep; but if it does not promise too much, it does not take up its task and evades the healing requirements of its most needful clients.

The sideways glance at religions of salvation and mediation thus contains an instructive lesson for therapeutic ethics. Such religions give form to the conviction that, for people of hot cultures—which means as a rule: for reality-sore subjects deformed by the pain of civilizing dressage—there is no path from Dasein to the full affirmation thereof that can be walked by their own power. Wherever salvation gains power as a motif of high-cultural life—above all in hegemonic states and empires, where the wretched of the earth grow numerous—there, religions of this type swear an oath to disclose humanity's metaphysical weakness. For just as humans can come into question only as receivers of their procreation or creation, so too their salvation depends, according to these doctrines, on help from above or beyond.

Salvation amounts to that second creation that the mystery traditions call rebirth. If the emphasis of Western-style soteriologies is placed fully on the necessity of committing oneself to alien or external aid to reach a new beginning, then the concept of salvation can be reformulated in philosophical language: salvatory work is peculiar to interventions that eliminate otherwise unsurpassable impediments to the retroactive affirmation of existence. Following this reformulation, it is hard to see why [286] such aid should be given only under religious auspices. Any aid that is translated by its receivers into self-affirmation and existential illumination would be "saving enough" from this point of view. Thus, it would be natural to suspect that a large part of modern Western psychotherapeutics operate an incognito soteriological practice—that is, the continuation of a defunct Christianity by other means. Psychotherapeutics succeeds soteriology in many aspects—especially when it does not content itself with the minimal therapeutic aim that is called survival capacity, but an eye on the maximal one, defined psychologically as self-integration, philosophically as maturity. Psychotherapy also parodies soteriology in that, like the original, it is most accommodating to those who need it least. In Christianity, did not the most favorable salvatory prognosis belong to cheerful minds who also would have been blessed without Christianity?

3. World-hatred and new beginning

The publicity successes of psychoanalysis have given rise to the delusion in public opinion that psychotherapeutic forms of self-care *eo ipso* imply a journey into childhood. Against this general trend, one must explain ever again why such ideas represent one of the harmful misunderstandings of modern psychological ideology. The arrow of time of well-understood psychotherapeutic work must always point strictly ahead—psychotherapy is no trip into the past [287], but rather the past subject's journey to catch up with its present. This catching-up can be rendered by the term *presentification*—a paradoxical enterprise, to be sure, for how are individuals, who anyhow can only exist in the present, supposed to re-arrive in the present? The sentence "become who you are" is not so much deep as it is comical. Not without reason do successful therapies end with the participants laughing at themselves. Occasionally one thinks one perceives a winking in the eyes of some Indian and Japanese teachers of man, that is: if only you knew that you are there. Now the expression "taking oneself over" can be given an extended meaning: to take oneself over means to overtake oneself, to catch up with oneself. To catch up with oneself means to perceive how one is with unlimited attention. All therapy is therefore self-catchup, and everything that leads to self-catch-up *ipso facto* has a therapeutic effect. This may be one reason cures, as a rule, are not precise effects of explicit therapies or exact techniques but result from new run-ups to life under improved constellations, with the help of psychologists' knowledge—the rest is patchwork, or worse.

Whoever wants to reach the end—one possible end—of this path of considerations can probably do no better than to revisit the approach of the depth psychologist Gustav Hans Graber. Graber has become known—or rather, remained unknown—as one of the fathers of prenatal psychology. Along with Otto Rank, he was the first psychologist of the generation after Freud who took the genetic idea of psychoanalysis seriously enough to reconstruct the life of individuals [288] from the intrauterine stage. For Graber, the life of the human soul self-evidently begins in the Mediterranean vastness of the mother's womb—as a continuum of euphoria out of which the born being is more or less abruptly thrown. One of the features of feto-gnostic self-development is—as one knows today—a depth-musicological aspect that co-constitutes[9] the tonicized creature of mood [*Stimmungswesen*], man, and a placentological dimension that comprises the original orientation of the self toward a covering shell, a genius, a guardian angel or a proto-"object."[10] This decisive, oldest layer of the psychic would thus be this non-objective yet extremely real vibration that emerges from the selfless self of fetal antiquity. Even the increasing adult rigidity and increasing objectification of the world can never fully extinguish it. In it rests the genetic ground of "soul" and sympathy. However, at birth we are abruptly and momentously separated from this vibration and its "soluble" [*löslich*] mode of being, according to Graber's insights. All the needs with which psychotherapists deal in their praxes are therefore consequences, mediate or immediate, of our early departure from the sea.

[289] *The ambivalence of the child*[11]—and equally of the adult—begins with the unwelcome fall into general duress, that is, into the conditions of the external world. Insofar as the child is permeated sooner or later by "the disadvantage of being born,"[12] the germ of an archaic and comprehensive

negation forms within it. Often the birth is already the primal scene of the No, which can connect, like an amplifier, the oldest experiences of displeasure to later, present ones. By a powerful impetus toward the displeasing side, the pendulum of the pleasure-displeasure principle is set in motion. The child's first active position in relation to the world would thus be a global negation—indeed, a negation before negation, a rejection and extinguishment that throws its shadow ahead onto everything that will be the case. The world can basically never be forgiven that its objective presence has displaced the pre-libidinal, pre-objective serenity [*Gelöstheit*]:

> The child experiences the object-world as, so to speak, the bearer or guilt for his new unfavorable being. It is therefore repudiated *"in globo"*; it (or the entrance into it) has indeed brought about the ambivalence of pleasure and displeasure.[13]

In all the displeasing experiences of later life, an "inarticulate primordial no"[14] is mobilized, without whose dramatizing effect the emergence of neuroses and other severe mental disorders would remain [290] energetically inexplicable; at the core of psychical disorders, we always find "over-reactions"—that is, powerful displacements of energy and affective fallacies which produce excitations in the wrong place. Hatred, in its hot forms as in its frozen masks, is therefore always also feeding off of retroactive bundlings in objects of later experience. According to this view, all object-relations, even pleasurable ones, remain latently colored by an originary hatred, since the fatal taste of the world adheres to each object as such. Therefore, no being-in-the-world is free from ambivalence. Even in the phenomena of the positive erotic life of the soul, psychologists who "look upon" existence from the worldless edge of the world must perceive the trace of the negative: what men call love is the guarantor of the infantile "originary compromise with the world."[15]

> The child loves only because the object forms a paltry substitute for the true object of desire, but the originary hatred is preserved at all times, since the object, which from the perspective of the infantile soul shares blame with the hated Being itself, can never provide full satisfaction.[16]

The soul's desire, ineffable as it may be, undeviatingly approximates the state in which the desire would be extinguished. Wishing is inhabited by a nirvanic tendency that manifests as a tendency toward a state without tendency. In the libido itself, a pull toward the alibidinous is at work, [291] as if pleasure itself were an obstacle to salvation. Hence the libido is secondary in relation to the originary tendency that strives for the "state without end" [*Zustand ohne Einstellung*].[17]

Here it is not a matter of subjecting Graber's speculative elan to a critical examination. It is surely unnecessary to prove that, seventy years after the publication of the book, many of the author's theses have been repeated and surpassed in more elaborate terms—the names Klein, Fairbairn, Winnicott, Bion, Jacobson, Mahler, Kernberg, Kohut, and Grunberger mark stages on the way to a more complex view of ego- and object-formative processes. Still it is worth recalling Graber's early intuitions, because in a humble, almost casual and yet definite way, they discovered the long-sought passage between therapeutics and philosophical psychology. On this path it can become clear what individuals have to look for in their beginnings.

Nevertheless, one objection against Graber's conception of the world seems inevitable to me. What Graber called the "originary hatred" of the "world" in general is from the outset wrongly stylized by him following the pattern of affectual object-relations, as if the newborn were already a formed subject that could relate to the "world" as to a global object worth rejecting. In truth, the "originary rejection" does not yet involve any "object"-relation. The category of object, and even more the idea of world as object-totality, are heuristics that cannot correspond to the child's mode of being on the threshold between fetal and extrauterine life—a mistake that everyone makes. [292] That is how grown-ups talk about something they no longer understand. But who would have words for pre-egoic constitutions? As a symptom of not being able to speak otherwise, the expression "originary hatred" isn't just a misnomer; in its unavoidable failure, it reflects one of the most evasive problems of our grammar, insofar as the latter condemns us to deal with medial phenomena in a language that is made for the articulation of objective facts. That is why we speak about things that carry us, surround us, engulf and permeate us, no differently than about things that face us, with which we confront ourselves and which we imagine.[18]

But how should we think, in contrast, of a pre-objective negation or a rejection without object-relation? What is denial as disattunement [*Verneinung als Verstimmung*]? Conversely, how does a pre-objective affirmation take place—and how do we identify it? What is affirmation as attunement? In such a pre-objective yes lies the answer to the question concerning the possibility of an integral self-overtaking as retroactive consent to one's own existence. What it means to take oneself over would become evident if it could be shown how a speechless pre-objective and pre-egoic yes-mood [*Ja-Stimmung*] passes over into mature gestures of self-acclamation. Psychotherapy is the enterprise of releasing the flow from pre-predicative "affirmations" to reflective consent into [293] the self-projected life. This is probably the reason why truly radical healings come about only when the archaic is rejoined to the actual.

Dissolution [*Gelöstheit*] in a pre-objective Being means serenity [*Gelassenheit*]: it means dwelling in a sphere that is more a soul globe than a world of crystallized, fragmentable objects. This mode of being remains possible for grown-up, conflict-hardened adults only insofar as they release themselves into the world as into a stream of ongoing birth. The stream of my coming-to-the-world flows steadily "forward," just as the time-arrow of successful therapies must point unswervingly forward. The lucky natures—William James once called them the *once born*—step into this stream only once [*nur einmal*], the problematic natures twice or more. The more often one has to begin anew, the better one knows the reasons for rejecting existence [*Anstoß nehmen*]. The more a new beginning succeeds, the more likely an earlier failure becomes the catalyst [*Anstoß*] for another history.

7

Where are we when we listen to music?

A. In departure and in return

Philosophy knows a madness of which psychiatry knows nothing. Think of Hannah Arendt, otherwise famous for her sobriety, who in full earnestness wrote a treatise on the question "Where are we when we think?," or of Valentinus and Basilides, the gnostic theologians of late antiquity, whose élan was directed toward finding an answer to the question "Where are we when we are in the world?" Bizarre thoughts preclude noble forms as little as madness precludes method. But that reason also has something to gain from madness, beyond linguistic inversions—this could be one of the lessons to be drawn from depth-musicological reflections.

In recent years, the ear has entered into philosophical discussion—as if this stepchild of epistemology had suddenly won the attention of myriad adoptive parents. Indeed, the occidental philosophy of light and sight, in its brilliant days between Plato and Hegel, had a rather [295] condescending relationship to the realities of audition. Western metaphysics was, in essence, an optic ontology that emerged from the systematization of an outer and inner seeing. The thinking subject arose as a seer who saw not only things and archetypal images but also finally himself as a seeing soul—a local manifestation of absolute eyesight. One could designate the members of this guild argumentative visionaries. Perhaps the "end of metaphysics" discussed since the Young Hegelians can also be read as a symptom of the fact that the medial inflation of images leads to the approach of a maximum beyond which the absolutization of sight can no longer be sustained.[1] The Occidental prejudice in favor of the eye at the expense of the ear no longer deafens all the participants in the conversation about what the Greeks called the great things. In view of this progress, one can appreciate the suspicion that the popular auditory pietism is part of a renewed conservative revolution, through which an old European human type, clinging to remnants of interiority, is trying to delay his decline into the deinteriorized media civilization for a few generations.

The difference between a primarily seeing or listening relationship with the world is of immediate significance for the peculiar question of where we are when we listen. To see something, the viewer has to face [296] the visible from an open distance. This spatial being-apart and being-across suggests the assumption of a rift between subjects and objects that is ultimately not just spatial but also ontological. As a consequence of this, subjects understand themselves as worldless observers who take up a relationship to a cosmos that is always already removed from them, a relationship that is, as it were, merely external; in that case subjectivity would be, in analogy to a mostly theoretical divinity, primarily contemplative, secondarily practical. Insofar as the world of the eye is a world of distance, ocular subjectivity implies the tendency to interpret oneself as an ultimately unengaged world-witness. The seeing subject stands "on the margins" of the world like a worldless and bodiless eye before a panorama—Olympic contemplation and optic theology are only two sides of the same coin. Thinkers, on the other hand, who want to interpret being from the facts of listening could not have conceived of the removal of the observer-subject to the imaginary outer border of the world, for it is in the nature of hearing not to occur except in the mode of being-in-the-sound. No listener can think to stand on the margin of the audible. The ear knows no acrossness; it develops no frontal "view" onto distant objects, since it has "world" or "objects" only to the degree that it is in the midst of the acoustic happening—one could also say: insofar as it floats or dives in the auditive space. A philosophy of hearing would therefore from the outset only be possible as a theory of being-in—as an interpretation of the "intimacy" in which human awakeness becomes sensitive to the world. That the relationship between ear and intimacy [297] in turn cannot be an exclusive one is recalled by the fact that humans for the most part behave toward the audible with the same attitude that prevails in their visual handling of remote things—namely, objectifying and scattered, non-intimate, untouched, in the mode of self-preservation and of distancing. Thus one cannot infer from hearing itself to wakeful intimacy—any more than one makes mystics of men by telling them that they are beings-in-the-world.

Where are we when we listen to music? The question is bizarre enough to evoke the transition from the representation of objects to the inhabitation of media. Inhabitive behavior is often revealed not by signs of participation in all that surrounds the subject but by the subject's sunkenness into itself. Recall the Socratic absences that still mark the beginning of European philosophy like inscrutable question marks. Both Xenophon and Plato report that Socrates had the habit of suddenly "directing his spirit in upon himself" and becoming "deaf to the most emphatic address"; at the same time he would continue his respective activity. On one occasion, during a military camp, he is said to have remained standing, immersed completely in thought, for twenty-four hours, inaccessible to any appeal from the outside world. One will hardly count such episodes as proof of musicality—but the question of where the thinker sank to during his absences can hardly be answered without talking about a world of inner voices and sounds, whose presence can be more powerful than every external noise. If philosophy [298] is engrossed in a sphere that to ordinary mortals seems not of this world, nevertheless its immersion in a state without external audition maintains a depth-acoustically relevant meaning. This is so essentially connected with animation and being-in-oneself that one could not specify what soul is supposed to be, if not always also a self-referential hearing. Had Socrates given an account of his raptures, he would have reported about states in which the world temporarily goes down without disrupting the continuum of psychic self-presence. I hear voices; thus the god is making me think; it whispers in me, therefore I concern myself with the great things. Perhaps Socrates would have described himself as an expert in discrete ends of the world. The enstatic trances of European proto-philosophers were a sleep of reason that produced not monsters but inner voices, ideas, and theorems. Being far away from everything else that is the case sets the stage for the awakening that makes us wonder at the fact that something is.

One needn't be a philosopher to let the world intermittently go down. Each mortal has a sufficient amount of doomsday experience—and not only because he or she occasionally gets carried away by apocalyptic moods.

Humans are beings that cannot not let the curtain fall on the world-theater for a number of hours each day—even if, during the day, they define themselves as rational beings, and reason wants to be the faculty of keeping oneself in a permanent wakeful relation to an ever-present world. Were not philosophers *ex officio* martyrs of the illusory possibility of permanent wakefulness? [299] Therein we can see one point of post-metaphysical thinking: that contemporary subjects, following millennia-long experiments with phantasms of perpetual wakefulness, convert in active resignation to a positive theory of not-always-being-able-to-be-awake-in-the-world. A new type of philosophical anthropology proceeds from the principle that humans are beings that appear within rhythms of world-rise and world-fall—existing, inexisting, present, absent. The idea of anthropology as onto-rhythmics yields a twofold program: on the positive side, a metaphysics of triviality; on the negative side, an ontology of discrete or gray nothings.[2] A rhythmological point of view brings to light a secret affinity between various areas of human life, which as a rule are never thought together: sleep and stupidity, the oldest refuges of world-remote existence, touch the cultures of drugs, meditation, and speculation—and music, the noble art that, as they say, transports us from gray hours into a better world. They follow one another like the lineaments of an immune system defending against an infectious, overwhelming world.

A passage in Erhart Kästners' book *Die Stundentrommel vom heiligen Berg Athos* [*The Hour Drum of the Holy Mountain Athos*] suggests how nocturnal acosmism can unite in a common pattern with the world-distancing power of monastic silence and the ecstasy of listening: [300]

> The hour drum, the wooden board, is struck at the beginning of the canonical hours [Horen], for example at the midnight service, so at the Orthros soon afterwards, so at the Proti. The hammer makes quick high and deep tones on the cypress beam, depending on whether it is struck in the middle or more towards the edge. The monk carries the beam in front of him. As he drums and walks, it echoes from here and there through the night, coming closer, receding, being swallowed by the dark gateway. This is the call to prayer of Athos: so much East, so much desert. So osseous, so arid; taken from the herbarium of ten thousand identical and ever-identical nights. And yet what captivating power in such clatter... Like the tip of a needle the drumming weaves itself into sleep and half-sleep... like an ivory tip, the wooden stanzas stitch themselves energetically to the black woolen fabric of the night.[3]

From here, it is only a short step to Emil Cioran's remarkable music theory:

> We carry within us all the music we have never heard in our life, which lies at the bottom of the abyss of memory. All that is musical in us is *memory*. When we did not have a *name*, we must have heard *everything*.[4]

If we succeeded in illuminating this gnostic aphorism, we would possess the key statement of a depth-musicology adequate to the tone-art of the past as well as the contemporary. I content [301] myself with breaking down Cioran's remark into two partial claims to amplify them. First: prior to individuation, we listen ahead—that is, the fetal ear anticipates the world as a totality of noise and sound which is always incoming; it listens ecstatically from the darkness of the sound-world, mostly world-oriented, in an irrepressible leaning toward the future. Second, after the formation of the ego, we listen back—the ear wants to undo the world as totality of noise, it yearns back to the archaic euphony of the pre-worldly interior, it activates the memory of a euphoric enstasy that accompanies us like an afterglow from paradise. One could say that the individuated or unhappy ear irresistibly strays from the real world into a space of intimate acosmic reminiscences.

Accordingly, music would always-already be the combination of two tendencies that mutually produce each other like dialectically related gestures. The one leads out of a positive nothing, out of the worldless, inward, womblike, into the manifestation, the open scene, the world-arena—the other out of the fullness, the dissonance, the overload back into the worldless, liberated, interiorized. The music of coming-to-the-world is a will to power as sound, which is brought forth on the line of a continuum coming from inside and which wills itself like an indispensable gesture of life; the music of retreat [*Rückzugs*], in contrast, after the breaking of the continuum, strives back into the acosmic floating in which the injured life gathers and heals itself as unwill to power. Therefore, in the primary gesture of all music there is a dualism of departure and return. [302] The first pole represents an adventistic motif that is entirely geared toward exodus, the desire to ring out and to step onto the ramp; the second represents a nirvanic trend toward turning inward and coming to an end, toward extinguishment and rest. Undoubtedly, the phantastic development of modern European music is grounded in its extraordinary power of embodiment, which was able to reconcile these basic tendencies anew at each stage of compositional technique. Western classical music magnificently orchestrated the emergence of subjectivity into the world as exit; at the same time, on high levels of melodic individuation it journeyed homeward to the innermost, the most distant—back to the islands of the blessed and into the gardens of the intimate Two. Where European music gave its best as an art of embodiment in the bodiless, it felicitously balanced subjects' yearning for dissolution with the work of ego-formation in a sounding body. Where it threatened to become too loud, it counterposed the positivism of orchestras and the machismo of composers with restraint, mellifluousness, mystery.

The synthetic energy of European high music seems to have been lost in the contemporary music business—for reasons that we will not discuss here. It would be pointless, under contemporary conditions, to try to conjure up the good old days of an integral music, in which what is now decomposed and differentiated was still united. One could say that the musical partial drives have become autonomous; each subculture listens to their own. Even the ear has discovered its polymorphous perversity and one single partner can hardly meet its needs. [303] In the following, I distinguish four types of current music, each corresponding to different auditory attitudes.

1. Authentically New Music exists primarily as an expert practice that is hardly a matter of singing and playing in the sense of traditional naïve musicality, but rather of exploring the means of sound production and compositional processes. It is the practice that most strongly accentuates the site of composition or first creation. The musical libido is bound up in the adventure of the score or in the allure of new generative techniques—its transmission to the site of performance and listening remains, as a rule, weak. This is also indicated by the fact that for New Music the criterion of immediate appeal is almost completely suspended. It is replaced by technical recognition and appreciation by the profession—vague feelings of accomplishment and indirect applause. As a result, New Music has largely decoupled itself from public audiences and retreated into solitary escalations. While Kafka's parable of the hunger artist has no longer applied to modern painters, sculptors, and writers for one or two generations, it retains its meaning for modern composers until further notice.

2. Performance music tries to make its way to the audience by offensive means. It, too, adheres to the primacy of production by aggressively superimposing the stage- and sound-events over the listeners' expectations; yet in the aggravation of the performance it still fights for the audience's response. As music with arena qualities, [304] it places the highest of premiums on the

burst of tone-gestures and on the musicians' stage presence. As risk music in action, it offers the best and the worst that contemporary ears can hear, whether it be pop vitalism *à la* Prince or aristocratic free jazz. No wonder that composers of New Music, if they ever break out of the festival reserve, are most likely to cross over into the performative field.

3. So-called light music [*Unterhaltungsmusik*], which should really be called diversional or sedative music, can be sure of a mass audience because it performs the function of protecting listeners from the risk of hearing something new. Who turns on sedative music does so in order to tune into surprise-free sound-worlds, of whatever quality. Through its sounding and resounding, it transmits the gospel that the known has eliminated the unknown. From this perspective, there are only disturbingly minor differences between the classical concert scene and light music [*U-Musik*]. Both stage music as a medium of the oldest conservatism, which promises harmony and repetition in ever predictable syntheses.

4. Functional music carves out partial effects of musical structures and makes sounds usable for defined purposes. Traditional pieces for marching, for winding anchor winches or for lulling children to sleep anticipated the functional tendency of music. Modernity submits effects of this kind to an explicit music-psychotechnical calculation. This is evident in the use of certain pieces in department stores, surgical operating rooms and lobbies, [305] as well as in hypnotic and meditative proceedings, telephone services, and the like. In each case, musical agreement-formulas are deployed between listening subjects and sound environments to preempt consent. In these practices of harmonic appropriation, the peaceful oases of music-based deep relaxation lie close beside the soundscapes of smiling totalitarianism.

Now it can be shown quite easily that the first two types of music go together roughly with the tendency of progressive exodus-music, whereas sedative and functional music can be assigned to the pole of reminiscence and retrogressive listening. Where the performative gesture and the experimental sensibility of New Music are at work, the tendency of coming-to-the-world in tonal gestures—progressively acosmic—remains clear; such music is fearlessly on its way from the formless to the formal, from the empty to the complex, from the silent to the manifest. It throws itself birth-mimetically forward, worldward, toward horizons that are never defined. The paths of being are strange, from the womb to Donaueschingen,[5] how is it possible?—but who are we to marvel that realizations are as they are? Progressive acosmism as music can tolerate the so-called outside world to the extent that it remains capable of filling the current world-space with its own tones. Auto-audition is enough; the rest will come. Such music therefore remains centered on the site of composition or production. Many composers of New Music make no effort to conceal their indifference as to whether there will still be an audience for the outcome of their experimentation. Even if the site of listening remains [306] empty, this is no reason for resignation. The story goes that the composer Edgar Varèse had sympathy for youthful moped drivers because they showed how it's done when it comes to heedlessly emitting a sound.

Sedative and functional musics, in contrast, from the outset relate only to the site of listening—they do everything for the listener, even if they do nothing for music. Pieces of this kind know little of the solitude of composition before the crowd. In the listening site targeted by light music and mood music, the regressive or nostalgic acosmism always already prevails. One only has ears for what aids in not hearing the world and otherness. Music for the unhappy ear replaces listening-ahead and approaches to new sound-worlds with the great turn back: it serves the urge to listen away, to listen prejudicially, to listen oneself out of dissonance. To this extent the history of music is always also an indicator of the transformations of the unhappy consciousness.[6] From the ancient veneration of Orpheus up to Schubert's praise of gentle art [*holden Kunst*], music has been ascribed a power to release the spell of reality and to transpose the listener into something that they—prematurely or not—call a better world. Conversely, in an era in which the unhappy consciousness is harnessed as a productive force for world-improvements, consoling and conciliatory music comes under suspicion of being opium for [307] the people. In fact the producers of tonal sedatives often act as cynical purveyors of fiction—like tabloid journalists with triads. For what do the people want?—nothing but musical devices for world-distancing: sweeteners, repetitions, simplifications. Tonal populism as consensus machine.

So where are we when we listen to music? The location remains vague—all that is certain is that one cannot be entirely in the world when listening to music. Listening in the musical sense always-already means: either moving toward the world or fleeing it. Thus the approach to an ontology of the ear gives way to the question of the ancient gnosis that in modernity can only manifest itself anonymously. Human being-in-the-world is, according to gnostic insight, to be represented as a being on the way or a being on the way back[7]—never as an insisting and dwelling, even if Heidegger in his late crypto-Catholic turn tried to readdress the human as an uncanny being of dwelling. The angels are rightly represented as playing music—they only sound; they do not listen. If they were listeners, they would resemble us. But we are condemned to music as to yearning and to freedom. As art of the condemned, music remains, per a saying of Thomas Mann, a demonic territory until further notice. [308]

B. In Percussion

1. *The sonorous cogito and the deaf spot—or, Descartes' attempt to think soundlessly*

To speak of a musical space makes sense only if there are borders of the musical. If all that is audible is to be designated as music in some sense, then the border between the musical and the non-musical falls away. Discourse about music—even the present one—would lose its object, would itself be music, transposed into the phonological score of normal speech. Do you hear? In a totally unbounded musical space, you would have to accept that, a piece of vocal philosophy for *solo cogito* is being premiered, without subtitles for the hard of hearing:

> LimaNeli Haschmu WaNschbok.
> Tama Haschmu: Portolabi Paehu
> Mui Pianeti
> Tamiba Temibo
> Temibanu Karuzu
> HaifatuNeti
> Haifatusolum RofuNo.
> Hoi Kirwimme. Katosta Healobe Kepipi
> Schamfuso ...

One could not say it more clearly.

Consequently, we were right to pose the questions of what musical space is, how to enter it, how to secure one's stay in it, and how to get out of it upon exiting into the nonmusical. An answer would [309] only be possible if the entire circumference of the musical could be traced back to an unmistakable basic experience, which, like an axiom or a sonorous cogito, supplied the inconcussible fundament of musical certainty. However, nothing is known of such a foundation, as little as of the musicological views of Descartes. Nevertheless it seems useful to me to repeat the Cartesian thought experiment, to sound its psychoacoustic aspect, which hitherto has remained unnoticed. Let us follow the author Descartes into his delirium of doubt and observe him as he tries to advance into a self-presence wherein a worldless, absolute, self-certain ego, without bodily proprioception, without organs, without exterior world, wants to attain itself as an inconcussible foundation of truth:

> I shall consider that the heavens, the air, the earth, colors, shapes, sounds, and all other external things are naught but the play of dreams... I shall consider myself as having no hands, no eyes, no flesh, no blood, no senses at all, but as having falsely believed that I had all these things...
>
> ... I have no senses; body, shape, extension, movement and place are nothing but chimeras. What, then, remains true? Perhaps just the one fact that nothing is certain...
>
> ... Am I something so bound up with a body and with senses that I cannot exist without them? Now that I have convinced myself that there is nothing in the world—no sky, no earth, no minds, no bodies—does it follow that I don't exist either? In no way does it follow; for if I convinced myself of something then *I* [310] certainly existed.—But there is a supremely powerful and cunning deceiver who deliberately deceives me all the time.—Even then, if he is deceiving me I undoubtedly exist: let him deceive me all he can, he will never bring it about that I am nothing as long as I think I am something. And so after thoroughly thinking the matter through, I conclude that this proposition: 'I am, *I* exist,' must be true as often as I assert it or think it...
>
> I exist... But for how long? For as long as I am thinking... I am a real and really existing thing, but what kind of thing? I have answered that: a thinking thing.[8]

The text can be read as a template for the exercise upon which idealistic philosophy—if not philosophy in general[9]—is based: the exercise in thinking away [*Wegdenken*].[10] What [311] is supposed to be thought away in this case is no less than the world as a whole, insofar as it is present in spatial and sensual representations. The ego of the exercise grasps itself as the irreducible remainder that is left when everything that can be thought away has been thought away. The Cartesian ur-sentence *Cogito, sum* can thus be reformulated: I think the world away and thereby attain myself. Or: I subtract all content from my representations—what remains, with absolute certainty, am "I"—that is the active principle of the representing life.

One can easily show that the cartesian exercise of subtraction centers around a blind spot—better: a deaf spot. The thinker assumes that he indubitably *is* insofar and so long as he thinks. But he does not notice—or, if he does notice, does not appreciate—that his coming-to-himself is dependent on his hearing-himself. It is not apparent to him that he can be certain only of himself and of his thinking because a hearing-himself precedes his "thinking-himself." The cartesian cogito presupposes a non-hearing that considers itself a pure thinking, or one could also say: a being-with-itself without any deceptive sensory mediation. This non-hearing applies to the mental voice that wanders through the thinker. It's as if the philosopher had found a method for bringing clairaudience and hardness-of-hearing to a common denominator. He stares into the content of thought without ever [312] paying attention to the sound of the voice in his thinking brain. Only in this way can he manage not to perceive that his I-think-I-am is in fact an I-hear-something-inside-me-talking-about-me-and-others. If this is noticed, the meaning of the cogito is altered from the ground up. The minimal inner sound of the thought-voice, if it is heard and thereby becomes intimate, is the first and only certainty that I can obtain by my self-experiment. One could call it a sonorous cogito. I hear something in me, therefore I am—at least I have sufficient reason to assert that I can safely "infer" my existence from this hearing in me. This I-hear-it-talking-in-me appears only when I have no intentions for myself or my thoughts. If I want to establish, prove, achieve something, this intent distorts the listening relation to the thoughts currently passing through me. I am already thinking of something other than the whispering tone of present thought. I would be—like Descartes— enslaved [*hörig*] to my search for foundations to such a degree that I do not notice how inner voices, presently certain, work within me. Ambition deafens—even in epistemology. There seems to be a radically exclusive relationship between constructive ambition and meditative attention. He who constructs does not hear himself; he who hears it sounding or talking in himself cannot simultaneously construct.

We thus convince ourselves that Descartes' "certainty" is grounded in the conviction of being able to construct oneself. Constructing is hearing-impaired action—self-assembly and self-foundation in one. The cogito finds itself in self-production and produces itself in finding itself. That is what is called the *fundamentum* [313] *inconcussum veritatis*. At the moment when constructing separates itself from hearing, the specifically modern science begins as a program of action for a hearing-impaired reason. To achieve security in the absolute, this thinking sacrifices the one true security, immediately given—the sonorous cogito as inner hearing—which admittedly offers a kind of certainty with which nothing at all can be done and with which nothing may even be begun as long as the musical intimacy of self-hearing persists. The sonorous cogito is the exact opposite of what Descartes demands of the logical cogito; it is neither a fundament—for it carries nothing—nor is it inconcussible, for it cannot be fixed. The most certain is, in truth, the most inoperable. Attention to inner voices and sounds means pure concussibility—availability for incoming acoustic presences; it is not I who gain a fundament from them, but they who submit me to their sounding. Who listens to the voices of thought is immersed in a sphere that is always-already quaked by others. Thinking is *in* the subject like the tone in the violin—in virtue of a vibrational relationship. Human beings, insofar as they think, are as it were musical instruments for ideas which represent the world. If the "instrument" takes heed of itself, it becomes clear to it: I am no *fundamentum inconcussum* but a *medium percussum*.

Because these depth-acoustical reflections concern an inner awareness that precedes the distinction between hearing music and hearing voices, our remarks on the sonorous cogito can be rendered fruitful for musical phenomena as well. [314] Music is music only in the self-audition of the "instrument," that is, the subject, insofar as one now understands it as an audio-sensitive medium. Music exists only in the listening subject. This sentence, of course, is valid only when paired with its inverse: the listening subject exists only in the music. The subject can thus be with itself only if something is given to it that lets itself be heard within it—without sound, no ear; without other, no self. It is only conscious of itself as a thinking and living being insofar as it is a medium vibrating with tones, voices, feelings, thoughts. This is, of course, not a new thought. For over a hundred years philosophy, on its way to radical modernity, has taken pains to purge the idealistic mirages of Cartesianism and the chimeras of absolute subjectivity in favor of an embodied intelligence. Existentiality instead of substantiality; resonance instead of autonomy; percussion instead of foundation.

Can listening thinking be brought about by logical measures? Is listening something that can be produced or caused at all? Can we ever do more than request a hearing? Judge for yourself:

> I éja
> Alo
> Myu
> Ssírio
> Ssa
> Schuá
> Ará
> Niíja
> Stuáz
> Brorr
> [315] Schjatt

> Ui ai laéla—oía ssísialu
> To trésa trésa trésa mischnumi
> Ia lon schtazúmato
> Ango laína la
> Lu liálo lu léiula
> Lu léla léja hioleíolu
> A túalo myo
> Myto túalo
> My ángo ína
> Ango gádse la
> Schia séngu ína
> Séngu ína la
> My ángo séngu
> Séngu ángola
> Mengádse
> Séngu
> Iná
> Leíola
> Kbaó
> Sagór
> Kadó

Kadó? *Cadeau*? Perhaps it comes down to learning better the art of accepting presents or pure gifts. The above text forms the last "sentence" or "movement" [*Satz*] of the *Ango laïna,* a kind of phonetic cantata for two voices from the year 1921 by Rudolf Blümner—designated by the author as "absolute poem." The *Ango laïna* shows what poetry can be after the emancipation of the vocabulary, grammar, rhetoric and phonetics of the German language. The poetological reflections of the poet show that [316] his antisemantic attack invokes the precedent of New Music. He wants to finally free poetic language from the curse of signification. The spontaneous combination of vowels and consonants is supposed to restore an original word-building power. Released from semantic slavery, sound steps out of the shadows and gives itself to audition with an unheard-of freshness and nakedness. Since it reminds us of nothing meaningful, the poem can appeal to an ear which it penetrates as if for the first time. But in appealing, it brings forth a new meaning: I am to be heard only; I am a text that brings the glad tidings of non-meaning to the world. Thus the poem, coquettishly, perhaps even a little decorously, carries its audibility before it and presents it to the public like a piquant gift. For most possible listeners, however, it falls out of earshot precisely by this procedure, for at the outset only two basic reactions are open to them: either they listen away from the phonetic structure, since after short time they "see through it" as a nonsense text, or they listen past the presence of the fresh syllables, since they always already, amused or not, "understand" the text—which here means as much as: acquiesce in the correct notion that the text signifies insignificance. What follows from this? Only that even such a poem, with its wager on pure audibility, can under no circumstances compel audition. The "phoning" of the phonemes must await the hearing of the hearer—with the usual risk of being in vain. Even the audial imperative of poetry—hark, thou shalt do nothing at this time but listen!—must ultimately [317] fall back on the question: are you listening? Did you hear? One cannot make a command of a question without annihilating listening. The sonic offering remains free. Even the moralizing demand for a "New Listening"—which has long polluted the atmosphere of New Music—just leads to the experience that the ear can only be touched in the mode of an offer to hear itself with the new sound.

2. Percussion, vibration, levitation

The insight that subjectivity is not of a fundamental but a medial nature was not reached overnight. I would like, on the basis of two eminent texts by Hegel and Heidegger, to call to mind traces of the great mediumistic dawn, in the course of which a resonating and quaking thinking sets itself apart from the reasoning and constructing intellect.

In the anthropology chapter of Hegel's *Encyclopedia of Philosophical Sciences,* 1830, the paragraph about the "feeling soul" contains several formulations which, by means of philosophical psychology, anticipate the developments of modern depth-psychology by more than 150 years. Hegel articulates for the first time the idea that a still utterly empty, experienceless, painless, and therefore indeterminate soul is permeated by determining and formative vibrations of the motherly medium. In §403 it says:

> Every individual is an infinite treasury of sensations, ideas, acquired lore, thoughts, etc.; and yet the ego is one and uncompounded, a deep featureless characterless mine, in which all this is stored up, without existing [318] ... The soul is virtually [*an sich*] the totality of nature: as an individual soul it is a monad.

This is followed by a logically stimulating explanation in §405:

> Though the sensitive individuality is undoubtedly a monadic individual, it is, because immediate, not yet as its self, not a true subject reflected into itself, and is therefore passive. Hence the individuality of its true self is a different subject from it.... By the self-hood of the latter it ... is set in vibration [*durchzittert*] and controlled without the least resistance on its part. This other subject by which it is so controlled may be called its genius.

What may have been obscure here, becomes translucent in the corollary of the same paragraph:

> In the ordinary course of nature this is the condition of the child in its mother's womb:—a condition neither merely bodily nor merely mental, but psychical—a correlation of soul to soul. Here are two individuals, yet in undivided psychic unity: the one as yet no self, as yet nothing impenetrable, incapable of resistance: the other is its actuating subject, the single self of the two. The mother is the genius of the child.[11]

In the midst of the idealistic construction, the word *vibration* registers an existential and depth-psychological quake that, against the fiercest opposition, grew increasingly vivid in the course of nineteenth- and twentieth- century psychological research. Absent participation in such tremors, there is no intellectual contemporaneity. [319] What Hegel still mistakes, however, is that the child in the womb is by no means just a passive vibratory medium for animation by the mother-spirit, but that through an early unfolding of the ear, it floats, as if spontaneously, pre-actively, from itself toward the sound-world of the coming life, as mother as well as not-mother. The auditive birth of the child, we now know, precedes the physical exit by several months. Hegel's philosophical embryology makes a bold connection between the ancient concept of genius and the most advanced state of bourgeois psychical research, the so-called animal magnetism, which goes back to Mesmer and his school.[12] Hegel listens back through the modern concept of the genius to the Latin source of the expression, and renders its psychological structure transparent. For ancient thought, having a genius means being another spirit's mouthpiece with one's own inner being. The genius is the host of a resonating force, and can utter extraordinary things, provided the indwelling of a high spirit in a profane individual makes epiphanies possible. On this background, we can understand the boldness of Hegel's transferral of the genius-soul-relation to the mother-fetus-relation. With the formulations of paragraphs 403-405, Hegel suggests the possibility of a bourgeois mediumism. [320] This of course would have remained impossible without the shocking effect of Mesmer's discoveries; only in consequence of mesmerism did a disenchantment of the womb-relation enter the realm of human possibility; ever since, critique of religious reason, still unformulated today, has been hanging in the air of the bourgeois world. A democratic esotericism—as authentic depth-psychology—has, in the wake of the discoveries of magnetic trance, of artificial somnambulism and hypnotic rapports, been brought into the world at least as a possibility. Now the mode of being of the child in the womb can be articulated publicly, without the discussion of these things needing to drive the soul out of what's being discussed. In Hegel one also finds statements, probably inspired by Nicolas Malebranche, regarding the natural magic of pure psychical transfusions, which can be traced to the model of fetal indwelling. In fact, the discovery of hypnotism had proved that this suggestive mode of being is not dispelled once and for all with birth and with subjects' entry into adulthood. The application of magnetism to adults demonstrated clearly enough that the fetal vibrational plane can have a persistent afterlife—and the contemporaries of the first hypnotists may have shuddered at the thought of the possible abuse of magnetic rapports.[13] As for philosophical pedagogy, then as now it could think of nothing but the necessary demise [321] of magnetic suggestibility; its goal was the erection of the autonomous subject, shielded from vibrations. Typical in this regard is the passage in which Hegel says that the purely passive, i.e. fetal soul was "as yet nothing impenetrable, incapable of resistance." In the word *impenetrable* one hears an echo of the cartesian *inconcussum*—while the phrase "not yet" makes clear the meaning of all self-education: the attainment of inconcussibility.

After Hegel and Mesmer, the rapping on the posts of impenetrable subjectivity never ceased. An age of music and psychology dawns that relates the glass palaces of rationality to a seismic below. The principle of self-preservation is challenged by a principle of concussion. Young Hegelian philosophers, especially Bauer, Kierkegaard, Marx, violently set the metaphysical treble onto the bass of reality. Thought is all at once looking for ways out into the real, the noisy, the emancipating—as if it had acquired from somewhere the strength to stop thinking away the below. If ever there was a "new hearing," it came to pass in Engels' reports on the situation of the working class in England. Post-idealistic philosophy grew ears for what cried out to heaven and eyes for what can no longer be passively witnessed. What had formerly been the pride of metaphysics suddenly appears as just a vain overtone above the root-tone of real human life. [322] With Schopenhauer a breakthrough takes place, after which the ground of the world, the will, is presented as purely musical. Schopenhauer still remains caught in the spell of classical aesthetics, insofar as he ascribes to music primarily the role of a remedy; he underestimates its capacity, proven by modernity, to participate in the emergence of the horrific in the sounding medium itself.

Heidegger's new approach to thinking means at the same time an advance along the line on which the epochal break-in of tones and moods into the post-idealistic basic conception of existence takes place. What in Descartes' meditation on thinking-away might still look like a methodically controlled effort of the subject turns out to be a passion and a horror in Heidegger: the involuntarily suffered withdrawal of the world. In his analysis of existential moods, Heidegger raises the question whether there is one among them in which "the nothing reveals itself according to the sense of disclosure"—and answers it in the affirmative, by indicating how the features of being disintegrate into nothing in "deep boredom." What Heidegger says in his description of anxiety remains decisive:

> Anxiety is indeed anxiety in the face of . . . , but not in the face of this or that thing. Anxiety in the face of . . . is always anxiety concerning . . . but not concerning this or that. . . . In anxiety—we say— "one feels uncanny." What is "it" that makes "one" feel uncanny? We cannot say what it is before which one feels uncanny. All things and we ourselves sink into indifference. This, however, is not in the sense of mere disappearance. Rather, in their very receding, things turn toward us. The receding of beings as a whole, closing in on us in anxiety, oppresses us. We can get no hold on things. In the slipping away of beings only this "no hold on things" comes over us and remains.
>
> Anxiety makes manifest the nothing.
>
> We "hover" in anxiety. More precisely, anxiety leaves us hanging, because it induces the slipping away of beings as a whole. This implies that we ourselves—we humans who are in being—in the midst of beings slip away from ourselves. At bottom therefore it is not as though "you" or "I" feel uncanny; rather it is this way for some "one." In the altogether unsettling experience of this hovering where there is nothing to hold on to, pure Da-sein is all that is still there.[14]

[323]
Certainly even Heidegger's convulsion [*Durchschütterung*] is not an immediately musical moment in the sense of music-making—no more than Hegel's passively trembling childhood. And yet this theory of anxiety deals with a pre-tuning of the subject as *medium percussum,* whereby the self reveals the properties of a resonating body. Moreover, Dasein's being held out into the "nothing" has a direct depth-musicological consequence: Heidegger's anxiety points to a catastrophe of hearing that is partly responsible for the emergence of music. The original auditory accident is the foil onto which all later rehearing of music is set. When during "rare" experiences of great anxiety the presence of nothingness [324] occurs to us, the sound of being as a whole also vanishes and withdraws. Being-there [*Da-sein*] in the world always-already means being exposed to a sphere where non-music is possible for the first time. Who is born has fallen out of the depth-acoustic continuum of the motherly instrument. The acute convulsion of anxiety arises from the loss of such music, which we *no longer* hear when we are in the world. A precise reading of Heidegger's dark speech makes us recognize that the anxiety in question can be none other than the anxiety in face of

the death of inborn music, the anxiety of the horrific silence of the world after separation from the maternal medium. Everything that will exist later as made music originates from a resurrected and retrieved music, that testifies to the continuum even after its destruction.[15] Retrieved music is a connection to the continuum after its catastrophe. When the heartbeat and the visceral noise of the primary musical instrument are no longer audible, the emergency of existential panic arises. For only there, in the empty levitation "in the world," does an uncanny silent vastness unfold, in which the acoustic continuum of the *musique maternelle* is sublated; only through an imperiled acoustic Ariadne's thread does the unbound individual remain in touch with the bearing force proper to the first, the inner, the shared sound-world. One understands why Heidegger could be convinced that beneath the soundscape of busy day-to-day life the old panic "sleeps": what is normally sleeping [325] possesses the authenticity of the horrific, which, if I withstand it, leads me to myself as an "existing" being. That is why Heidegger cannot emphasize enough that the inauthentic life passes in noise and idle talk, while authentication involves anxiety before a terrifying silence:

the originary anxiety in Dasein is usually repressed. Anxiety is there. It is only sleeping. Its breath quivers perpetually through Dasein.[16]

To its essence belongs a "peculiar calm," an "entranced calm," and the urge to drown out the "vacant silence."[17] One could call the hearing of silence a panic cogito, since it entails Dasein's hearing itself in intimacy with the uncanny. I hear nothing more, therefore I am there. Being there in the silence of the world is a string that vibrates with its own tension. It may be that the meditators of all ages have sought silence and stillness because the self-hearing of existence in the quieting of noise helps tense the string. Therefore music not only celebrates the reconnection to the continuum but also, if it is more than sedative or narcotic, always recalls the cosmic silence of existence.

8

How do we stir the sleep of the world?
Conjectures on awakening

> Today religious experience has again become universal ("catholic") and abyssal. It expresses itself in every experience as the lack of a ground.
> —Vilém Flusser, *The Ground Underfoot*

> Sleep is at bottom only the most consistent of your disappointments.
> —Henri Michaux, *Tent Posts*

Again a morning takes care that there will be me. A light breeze moves through the half-darkness; in the room appear omens of a something that intimates itself through rustlings. This being—or whatever else what stirs there can be called—behaves not unlike parents who no longer bother to be quiet when the time has come for the kids to get up. The noises become aggressive, not to say inconsiderate. Thus, whatever else the world may be, all that is certain is that it's something that starts running before I do. Flies of light land on the eyelids; they won't stop administering their torments until they've forced the eyes to give up their resistance to the day. I am permeated with a sense of where the scene is heading. [327] I have experienced what's coming too often for there to be any misunderstanding about the outcome of the case. I know what they are up to—they intend to bring me, there's no doubt about it, back to myself. Long have I understood that during the night the dark-clad bath attendants walk up and down between the sleeping-tubs and, toward morning, or whenever they think enough is enough, pull the plug. As the sleep water runs off, the body comes slowly back and senses itself as a vague tendency that soon will be doing this and that—one will call it acting, once one is back on one's feet. I would have to be ill not to draw conclusions from the return of the body; one doesn't stay long in a drained tub; once the body has returned as a clue and an assignment, I can't be far off; after my arrival, the first thought and first gesture aren't long in coming. From the tub-warm darkness rise preforms of personality. No one has to tell me that the goal of the exercise is verticality; and this morning something in me is ready to conform to the genetic fate that made us risky beings, on two legs, with free hands—the head set at the highest point, favorable to cool overviews. No one will be able to say that this morning I did not respond to the call to human dignity. The improbable—it's happening now, the upright walk, now it's an event, my standing-there on no more than two legs is an accomplished fact, from here, it will be a matter of course to rehearse an abridgement of mankind's ascent to the height of consciousness. If the phone were to ring, [328] once, twice, the third time I would already pick up the receiver, a caller might ask for someone by my name, and at that time I would be able—I guarantee—to produce the words "It's me," without any pathos, in the tone of a saddled world-denizen who knows not a weak minute. "You're speaking with whom you seek, what is it?" I might say, as if any suspicion that I'd been world-remote for even a moment were in bad taste. I would make the early-morning caller understand that I persistently hold this established post of creation, even at an hour when other, hollower beings, gnawed by absence, wouldn't yet be able to maintain their identity with themselves. But even when no ringing prompts me to early upswings of self-assertion—there will be no going back, and I go, as an old-fashioned room crosser, to confront the first tasks; of course, when there is no call from the outside, self-consciousness takes longer to find me; being remains formless and familiar for a while. Should I be proud to be someone who has just emerged from bed? Unable to represent the night behind me as a meaningful past, I behave rather like a refugee who steps listlessly off the boat, at best a regular passenger who, without looking back, leaves the ferry to rush toward his tasks on land. There is no longer any doubt about the victory of the vertical.

Now it is noon—there is no alternative to day and doing. My alertness is like a Great Dane trotting loosely beside its owner. I sit at the desk as if at a conductor's stand, [329] I have access to an active vocabulary of fifty thousand signs, judgment oozes into the finest crevices, no problem is safe from my perusal, the brain works like the UN telex center. Surrounded by monitors, telephones, magazines, and bookshelves, I enjoy my encirclement by an informatically processed reality. The cosmos of problems besieges my desk; I'm not far from top form. Like a bishop, I officiate in a cathedral of difficulties. In the course of a few hours, I talk over the lines to more people than a bushman will meet in a lifetime, and yet a kind of material contact occurs with each partner, a couple minutes of shared reality unfold—beyond nearness and distance, beyond intimacy and estrangement. For the likes of us, existing means being kept awake by universal questions. Am I mistaken? It seems to me as if all facts and truths target these bright moments—the midday wakefulness is magnetic. All problems come to her and cajole her, as if wishing to ride on her back. Is politics not in fact, as the Greeks said, a child of attention and care? That is what it means to be a member of the universal class today: whoever knows something about mankind becomes, possibly against his will, its agent or official. Who said that officials are absent-minded and dull? And what if the opposite were true? Are there not in fact offices that make the mind? The troubles of mankind line up at the world-official's head [330] and press for their solution. Who could blame us if our eyes get tired at some point in the afternoon? The gaze wanders to the window—not because there's something special to see there, but because constant readiness for the great issues instills apathy; there arises a need for pauses, and in the pauses, doubt. What is it that compels us to diligence? What cruelty in the ground of the world necessitates so much circumspection, so much administration? In the wakefulness of the world-official shimmers a trace of resignation; his eyes stare at the horizon as if seeing in the distance a trench in which the losers of millennia lie side by side.

Toward evening a sense of distance sets in; it's as if one had been on a long train ride and suddenly noticed that the landscape has changed. How shall I describe it? Among non-intellectual colleagues, I might say that it was a long day. Among friends, I might ask, don't you feel the world is disappearing behind a bend? I no longer see problems, only stimuli. How did beauty become so important? Now there is much more wakeful life than there are serious topics to fill it. I drift on the raft of time toward the frontier;

I perceive the clouds, the passersby, the neon signs, the leaves of the poplar tremble outside the window, we are synchronized. I am as awake as during an alarm, even though I expect nothing to happen. In a way that I barely understand, I hover in mortal danger. What keeps me on my toes is a threat so vague that it might as well be a promise of bliss. For ten minutes I have been sitting still as if in the presence of a classical painting. [331] Now I realize that the blackness of the sky is a measure of its distance. My room is a middle floor of the universe, the walls shouldn't be taken too seriously. Most promising is the door, since the beloved could come through it. Is it a consequence of overstimulation if the room seems to me emptier than usual? Perhaps this wakefulness in me is the remnant that was left when, long ago, I gave up waiting for the lost one. In her place came innumerable impressions. Oh, the whole world was able to enter me because she didn't return. Since we became two, there is too much space for experiences; this has been going on for too long; the term *world-picture* gives only a vague idea of the effort it takes to crudely fill the void our separation left behind. I am wakeful because I am merely a remainder of two. If she came in now, I'm sure the world would go down in an instant. Something tells me that she will come; something else in me knows she won't. The attempt to believe both leads to exhaustion. So, at last, this day too shatters on the block of undecidability. Sleep, I know, will not solve any problem; it will disarm the problematic. Where are the issues that were so pressing on the stage of the day?—they no longer concern me. I cannot say with certainty whether I have ever understood what a problem is. The world no longer retains me—it passes out of me like a sister in a nun's winged cap and loose gown, turning off the light behind her. What can I do but let it go in good faith? That in spite of everything I am a child of the world—is this not proven by the fact that I trust it enough to accept its end without panic? [332] Until tomorrow, I am immortal. The world, it will come back—like an old star and a new promise; it will arrive young, untouched, unprecedented, at once familiar and rediscovered, and in both cases the experienced heart will say, it is always like that, I know it, it was the first that touched me. How could I not have the affair of my life with it?

1. Clearing—luxury—alert

What we call world exists only for creatures that do not have to be ready to flee at every second. If such a creature, which has world, lifts its head, it is carried by the sure expectation that the horizon will not suddenly split in two. There comes no enemy, there comes no prey. The watchers are in their places, no alarm signal has given any hint of danger. The stillness of the world can be counted on until the next event. Now the world-creature looks up and enjoys the earliest theory: seeing the field and not having to flee. No attacker violates the visual circle of the animal that has looked up; no moving threat compels action, no distress call compels intervention; some time will pass until the next hunger. The open horizon offers a field of visibilities that are not changed by watching. [333] What does change is the eyes, which open wider than usual in view of the stillness of all things. It's as if they had a little extra vision left to waste. An unknown shine enters the eyes, and although it would be too much to say that they celebrate, still they are brighter than those of animals. Animals live on a spectrum between fear and indifference, sometimes they are merry in a blind way. We, however, have access to the clearing. With the serenity that rises in the eyes of the early world-viewers, the history of luxury begins. Nothing will ever again be as generous as the first lavishing of attention on the things that surround the protected human animal, representing neither danger nor benefit; from then on, serenity takes over in him. Pleasure rises from the belly into the eyes and turns into glances. Serene awakeness makes man the patron of the universe. He has an attentive glow to give, from which all interest in successful things—indeed in all that is—will issue. The world can become cosmos, jewel, beautiful present, because a seeing power fancies it. World is now all that from which we no longer flee. The stones rest, the plants radiate constancy, there is nothing to fear from the birds, the earth will not withdraw under our feet; at night the stars attract attention by glittering, [334] as if they wanted to imitate the luxurious glances that look up at them to read figures. The fact that they are exposed to observant glances hardly seems to trouble the things themselves. They keep to their way of being, coming, staying and going as is peculiar to them. Things are thus beings that show less tendency to flee than their agile observers. Their stability is the stuff of which our certainty of knowing them is made. Their good-natured self-display creates a ground of trust on which watchfulness turns into knowledge.

On it, the alert, luxurious animal crosses over into the human field. There grows the world as all that with which we are familiar. Humanization occurs in virtue of a metamorphosis of animal wakefulness into shared knowledge of things and of their epitome, which will one day be called world.

Luxury makes human beings possible, and in them the known world. Because humans are from the beginning the animals that spoil and release each other; because all along they keep watch for each other and give themselves more security than any living being enjoyed before, they hold the external world at bay since the dawn of time. Mankind originates in a secession from the Old Nature. One could speak of a birth of man from the spirit of vigilance. In the age of primitive hordes, the species waxes in an incubator of attention, empathy, complicity and emotional surplus. In the beginning, we set our collective intelligence against the world as the totality of dangers. Being smart together: the stuff the species is made of. "God," "love," "enlightenment," "wisdom:" later names for the miracle, intense from the start, [335] that waking life finds itself secured and energized by other waking lives. We are immersed in the conspiracy of neighbors. Group vigilance initiates the adventure that humans can become promoters of more delicate, more imaginative, "higher" humans. All luxury arises on the watch of others. What we call culture is the late consequence of the fact that hundreds of thousands of years ago, one animal—more awake than all the rest—put more clearance around itself than all the others. In the distance from the environment guaranteed by the collective alertness of the ancient horde, the superfluous, the charming, the risky began to bloom. Man became the theoretical and frivolous animal. In the theoretical species, skins became more sensitive than was advisable, women more pretty than was necessary, brains more open to the world than was safe. When the first people introduce the first word for world, they draw an imperceptible line around all that is, such that the eyes of the luxury-animals have something to grasp as the whole—their whole—with their free, overflowing vision.

That the world dawns in man presupposes the precarious openness to the world that takes place in the luxury development of the attention-animal homo sapiens. From the primitive communism of attention, the riskiest of all mutations: the individualism of late world- and self-consciousness could unfold. [336] In this respect, culture, "high" as well as early, is always-already a descendant of patronage—that is, an effect of man's favor for man. The originary patronage consists in the mutual gift of vigilance, which stabilizes a climate favorable for improbable developments. In later times, which we now call antiquity, the primal gift of attentiveness is thematized under the title of friendship—suggesting that intimacy has become problematic in the ancient metropolitan and imperial traffic worlds. Indeed, it is not a power-protected insularity that creates the optimal early high-cultural atmospheres—as Walter Benjamin suggested in a dangerous remark about late bourgeois culture—but rather an attention-protected intimacy. The connection between high culture and the office of guardianship is still evident in Plato's ideal polis.

If it is plausible to understand humankind as a whole as a product of its revolutionary-luxurious augmentation of attention, then obviously [337] human subjectivity is to be grasped not from the fact of egoic self-consciousness, but from the primitive coalition between the awakeness of the individual and that of its co-wakers. The smallest unit of self-consciousness is already a dyad: the self and its guardian, or also: the guardian and the other whom he or she watches over. That this applies genus-wide to all not completely failed mother-child relationships of the specifically human type needn't be discussed in detail here; fathers are also important in a cultural-evolutionary perspective, especially as guardians of their children's chances in life; this too seems all but self-evident. In contrast, the unconceived relationship between self and guardian deserves some comment from a psychological perspective; it is not sufficiently known that it conceals the keys to the history of mind, subjectivity and soul. The Occidental ideology of independence, which stretches from the Stoics to the liberals of our day, has blocked a meaningful discussion of the original division of wakefulness in intimate dyads and triads; from the outset it unjustly elevates the individual as the self-caring subject. In doing so, it points, more involuntarily than consciously, to the fact that for two or three millennia typical adult urbanites and statists have been forced to live in a permanent state of self-preservation, transfixed in themselves as in a glass dome, at a persistent distance from solution in old human watch-group solidarity. Even Michel Foucault's rediscovery of the late-ancient "techniques" of *souci de soi* [338] stands in the penumbra of this early individualistic blindness.

Nevertheless, the ancient tendency to shift attention from group vigilance to self-observation was one of the conditions of possibility for the first discovery of the mind in the advanced cultures of the axial age, namely in Greek philosophizing. Thinking can only unfold into a culture of argumentation, that is, into philosophy, when a newly canalized self-attention frees individuals to concern themselves with the denser or "logical" connection of thoughts to their predecessors—then the hour of the "text" and "internal consistency" has arrived. There can be philosophy and rational worldviews only when more attention is paid in the thinkers' consciousness to making propositions appear interconnected than to making them plausible to listeners or correspondent with states of affairs. From then on, non-narrative great texts emerge that introduce consciousness to sentences that consecutively "follow" from one another, while at the same time dirempting it from circumstances and referents. Thus begins the history of metaphysics as the victory march of an absent-minded concentration on truths to be developed argumentatively. The philosophers' gaze goes out to structures that only show themselves to linear, "consistent" thought—not to the free-floating synchronic perceptions of the watchmen, [339] who keep to the arch-human awareness of the eventful world-field before the city wall. All traces of watchful lurking for prey and danger tend to vanish in philosophical speech; its bliss is the melting of the soul at the revelation of eternally true structures and traits. The adventure of mathesis starts from here. It is the triumph of the city, of the temple, and of the philosopher's garden, that discourses could arise there that were able to draw all attention to their inner or logical progression without an alarm or an objection from outside being allowed to break the coherence of the sentences. As long as there have been great texts, the luxuriant contemplativeness of the urban wakeful animal has oscillated between the silent synchronic view of the total circumstance "world" and the critically listening comprehension of deep speeches about the structure of the whole. This state of affairs has not changed substantially up to present times; even today we experience intelligence in its most awake forms as a hovering between speechless regard for overall situations, especially in art, and precise following along with coherent world-interpreting texts. At the same time, we take it for granted that being awake is an achievement of the individual alone, as if he could have carried out the transition from vigilance to knowledge entirely by himself. That even our attentive hovering between situational awareness and textual comprehension is a waking that owes infinitely much to the unnoticed patronage of invisible co-watchers—this is a thought that must evade even the brightest consciousness, as long as the latter remains in the individualistic daze that thinks it is only watching for itself. [340]

If we go back before the individualistic semblance, we immediately discover the traces of an older order of wakefulness, in which several disparate intelligences must always be combined in order for something like human life, and that means at first and for a long time: life in hordes and tribes, to become possible. This is particularly true for the prominent ethnic groups of high-cultural ages. In a psychohistorical and religio-philosophical perspective, high culture could be characterized as a formation of human intelligence that excels in metaphysicizing the shared wakefulness of ancient hordes. Ethnic guardian spirits now transform into world-knowing sky gods. "God" is no longer just an energy field or a good shepherd of his human herd. The early theoplasm now condenses into penetrating, integrating, balancing, and equalizing superintelligences, which position themselves as ever-open world-eyes at superior distance and in innermost intimacy with beings as a whole and, in the first place, their living center. One could speak of a cognitive revolution of the divine, which changes from an active power into a power of consciousness. As if under an evolutionary pressure, the early history-making or state-building peoples, namely Egyptians, Greeks, Persians, Jews, and Romans, set over themselves during their people-forming periods wakeful total intelligences [341] that see through and govern the coherence of the world as a whole; such peoples must learn, from then on, to live under the precarious, mostly veiled presence of judgmental deities of wakefulness. The attempt to bring these deities closer to human imagination mobilizes the peoples' priestly and philosophical intelligence in an unprecedented way. The ancient Mediterranean theologies represent experiments in placing the world under the monarchy of principles which, through all-attention and all-knowledge, ensure the coherence of all things. Most bluntly, ancient Rabbinic and prophetic theology addresses the Jewish god as guardian, leader, and judge of his favored people. But similar traits also appear unmistakably in the Egyptian gods Horus, Re and Aton, in the Olympic Zeus and the Capitoline Jupiter. Where the idea gains strength that the omnipresent and sleepless world-witnessing god has always-already grasped the coherence of things in his synoptic knowledge, human intelligences can feel encouraged to attempt more momentous world-interpretations in imitation of the divine knowledge. In this formation, every human knowledge and every human awakeness is towered over by a watcher in the foundation of the world who co-knows and completely pervades everything that happens here in the front stage of being. Once the concept of a wise and ever-wakeful god had been established, it must have been obvious to understand far-reaching world-affecting thought—which now means more than a prelinguistic awareness of the [342] overall circumstance—as a mode of presence of the co-knowing and judgmental god in human consciousness. The exemplary thinkers would then not be mere isolated speculators, as the moderns are tempted to think. Rather, they, along with all that takes place in their illuminated heads, would be branch consciousnesses of the world-knowing god and waking locales of the absolute witness, who splinters and separates into as many perspective self-perceptions as there are eyes and souls. What knowingly wakes in the thinkers would then not be just the old sensitive and animal life procuring extended prospects by means of higher speech symbols; rather, what wakes in us would be the divine knowledge of the status quo of the world process, which has individualized itself in us as its focal points. The "divine knowledge" can be interpreted, in a persistent anthropological perspective, as the metaphysicized intelligence of peoples setting out into history. The intelligences they project into the sky or into the world-ground are at the same time the bases of security whose clearing and clarifying effect will make the risk of the macrocosm bearable for high-cultural subjects. How else could I accept that I am now myself a window onto the immeasurable and the inhumanly great? Only if it is promised that what wakes in me is an intelligence that has always permeated the world can I have the courage to accept myself as a stage for world-affecting thoughts, indeed as an eye of the world at all. What appears psychologically as ego appears ontologically as a here-now site of cosmic openness. [343] If the watcher-consciousness is exaggerated to the extreme, as in certain Indian systems, the conclusion is inevitable that in the meditations of the truly thinking, indeed potentially in every human consciousness, "the universe itself" opens its eyes—assuming that the universe as a whole is moving, as it were, humanward and knowledgeward. Human vigilance that becomes knowledge would then be a relay of the absolute, which comes through with us. The reed that thinks is the reed in which all non-reed comes to itself. What wakes in the awakened is always the greater intelligence, which uses mine as a window for its shining-through.

Even on this level, where the Other who watches through and "over" me is conceived only in high metaphysization, one can easily recognize the arch-human coalition of attentions and the originary division of watches in the hominizing dyad together with its social extensions. Only now, the embedding of each consciousness in a milieu of canny companions has become the meteoric metaphysical relationship between the meditator or thinker and the world-overlooking god who lets himself be known in him. But this metaphysicized knowing and waking of the god "through me" actualizes more than ever the ancient principle, that only through the patronage of [344] the wakeful other is my own consciousness freed for the possibility of serenely lavishing its attention on the coherence of things. As strict as the god of the metaphysicians may often seem to be, his decisive importance for the evolution of human consciousness lay in his agreement with the luxury of great views; with them, he "supervises" his world in the thinkers. The *sophon* as the wise divine is an index of the dose of favoritism by "super"vision that the intelligence of the individual must experience in order to become more serene and more serious than that of the primitive which he was.

2. Joining the community—Toward a political ontology of the watch-room after Heraclitus, Zarathustra, and Isaiah

As diurnal creatures, humans have always tended to mythically exaggerate the light that illuminates the world-field as their sphere of action. But a radical metaphysization of the day can only come about after the turn to [345] the rational world-picture in the axial age, in which the surveillance of the world by the overwakefulness of the wise and "all-separated" god is to become permanent. The most important agent and witness of this turn, as far as the narrower European tradition is concerned, is Heraclitus of Ephesus. The fragments of his teaching contain encrypted traces of a process that could be described as a high-cultural watch-room revolution. Heraclitus enters and opens a zone of continuous knowledge-brightness, which is placed like a higher floor above the changeful light-dark world of mortal states. On this upper floor the adventure of generalization articulates itself; it claims to juxtapose the concretism of small-scale everyday life with a new teaching whose basic motif is: to belong together in the conceived great. For there to be greatness, the coherent totality of things must always already exist as the greater, the greatest. Precisely this is the cosmos of cooperating polarities. For the Western Hemisphere, this marks the beginning of the age of the world concept—the age of logical and moral bridgings from the narrow into the wide, from the domestic into the enormous, from the touch of things at hand to the view of the whole. This deep agitation of intelligence by the exodus into the greater is what initiates the becoming-philosophical of the world itself. The lighting of the higher zone springs from the *logos*, which is said to administer the universe. To think in accordance with the *logos* is to enter a heightened state of wakefulness as the logical antenna of an extended affiliation with great contexts; this new logos-awakeness relates to the awakeness of the bad multitude (*hoi polloi kakoi*) as to another sleep. [346] Heraclitus has in mind the image of a crowd who do not want to awaken even during the day, insofar as their awakening does not reach the *koinon*, the communal, the general, the day of *logos*, but remains stuck in "private thinking," in old wives' tales, children's toys, obsessions. Never before had one spoken so sharply of the "idiocy" of men who do not grasp the wide generality because they are full of miserable personality. Heraclitus denounces the civil somnambulism that poses as urban life. Nor is the *polymathie* of poets and singers safe from his sarcasm. Even the intelligent Pythagoras is accused by Heraclitus of bad "personal wisdom" that turns its back on the *koinon*. His sharpest hatred, however, is directed against the shamans and sorcerers' apprentices of folk culture, who perform as illogicians and revel in the obscure and uncommon; he calls these "magi, bacchae, maenads, and mystics" the "wanderers in the night" (*nyktipóloi*); he threatens them with hellish things after death. One could imagine that Heraclitus' nastiest remark, that pigs bathe in manure, refers to them. What, in contrast, does the Heraclitean day signify? It is the divine wisdom (*sophon*) which holds itself by itself in uninterrupted brightness as knowledge of the One composed of opposites. Such wisdom alone is God—not for nothing does Heraclitus speak as the theologian of Apollo. He, separated from all yet forcing all things together, is a day beyond day and night, a light beyond inflaming and extinguishing, a logos beyond expression and secrecy, a wakefulness beyond waking and sleeping—[347] where the word *beyond* could always also mean *through* both or *in* both.

I now want to show that the Heraclitean logos-day essentially signifies the metaphysicized watch-room of the Greek polis—and beyond this, the everyday concern-space of all later European and world "politics." The discovery or proclamation of the logos-day marks the advent of political or polistic ontology; for the being of the city can only rise with the opening of the *koinon*, the common ground of open and bright speech. Common here denotes the condition of an ordering intelligence that, as "law," *nomos*, watches over the city and its members. For this diurnal waking consciousness of the common, the night necessarily presents itself an adversary. Night is the state in which each and every civilian leaves the *koinon* to descend into his "own world," into his idiocy, into his dream dialogues with the dead. The sleeping are anomic, apolitical, amathic, alogical. Asleep, the citizens sink into the Hades beneath the city. A first critique of the political night is alluded to in an obscure fragment of Heraclitus that was passed on by Clement of Alexandria:

In the night man kindles a light for himself, dying, his vision is extinguished; still alive, he stirs the sleep of the dead, his vision is extinguished; when awake, he stirs the sleeping.

[348] If the world is that which can be spoken of in the watch-room of urban communality, then it goes without saying why in the city night the world is at risk of going under. People cease to be citizens and gather to their dead; in privacy they relinquish what they have in common; they sleep, they believe, they toss and turn, they dream. Each for himself, none for the city—with one exception, on which everything hangs: the wise God and his vicarious accomplice, the philosopher, hold open the wakeful urban "outer" space, even when the beastly privacy of the many seems to prevail. The god above the city and the philosopher within it sublate the night along with its tendency to annihilate the universal. Therefore the city can be completely itself only in the thought of its awakest and strangest citizen—the philosopher who meditates and affirms the law, the invisible harmony, the logos of the whole. It could happen that in a city of sleepwalkers, drunks, and wet souls only a single citizen keeps the general and common before his eyes; then it would be true what Fragment 112 says: "It is law, too, to obey the will of one."

Because the Heraclitean doctrine of the *koinon* is a doctrine of being that applies to the agora and the temple, not to the sectarian gardens and hermitages, there is little of the spirit of leisure or the struggle for transfiguration in the thought of the logos-philosopher. Ephesus is not yet Athens, but neither is it the *Thebaid*. Heraclitus' depth is not so much academic-luxurious or religious-numinous as political-tragic; his thinking has the severity of a life-and-death municipal service. [349] As interpreter of the world, he also always remains guardian of the city and interpreter of war (*polemos*), without which no life in the *polis* was conceivable in his time. In the world-alertness of the metaphysician of Ephesus, a spark of city-soldierly readiness remains present. Whoever wants to hold open the urban space of vigilance and truth must also be prepared to defend the wall. Perhaps the Greeks of the *polis* period only called men mortals because they were supposed to be ready to lose their lives in the battle for their city. In this respect, even the highly original Heraclitus conforms to the most powerful Greek norm: "Those killed in battle are honored by gods and men." We now know: the city is the form of the world; but the world is the epitome of all seriousness because it is the scene of elimination battles for the fateless. The doctrine of human being as being-mortal-for-the-city is serious enough to pose the question of the city martyrs and their reward by the ever-wakeful god. Perhaps it is to them that the dark fragment (Fragment 119) refers:

they rise from (death)-sleep and in waking become watchmen over the living and the dead.

In Heraclitus' thought, the primordial communism of attention unfolds in a specifically high-cultural way. The city, the Ephesian seems to know, can only survive as the form of the world in general if it makes the transition from vigilance to knowledge in its own way. This implies that city-born knowledge, even where it is theoretically or aesthetically luxurious, must never [350] completely stop being a danger-conscious awakeness, thus a political readiness for trouble and alarm. The watch-room of the city is a room of peace supported by conviviality, which must continuously set itself off against war and madness. Thus Heraclitus observes with anger all tendencies that lead to the destruction of the communal waking world: people's propensity for the night of private opinions; the appearance of sorcerers and trance artists, who schlepp knocked-off rural ecstasy gods into the city to undermine the bright speeches in the agora; the procession of drug maestros and illusionists, who, under the pretext of offering magic illuminations, lure citizens away into ever deeper and more vicious blackouts until they are completely lost to the objectives of urban coexistence. Where such forces take the helm, it is all over for the ideals of polis-life, wherein civic liberty is a function of civic wisdom; then the main clause of the oldest political ontology: "prudence is the most important virtue" (*sophronein arete megiste*) (Fragment 109), no longer holds. The occult powers rise from the night and take one citizen after another. The religious re-enchantment movements of the Roman imperial period show how far this can go; then, of course, the spirit of the city has long since been replaced by the imperial program of the god-emperor. When Heraclitus warns against *hybris* in some grave phrases, we should understand these statements as defense theses on the protection of the polis-watch-room. *"Hybris* should be extinguished even more urgently than a great fire" (Fragment 100). Hybris is the aberration of claiming to lead the city on the basis of nocturnal inspirations by private demons. [351] It prepares the flooding of the public by the insignia and power-words of an ultimately idiotic, uncommon and exorbitant magic will. It disintegrates the primal coalition of human intelligences that are supposed to come together for the good common life, and presents acting out madness as a public possibility. Hybrid illusion-dealers threaten the city from its own center and conspire to ensure that ultimately "every man remains in his own night." Who could deny that these observations are relevant not only to the decadent phase of ancient Mediterranean polis culture? They apply equally and even more to the construction and destruction of political waking worlds [*Wachwelten*] in the age of bourgeois nation-states and their present-day successors. It would be misleading to interpret the turn to the political ontology of the watch-room only as an affair of the Greek city and its philosophical genius. Wherever peoples cross the threshold of high culture, they begin to illuminate the world as the whole that vaults over the state or empire; then emerge rudiments of alternative political watch-room determinations, sediments and fragments of which have remained in force to the present day. Beside the "Greek Awakening," the ancient oriental peoples' stirring to macrocosmic existence remains eminently worthy of mention. As Jan Assmann has shown in his infinitely praiseworthy book *Ma'at—Justice and Immortality in Ancient Egypt*, pharaonic Egypt possessed in the concept [352] of *ma'at*, the linking justice, a profound model that illuminated the moral connection between the people of a great "empire." For the Egyptian consciousness, the connection between people in the world at large, especially between the people and the princes, can only be kept flowing by means of a prudence equipped with a strong memory; *ma'at* springs from a continual living effort of thinking about and acting for one another. By virtue of *ma'at*, society remains open as a watch-room of vertical solidarity; it generates, thinking ahead and thinking back, an ether of moral attention that must flow from the bottom up and from the top down so that the poles of the unequal social macrocosm are held together in a common striving for justice. An inscription on a royal tomb from the seventh century says:

> How beautiful it is to act for the active.
> Lucky is the heart of one
> Who has acted for one who has acted.

As an aura of moral and communicative effort, *ma'at* produces life-giving effects for those who perform it. Traits of this metaphysicized imperial intelligence are imprinted in the Egyptian notion of survival in the afterlife. For what "lives on" there is the eternalized result of the good, morally awake life in the cosmos of *ma'at*. A *ma'at*-filled language establishes among mortals the common sense that banishes violence and makes men into promoters of their kind. [353] If human speech decays, the ether of imperial solidarity disintegrates. Thus it is not surprising that the great Egyptian laments—for example, the *Conversation of the Life-Weary with his Ba*—speak in the bitterest tones of the barbarization of society through the loss of communication.

If the "Egyptian awakening" to the world of united empires is articulated above all in the great discovery of the principle of solidarity as a connective justice, the peak of the Iranian awakening pointed to the discovery and propagation of the principle of decision. In a world whose basic form is the war between good and evil, everything depends on choosing the right side. By interpreting the openness of the world as the arena of a still undecided battle of principles, Zoroaster keenly promotes the metaphysization of alertness as a style of wakeful existence. Persepolis, not Jerusalem, developed the sharpest antithesis to the Eleatic and Athenian theory. At the same time, Zarathustra's doctrine of Ahura Mazda, the Wise Lord who needs all possible support from the good-willed in his battle with the adversarial forces of Ahriman, reveals the onset of a new dynamic and expansive concept of the world; this conceives the world as a large space that is to be gradually permeated by Vohu Mana (good thinking) in the war against the cloudy, mad and ill-willed spirits. The Iranian conception of world-alertness as decidedness for the good thus also includes the idea of establishing the world in the first place through "world-mission"; that is the sole and undelegable assignment of the "party" of wisdom. "World" as the watch-room of Iranian day-consciousness is constituted [354] by the double call to battle on behalf of the "Wise Lord" and to the mission to convert those who have hitherto mistaken him. The question of whether Zarathustra's doctrine was actually the imperial religion of the expansive Achaemenidian dynasty of Persepolis can be left aside here. What was seminal was the new conception that the world as a whole will only reach a completely transfigured and definitive form through the final battle and final judgment. This "reform" will lead to an ultimate configuration—an idea which, after its recasting by Judeo-Christian apocalypticism, will have world-historical consequences up to the communist and fascist millenarianisms and the US-American phantasms of the New World Order. In the Zoroastrian vision, the transfigured final world will one day be coextensive with the field of being illuminated by the wisdom of god. But even in the vestibule of such imperio-eschatological world concepts, the Iranian king is seen as the protector of life, and thus as a potentate who is responsible for the conservation and regeneration of the world. Royal wisdom and world guardianship converge in him, politically as well as theo-ontologically. In this respect, we can [355] see in Zoroaster a "contemporary" of the polis-thinker Heraclitus. His impulse is also in a certain way "simultaneous" with the Upanishadic crisis of ancient Indian spirituality, which initiates the rationalizing and meditative clarification and dissolution of the old Vedic culture of ritual, trance, and sacrifice; of course the Indian fixation on salvation will later also smother every approach to a political ontology of the watch-room—as far as we exclude the rather unclear imperial ideas of the Ashoka kings. Zoroaster becomes an ontologist of the religio-imperial waking world insofar as his system teaches a "good thinking" that directs itself in a bright, sober, decisive, and alert manner toward the preservation of Asha, rightful order. Opposed to it stands Aêsma, the frenzy of rage, the furious confusion of the evil spirit. Thus, Zoroastrianism represents a doctrine of world-illumination through the connection of the rightly decided to their Wise Lord. As he himself originally freely chose the good, so too should his people decide for the good, repeating the original choice. For the first time in the history of thought, it seems, here "free will" is elevated to a factor that co-decides on the meaning of the world.

From this, an important conclusion can be drawn regarding the riskiness of cultural transition from vigilant to rational-cognitive life: because in high culture essential knowing can never only be a calm persuadedness by the unchangeable, as the eleatic ideal of metaphysical contemplation pretends, but always also contains—in Persia more than elsewhere—an element of alertness on behalf of a disputed order, [356] the knowledge-seeker must not only be taught about the basic truths but also must decide and "engage" himself for what he now knows. Wherever a culture's worldviews and knowledge-forms are articulated in close proximity to moral and political alarm, a manic trait enters knowledgeable speech; the knowledgeable then appear as if gripped and driven to compulsion by what they know. Especially in the near East, the proclamation of "truth" often becomes an affair of the excitable, who move in a spectrum between manic and panic states. From Persia to Palestine stretches a spiritual sphere in which manic semi-theorists could professionalize alarm—culminating in the ancient Jewish Nabi or cult prophethood, then again in the literary prophets and in the later apocalyptic panic-culture of the Maccabee and Jesus era. While Indian thought in its sublimest forms aims at indifferent awareness of the cosmic circumstance, the Iranian spirit interprets the meaning of wakefulness primarily as decidedness. In the Indian sense, "awake" alone is he who dies during life and achieves divine impartiality by melting into the world-ground—to the highest degree "knowing," to be sure, but alogical and apolitical. Iranian, in contrast, is the motif of an enlightened partiality that does not shrink from combat—good thinking has muscles and distinguishes friend and foe. Here begin developments that will lead up to the western mysticism of action. Not nature but decision grounds the distinction between good and evil spirits. Connecting oneself [357] to the Wise Lord thus implies a gesture of freely opening oneself to the principle of good, which, as far as its own camp reaches, must act at once as school teacher and army general.

In Zoroaster, too, we encounter the anti-orgiastic option; in him, as in the Jewish prophet Hosea, a high-cultural sobriety cleanses the well-ordered watch-room of the stupefying blood-sacrificial and trance practices of old time religion. This accords with what is said of the old Iranian gods, now interpreted as devas or daemons, namely, that they have entered the camp of the raging evil principle. That Zoroaster was supposedly murdered by members of an old Iranian possession cult wearing wolf furs also fits this picture; the demotic revenge of intoxication against holy sobriety accompanies the precarious history of higher political and imperial religious ontologies up to recent times. Satanisms are, for the most part, declassed cults that shift to counterattack through shame. As religions of resentment, they also play a role in what will one day be called "fascism." In the fascistoid neo-paganisms of the twentieth century, a violent mischief all too familiar since antiquity will rear its head, determined to reheat past obsessions.

From the eighth century AD onward, there appeared in Israel admonishing and menacing visionaries who in the historical crises of their people redetermined the meaning of being awake. [358] It is characteristic of the composite structure of the post-ancient European concept of the world that the contribution of Jewish prophetism to the interpretation of the high-cultural waking world remains virulent to this day. Along with Rome and Athens, the name Jerusalem too represents the draft of a "world" whose inhabitants conceive the whole of being in a distinctive wakeful tone that at first is unique to them. Through the world-historical effects of Christianity, motifs of Jewish "ontology"—namely the messianic element and the apocalyptic suspension toward the fall of the status quo—became factors in the planetary ecumene, or whatever else the sphere of Judeo-Christian presence may be called. Jewish prophetism conceives the wakefulness of being neither as Greek logos-day nor as Zoroastrian decidedness for the good principle; the Jewish watch-room is characterized, in its most important moment, by the idea of the covenant with a life-giving being, which hides in the always precarious name of god; in addition, Jewish waking always also means waiting for the coming of a savior in whom the hope for a better world will be fulfilled. Jewish covenant-consciousness is undoubtedly one of the most profound transformations that befell the hominizing communism of attention in high-cultural time; it testifies to the attempt to superimpose an unconditional fidelity-engagement between god and people over the unstable sphere of merely human fidelity-intentions. Rarely has the relation between social vigilance and its theological "super"-vision been conceptualized so clearly. Covenant (Heb.: *berith*) is the [359] period expression for the need to counteract, with a theological dunning-formula, the dereliction of attention in the masses and the murderous breaches of promise of collective life. Jewish awakeness, understood in its second aspect as awaiting, means: preliminary participation in the approach of the messianic age, in which the ethical world order will have become present. The waiting waking convoked by prophetic speech is permeated with the spirit of "moral futurism." The latter presents believers with a condition in which the bold moral provisions of Deuteronomy would no longer be disregarded, but followed with enlightened free will by all who remained.

However, the most significant of the ancient literary prophets, Isaiah (b. 765 BC, d. after 700 BC), initially determined the meaning of wakefulness vis a vis the future of his people in a much heavier and darker way: as preparedness for the disaster that will befall the unfaithful if they do not immediately remember their original "constitution," their religious covenant of faith:

> The look on their faces bears witness against them; / they proclaim their sin like Sodom, they do not hide it. / Woe to them!/ For they have brought evil on themselves. (*Isaiah* 3.9)

What often appears in translations of the prophetic books as a "punishment" of the unfaithful and unjust by the strict judge God, in reality signifies a kind of summary self-execution by those who, [360] in defiance of the holy instructions, continue to live unwisely and unjustly. The name of god reads like a religious caption for a retaliatory mechanism, inherent in the life of a people, which eliminates the wicked and blesses the pious. "God" is the aura or agent of a moral selection, according to which deeds return to the perpetrators or their relatives in the form of curse and blessing. What happens to you is what you yourself have been. Thus has the deserved downfall been so often predicted to the sinners of Israel; with the presence of mind of an executioner, the god-sent enemy will fall upon the indolent souls:

> Therefore the anger of the Lord was kindled against his people ...
> He will raise a signal for a nation far away,
> and whistle for a people at the ends of the earth;
> Here they come, swiftly, speedily!
> None of them is weary, none stumbles
> none slumbers or sleeps,
> not a loincloth is loose,
> not a sandal-thong broken;
> their arrows are sharp,
> all their bows bent ...
> And if one look to the land—
> only darkness and distress;
> and the light grows dark with clouds. (*Isaiah* 5.25–30)

In the light of the texts, the oldest scriptural prophetism appears as an attempt to cope with the vicissitudes of Jewish history through a theology of culling. For Isaiah, the people of Israel represents a multiple from which a *remnant* is singled out through summary, or rather divinely judged, extermination; [361] this remnant, by virtue of its sheer survival, evidences the claim to being spared by the divine guarantor of justice. Ancient Jewish prophetism thus signifies a metaphysization of the selection process that entangles peoples at the threshold of high culture, especially in the near East, in life-and-death struggles. The god of ancient Judaism is a god of battles—his work is revealed above all in the fortunes or misfortunes of his people in war. Of course, the theological genius of Judaism manifests itself in the fact that it was capable of moral internalization of defeats like no other people. The ability to internalize exterminations becomes the secret of the race's survival. Therefore, a Greek-style theory can never develop in Jerusalem, nor an Indian-style culture of contemplation, but a theological form of alertness, which rises to the highest sensitivity for the question concerning the right to survive. On the Judeo-Christian line, all theology tends to become a theology of selection; the term election is an alias for the panicked awareness that only a few of those who set out will make it. What keeps this thinking awake is the excruciating question of who will be allowed to live if all that happens is the work of a culling and sparing justice. The right to be spared [362] remains, in the view of the early scriptural prophets, the property of a very small group of righteous people—Isaiah addresses them again and again by the title "the remnant of Israel:"

> On that day the branch of the Lord shall be beautiful and glorious, and the fruit of the land shall be the pride and glory of the survivors of Israel. Whoever is left in Zion and remains in Jerusalem will be called holy, everyone who has been recorded for life in Jerusalem. (*Isaiah* 4.2–3)

> Ah, sinful nation, people laden with iniquity,
> Offspring who do evil, children who deal corruptly,
> Who have forsaken the Lord, who have despised the Holy One of
>   Israel...
> In your very presence
> Aliens devour your land;
> It is desolate, as overthrown by foreigners.
> And daughter Zion is left like a booth in a vineyard, like a shelter

> in a cucumber field...
> If the Lord of hosts had not left us a few survivors,
> we would have been like Sodom, and become like Gomorrah.
> (*Isaiah* 1.4, 7–9)

On that day the remnant of Israel and the survivors of the house of Jacob will no more lean on the one who struck them, but will lean on the Lord, the Holy One of Israel, in truth. [363] A remnant will return, the remnant of Jacob, to the mighty God. For though people Israel were like the sand of the sea, only a remnant of them will return. Destruction is decreed, overflowing with righteousness. For Lord God of hosts will make a full end, as decreed, in all the earth. (*Isaiah* 10.20-23)

The focal point of Jewish wakefulness, according to Isaiah, would thus be the concern for belonging to the number of the saved, who are spared for the race's next attempt at life. *Oh when the saints go marchin' in, I wanna be in that number.* Knowledge of the law of selection—which, thought with sufficient moral depth, should mean the self-selection of the righteous—translates into the hope of being spared due to a radically pious life. The leap into unconditionally obedient trust in god is supposed to save one from the culling panic; in the slaughterhouse "history," the prophets see a narrow exit into the future open for a few righteous ones, the *tzaddiks*. The watch-room contracts into the narrow tunnel of time, at the end of which the messianic light shines for a strictly limited number of chosen ones.

After the Christian turn, the principle of "world as selection tunnel" has overwhelmingly prevailed. The interpretation of the world as the leeway of salvation history has augmented rather than diminished the metaphysical terror of selection. According to Augustine's doctrine of grace of the year 397, it is not even a "remnant" that escapes the self-earned annihilation of the sinful masses; in [364] the world image of the bishop of Hippo, Christian wakefulness is completely set to fear and trembling; because of the original sin, no living being, not even one totally invested in its own salvation, can be sure of its election; if I am destined to beatitude, I cannot know it in my lifetime, even if I am a priest or a monk. Thus the watch-room of the Augustinian-Christian world flows into a salvation tunnel through which not even the remnant of a people, however decimated, can pass. Only by virtue of an inscrutable pardon do chosen individuals reach the other side; their lots are drawn exclusively from the lottery-wheel of the church, which in this respect represents not a chosen but a preselected community; hence, *extra ecclesia nulla salus.* The ecclesiological formula "communion of saints" means not the really existing folk of the church membership, but only the indiscernible selection of the few from their "midst." The communal [365] has now completely dissolved into something negative: the damnability of all due to original sin, and something incomprehensible: the mystery of injustice in the pardon of the few; nothing remains of the *koinon* but the common belonging of all men to the "lump of perdition," *massa perditionis,* from which some are lifted out and saved according to completely incomprehensible rules. Obviously, only a stump of Heraclitus' philosophical city-world-watch is preserved in Augustine; it survives as the episcopal office of having to take care of a most likely damned flock, with dark ulterior motives.

Looking back at these early high-cultural interpretations of being-in-the-world by historically powerful peoples reveals a millennia-spanning continuum of diverse political interpretations of "being" in the risk-space "world." Their legacy continues to be felt in the current civilizing process; it affects those living today in one way or another, with varying degrees of obligation, occasionally still with deadly seriousness. But how the regional exegeses of wakeful existence in the high cultures can be developed into a world-cultural hermeneutic of the meaning of wakefulness at the level of modernity and in the planetary horizon: this is one of the unsolved problems on which the world-interpreting intelligences of our time have to work. The only thing that seems certain at the moment is that all world interpretations along the lines of the classical urban and imperial [366] ontologies have reached the limit of their capacity. Urban or imperial world interpretations can no longer illuminate a watch-room of planetary scope, as is required by the current world situation; therefore, the US concepts of the civilization-policing guardianship of the "city on the hill," which still have priority at present, are at best provisionally meaningful but in substance obsolete; they do not go beyond the possibilities of the North Atlantic prophetic imperialism that left its mark on the nineteenth and twentieth centuries. It is also obvious, however, that the cultures of the earth are now colliding in a quasi-eschatological alarm, in which they learn to understand themselves as an ecumene of worldwide risks. Whether this alarm can result in sustainable knowledge about the rules of planetary coexistence: who would want to consider that a safe option in view of the fatal tendencies in the general course of the world? But conversely, who could rule out a priori that in future learning processes a new world-awakeness will generate a new corpus of principles of life knowledge? [367]

3. World pause

> He preached in his sleep. Awake he knows nothing of it. So much will be learned about sleep that no one will want to be awake anymore.
> —Elias Canetti, *The Province of Man*

On the path of consciousness from shared wakefulness to exclusive and systematic knowledge, thought increasingly falls into the temptation of wanting to turn off its trembling in alertness in favor of the great security that arises from essential knowledge and ultimate insights. Metaphysics of the Greek-occidental type can be characterized as the epoch-spanning attempt to turn world and life in their entirety into a day and a secure conception. As nightless thinking, metaphysics wants to reform the day and prevent it from being the interval between two nights; knowledge, too, should become more than a corroborated thesis between two uncertainties. A continuum of certainty should emerge that links everything to everything and presents each in sun-clear evidence. The reformed metaphysical day depolarizes being and places everything that is into permanent brightness. World altogether ceases to be a rhythm of coming and going. It is transformed into a gathering of things that meet in an everlasting plenum. Its convening principle is the wise god, whom the tradition unthinkingly calls the all-knowing—of whom we now know that he means an intelligence that rose above empires as [368] the guarantor of world reason—all-awake, all-observing, all-witnessing, all-connecting. His world knowledge holds the disappointment-free, unwavering, unsuffering, translucid view of all things. Indeed, in the assembly of being presented before the eye of the absolute conspirator, all that is the case is subsumed with triumphant completeness. No less than this would deserve, under metaphysical auspices, to be called world. However, the completeness of the plenary assembly of beings in Being is significant less in terms of perfection than as a sign that the present has triumphed over the absent, the revealed over the concealed; what has only been and gone, and what has not yet been and only may come to be, now becomes a non-being and an absurdity. When the world is all that stands together well-defined and summarized in the day of Being [*Seinstag*], absencelessness is enforced as an ontological principle. Being now means inability-to-be-absent. No essence can come to nothing, no thing ever loses its face; set up in permanent illumination, it forever has a look that characterizes it completely. What is prayed for in the formula of Catholic intercession for the deceased, *et lux perpetua luceat eis*, is always-already accomplished fact for the beings of the metaphysical day of Being. Just as the dead who arrive in a positive hereafter can never again be imagined as dying, so too the essences and structural moments of "Being" are to be thought of as quantities that "essence" ever-beingly, ever-luminously, ever-manifestly—incapable of decay and decline. The transfigured dead and the metaphysically conceived beings (substance, *essentia*) have in common that they [369] are displaced into immutability, where, existing without pause, they no longer have anything to fear from the coming and going of so-called transients. The eternal light achieves the synthesis of life and death. Thought beyond life, it protects against the vicissitudes of life; conceived beyond death, it is untouchable by death. Thus there is no flickering in the flame of eternal life—its brightness neither decreases nor increases. It denocturnalizes Being and demortalizes life. Like a silent reactor or a domesticated sun, it irradiates everything that lasts in ultimate uniformity.

As shown, these conceptions of eternal light never lead to a heightened wakefulness of existence but rather to an epochal light-narcosis; this accompanies metaphysical illusionism from the beginning; in the enlightenment concepts again becoming virulent among today's neoreligious meditators, light-narcotic phantasms remain in force. The long march of high-cultural mankind to the strongholds of knowledge brings us only paradoxically and apparently nearer to a heightened world-awakeness. It is true that the developments leading to metaphysical world concepts are inseparable from the expansionism of earlier peoples and empires, and cannot be imagined without an explosive increase in traffic capacities and knowledges. Without increased penetration of the world, no expanded world-pictures. But it seems as if the consciousness of the logical pioneers could only have been responding in self-defense to the political and geographical enormization of the world by investing its energies in metaphysical strategies of imperial and soteriological world-craftsmanship. Henceforth it wishes to see traces of the Great Order and entrances to paths of salvation everywhere. [370] The monstrosity of the face of being in general in world-historical time forces people to look away from the heart-rending ambiguity of what is coming and going. It is as if the night has become too dark, and death too bleak and violent. For the thoughtful, staying awake in the pulse of ancient human polarities becomes unbearable—the amplitude swings out too far into the extremes. Whoever now wanted to stay fully awake for the more and more self-unveiling known world would have to experience consciousness as a doom. The wonderful offspring of ancient human attention: love, help, and faith, can only withstand the extremes of violence and of terror if their bearers remain harmless and unhistorical. In historical time, the happy are always also the unworldly [*Weltfremden*], the spared, the marginal. For everyone else, the law of needing-to-become-hard applies. For them it is not true that love is as strong as death. It is natural for them to take refuge in wisdom or cynicism; thus the stoic works on his inner statue, the spiritualist on his astral body, the cynic on his impartiality. It now seems as if one could no longer let the nocturnal come and the dead go without assuring oneself of what neither comes nor goes, but endures and is ever-present: Being and nothingness. Thus metaphysics of this type would be the answer of thought to the pavor nocturnus of world history. World-terror provides motives for us to play dead in god, in stone, in the final formula. Where history becomes too hot, history, indeed time at all really ought to be no more [371]. At this point, metaphysical motifs touch apocalyptic ones; as the former settles true knowledge in the eternal day of a nothingness-free being, so the latter—according to the revelation of John 21.23–25—knows in the messianic Jerusalem "neither sun nor moon to illuminate it (the city), for the glory of God is its light, and its lamp is the Lamb ... Its gates will never be shut by day—and there will be no night there." "And they need no light of lamp or sun" (22.5)—waking in the eternal light nullifies the vigilance that, in the time of the old earth, makes us shut the gates at night and man the walls. Along with the last danger, enemy- and danger-related awareness too would end and merge into pure, celebratory theory. Only then would attention become the "natural prayer of the soul." Such things could only happen under a new sky on a new earth—in a messianic world where pain and anxiety no longer overpower waking. But here, where anesthetics are needed, the unity of knowing and waking in illumination has long since fallen apart. What remains are two mutually alienated stumps of consciousness—here unknowing wakefulness, there unwakeful knowing. The best among the cripples of one sort win Nobel Prizes; the others, the sorcerers and meditators, are followed by the bliss-seekers who want to hear nothing more of reality. In the middle, the artists operate as intermediate cripples, as vague guardians of the whole, driven by sporadic illuminations. [372]

Modernity is grounded in an ontology of experiment through which the self-sobering mankind of the West works its way out of the daze induced by the phantasms of day- and light-metaphysics. After the early nineteenth century rediscovered the night and allied it with the threatened ancient inwardness, modern technology sublated the archaic human fear of the dark altogether; a civilization that experiments with everything no longer needs to fear darkness either; it found a way to translate metaphysical illuminations into electric installations. It could therefore give the impression that the age of night-denunciation is essentially over. In truth, romanticism and technology together have only played into the hands of a colonization of darkness. Even the absent, the dark, has been experimentally broken open and functionalized by the day—the principle of nightwork prevails everywhere, from dream research to the circadian traffic of the globe. The metaphysical tendency to lift night into day, absence into presence, the non-world into the world, remains unbroken along the line of scientific and romantic attempts to rehabilitate the "other side." The fundamental positivism in the basic project of the Western "world" perpetuates itself overwhelmingly in post-metaphysical schools of thought of the pragmatic and realistic type. No beyond is safe from measurement anymore; night has long since become the paracosmic day; the night-sympathetic inclination of modern psychologies and parapsychologies [373] only executes the general positivist inclination toward the ontological disempowerment of absence, now reaching even to previously suspect and occult data.

A thinking that did not mask its dependence on waking states would immediately understand that it can be nothing other than a being-present at the rising of the world—and at its withdrawal. It would know that it is the world itself that opens its eyes in us, and in turn sleeps in us—wants to sleep, must sleep. When we go to sleep, it's not that it is we who take a time out, like boxers who sit in their corner and are quite the same as in the preceding round. Sleep is the "out" of the world; it is the discrete nothingness in which being is suspended and absent for us. In sleep, worldlessness is "given"; the phenomenal world is felled; in dreams the dark stump of the world sprouts paracosmic ancillary drives, which seldom become mundane durables. Crucially: it is not we who pause when we sleep, but the world that pauses when sleep temporarily removes us from it. We appear in rhythms of waking and sleeping times. Drawing the pauses into the ontological fabric of the world dissolves the positivistic block that embodies the compulsion to shut nonbeing out of life and admits only a prenatal not-yet-being and a no-longer-being after death [374]—both repressed and blocked by the continuum of imaginary permanent day that encompasses all that is the case. In truth, our "residence" in the world is a constant pulsation between being-there and being-gone. Were there no interruptions of being-there, regular as well as catastrophic, the world could never appear as something that is there at all; never would there be a new illumination of all things, never a new epochal morning. An ontological understanding of the pause brings down the metaphysical concept of a nothingness-free continuum—the day of false world-insurance comes to an end. World pauses are enablings of world through non-world—as the zeros in the number 10,101 articulate the value expression. When the world pauses, it forms the vowels around which the consonants of being cluster. If they understood themselves correctly, what would humans be but world-syllables in which discrete nothings and concrete profiles are united? The unity of the species speaks in universals of worldlessness. These sound the federal nothingness that mediates between the natal mortals like a deepest memory of what is not positively given to all. Memories of these nights, the discrete nothings, the pauses of the whole, the losses of stability are the real commons of the species. Who was prepared for the koinon to appear on the negative side? The pause represents the *deeper consensus* [English in original] against the competition of sounds. This Federal Nothing is the world peace for which the [375] people of metaphysical eras used their highest word: god. Who could forget that this expression, when it itself came into the world, became part of the positive plague ever since? It seems the best thing about theology has always been its wise concern to keep its basic word safe from the infection of empirical thought. Hence there cannot even be a "interreligious dialogue," if by religions we understand positive doctrinal systems, but only an ecumenical movement that agrees to wake and watch together in a new spaciousness; otherwise, an ecumenical monster would emerge, issuing standards for holy pollution levels. If one could finally cross out the word god, what would remain of him would be the "out" of the world itself—its pause, its discrete nothingness. That even the whole is something that cannot exist without its own disappearance and return—this indicates the rank of Most Discreet. It dies—it appears—there is something—there is nothing. The pause of the world creates the "ground" on which its sounds, its images, its positives can settle like inconspicuous figurines. Whoever is born on the night of the world's pause experiences the positive differently: the world is all that of which it is conspicuous that it is the case. [376]

4. World-watch in the age of One Earth: *Scienza nuova* of world citizenship

> The time is out of joint; O cursed spite,
> That ever I was born to set it right!
> —Shakespeare, *Hamlet* I.5

The fate of the earth's inhabitants depends today—more than in the time of cities and empires—on higher metamorphoses of attention coalitions. To the extent that older patterns of imperial world-surveillance prove inadequate, the need for an evolutionarily enhanced quality of world-wakefulness enters the horizon. In the transition to the totality of troubles of the coming world of worlds, an adult life must be one that newly determines itself in terms of a new division of labor in the world watch. Perhaps the meaning of growing up is becoming clear in its general content only today, as the species-forming drama of transition from the house into the world, from the familial horde into planetary coexistence, reveals itself to all in its inevitability. *Paideia*, or education, has hitherto been the effort to lead the playful, sensitive, pleasure-hungry and curious child of small-group humanity out into the world climate of cities and empires with their expanded vistas, difficult battles and hard grudging work against oneself. Grown-up was the traditional name for those who had learned to seek their fulfillment in luckless spheres. "He who is not maltreated [377] is not educated." Where philosophies or world interpretations of high-cultural type arose, they were always also schools of growing up in the sense of a relocation of the soul into the larger, the harder, the abstract. To describe such relocations as a possibility was the task of the ancient holisms; they thrived on a metaphorical *élan* for representing the self-disbanding world, despite its frightening vastness and strangeness, as something homelike; world, so the old sage voices say, is the larger tent, the encompassing house, the cosmic village. Because house- or home-conditions prevail even in the greatest, according to the first pedagogies the heart of the world within us never had to be completely broken; the initial heartbreak of growing up could be interpreted as a stress that must occur in the passage into the watch-room of imperial and urban worlds. Socrates, the obstetrician for adults, first confirms the woeful nature of the discomforts that attend the soul's breakthrough into political and logical worlds at large. The transitioners were always promised, however, that in the heart of the world the child's heart, however battered, could remain in good hands. Thus even the most extended world was regarded as the home of the grown-up spirit.

This projection of domesticity onto the world [378] as a whole faces its final test in the ecological crisis of the earth, which is at the same time the first crisis of humanity. This present crisis of worldliness goes deeper than the one whose pressure formed the soteriologies and older apocalypticisms. For the real common house of mankind first comes fully and truly into view at the moment of its destruction. As peoples try to move into it, they discover it as something already falling inexorably into desolation. This crisis of worldliness fundamentally calls into question the earth's ability to be a house and mankind's ability to dwell. Thus the early world-fugitives', the gnostics', and the monks' doubt about dwelling is now becoming a matter of all members of the ecumene of dangers. General house theory or ecology has become the timely form of the doctrine of last things. It is this planetary house doubt, this eschatological housing shortage of the half-attentive animal, that marks the present world-moment logically, politically and existentially. The crisis of the house-world equation gives contemporary wakefulnesses their unmistakably *present* quality. The alarm in the house, as knowledge and as wakefulness, is our time apprehended in thoughts.

Amid the terminal-transitional ecological stress, a new international division of labor in the world watch emerges both through us and before our eyes. The paradoxical task of moving into a world-house that is disintegrating precisely due to our moving in must start by sublating within every society the high-cultural division of labor between philosophers and politicians. [379] The ancient doctrine of world-wisdom is being transformed into a planetary world-watch faculty—in a new mobile university. In this respect,

How do we stir the sleep of the world? 213

Lester R. Brown's 1974 initiative of the Worldwatch Institute, 1776 Massachusetts Ave., NW, Washington, DC, 20036, USA, is more university-like than everything the academic thinkers have produced since 1945, indeed since 1914; there the world-spirit has one of its addresses until further notice.

What we call the One Earth signifies the geological monad that was conceived by the members of the species first as home and mother, then increasingly as burial place, workplace and stage, finally as resource and biotope. Today it stands before the uninebriated members of the species as a figure viewable in the image. It is the bearer of an as yet unthinkable complexity. Because the earth has now been discovered in earnest as the base-one of all hordes, peoples, nations and cultures, a new cycle of intelligence can begin worldwide, leading beyond the regional classics, perhaps even beyond the devil's pact between intelligence and globalized capital.

In this cycle, new entanglements between knowing and waking are generated —entanglements that correspond to the world-watch spirit of expanded international and interrational relationships. In the globalized watch-rooms, the major dimensions of multirational intelligence are explored and established—as New Politics, as New University, as New [379] Anthropology. All aspects of this *scienza nuova* of world citizenship reflect facets of a Second Education that not only moves the human child from the nursery room to the capital, but also from there to the nerve-centers of the global densification process. *Ci vuol filosofia*. Philosophy, however, will have to provide more in the future than during its metaphysical cycle, in which it—apart from the rational securing of the world-form as such—had to serve as the mental fitness-training for political and logical power-seekers. After the end of its regional-metaphysical main cycle, philosophy is again, as in its axial-age beginnings, a transition aid into an uncanny growth and awakening, medium of the exodus into transclassical world-forms.

At the end of our passage through the formal series of worldless states, we see the difference between mania and pathos in the styles of philosophical and political world-watch somewhat more clearly than before. In mania as Plato presented it, there was at work from the start a frenzy of homesickness that wanted to fly over the world to get nearer to some higher or deeper being-nothing. In the claim to beautiful madness, the imperious side of the old metaphysics was visible. When such high-altitude tendencies were mixed into human speech about great affairs, the hour of megalomania had struck—it is the madness of those who only talk of greatness in order to have something to let down and fly over. In pathos, on the other hand, we feel the weight of the world—and the soul, as world scale, sinks deeply when what the Greeks called *to megala*, the great, the inevitable, the un-overflyable things, are placed in it. [381] When people grow up, soul-expansion is always at play. What the Indians called *mahatma,* great soul, should by rights be an epithet of every adult, that is, of every life that has come sufficiently far into the world. The Greek-European title for the adult could be: megalopath—he who is affected by the great things.

Who could fail to see that what weighs upon the life of present-day intelligence is a megalopathic crisis? The habitability of the coming hypercomplex worlds is not proven, the steerability of political evolutions hardly more than a pious wish or pipe dream. What is in store?—a century of overtime, of doubt, of mass escape. But complaining counts for nothing, and it is indecent to belittle oneself. The duty to be happy applies more than ever in times like ours. The true realism of the species consists in expecting no less of its intelligence than is demanded of it.

Notes

Chapter 1

1. [English translation by William Lovitt, in *The Question Concerning Technology,* New York, 1977, 153.]
2. For a more precise definition of "primary process," see comments in this chapter on determination and passion.
3. [English in original—referring Donald Winnicott's concept of holding or containing.]
4. Cf. Otto Ranks' reflections concerning the heroic compensation in *The Trauma of Birth.*
5. Hugo Ball, *Byzantine Christianity,* Frankfurt, 1979, 19.
6. Cf. Manfred Sommer, *Identität im Übergang: Kant,* Frankfurt, 1988, 75ff., "Feigenblatt, Blendwerk und Selbstdarstellung."
7. The so-called philosophical anthropology of our century (e.g., that of Max Scheler) remained on the whole a failed attempt to win back the height of humankind by describing it. Limited by aestheticism it persisted patrician abstractions.
8. In two earlier publications I have laid out provisional exposes of a theory of essential speech as promise: *Zur Welt kommen—Zur Sprache kommen* [*Coming to the world—coming to language*], Frankfurter Vorlesungen, Frankfurt, 1988, ch. 5 "Die Welt als Poesie und Versprechen" [The world as poesy and promise], and *Versprechen auf Deutsch—Rede über das eigene Land,* Frankfurt, 1990.
9. [English in the original.]
10. Such a linguistics of the You, founded in a metaphysics of the appellative, unfolded in grand style: Eugen Rosenstock-Huessy, *Die Sprache des Menschengeschlechts. Eine leibhaftige Grammatik in vier Teilen,* 2 vols., Heidelberg, 1963, 1964.
11. This falling-into-a-role is a far-reaching, unresearched principle of spiritual history, or, better, spectral history. In the contemporary epoch there is a theosophical and pseudo-Indian motivated introduction of the thought of reincarnation into the occidental economy of ideas; it allows for countless obscure and prominent individuals to interpret themselves as revenants of great personalities. "Roles," in this perspective, are identical with significant names and forces, of which we are

informed thanks to our cultural historiography: we read them as if they were manic sample-catalogs from which we order our shipments [*Sendungen*].

12. That this clothing metaphor isn't just a superficial one becomes evident in the investigations of the new-testament and gnostic use of language, which often operates with an equivalence between clothing and the self.

13. Oswald Spengler, *The Decline of the West,* Munich, 1972, 818–19.

14. It is perhaps not superfluous to note that the expression *mania*, in this entire section, doesn't have a psychiatric meaning but alludes to the doctrines of Plato's *Phaedrus* that deal with the benefits of inspiration for humans in general and for philosophers in particular. Concerning the expression *Übermensch* it should be clear that we don't take it as the idiosyncratic idea of the megalomaniac Friedrich N. Wherever in the story of humankind the idea of theandry—that is, Godmanhood—appears, there exists *de facto* a thought of the Übermensch—in old Brahminism no less than in Lamaism or in the Catholic and Orthodox teachings of the saints. Nor does Judaism entirely lack a thought of the Übermensch, insofar as, in accord with the teaching of some "radicals" (e.g., Lubavitch Hasidists), the members of the chosen people are as different from the rest of humanity *toto genere* as normal humans are from animals. Cf. Gilles Kepel, *La revanche de Dieu: Chrétiens, juifs et musulmans à la reconquête du monde,* Paris, 1991, 251–52.

15. [English in original.]

16. A further step toward the explication of autogenous manias presents itself with William James pragmatic teaching about the "will to believe" (*The Will to Believe,* 1886); on the line of James' suggestions, since the 1960s a post-psychoanalytical neo-autohypnotism has been sweeping the entire psychological field, starting in the United States.

17. Franz Kafka, *Collected Stories.*

18. Cf. Thomas H. Macho, *So viele Menschen—jenseits des genealogischen Prinzips*, in *Vor der Jahrtausendwende—Berichte zur Lage der Zukunft*, edited by P. Sloterdijk, Frankfurt a. M. 1989, 29–64.

19. Oswald Spengler, *The Decline of the West,* Munich, 1972, 815.

20. This thought is laid out in Nietzsche's critique of the last men, if not explicitly stated; its polar opposite is Pascal's thesis from *Pensées*, Fragment 434, that man endlessly overshoots man.

21. For Indian culture, see the Eriksonian psychoanalyst Sudhir Kakar on the conflict between childhood and adolescence; cf. *Kindheit und Gesellschaft in Indien, Eine psychoanalytische Studie,* Frankfurt, 1988.

22. Hans-Peter Duerr has proved something similar in regard to the decline of shame in modern societies.

23. For one example among countless others, see Hans Urs Balthasar, *Prometheus, Apokalypse der deutschen Seele,* 1947, vol. 1.

24. Sigmund Freud, *Reflections on War and Death* [#2, "Our Attitude towards Death"; New York: Moffat, Yard and Co., 1918]. Behind the therapist's profile, the silhouette of the nostalgic moralist unmistakably emerges—as moral philosophy is older than psychotherapy. To the choir of those who grasp that man is a being who has to be talked into contentedness with the way of the world, Immanuel Kant energetically joined in: "But it is of the greatest importance to be *content with providence* (even though on this earthly world of ours it has marked out such a troublesome road for us), partly in order to pluck up courage even among our toils, and partly so that by placing responsibility for it on fate, we might not lose sight of our own responsibility, which perhaps might be the sole cause of all these ills, and avoid the remedy against them, which consists in self-improvement" (*Conjectural Beginning of Human History,* Concluding Remark) [English translation from I. Kant, *Anthropology, History, and Education*, edited by Zöller and Louden, Cambridge University Press].

25. Ludwig Wittgenstein, *Tractatus Logico-Philosophicus* 6.44 [English translation by C. K. Ogden, New York, Harcourt, Brace & Co., 1922].

26. Approaches, albeit inadequate, to an analytic of being-in in general are outlined in paragraphs 12 and 13 of Martin Heidegger's *Being and Time.*

27. What is here characterized as a womb-relationship has been interpreted by classical philosophy as an domestic relationship; the human spirit can dwell in the world without horror because since the Greeks he has "made a home of the world"; from Parmenides to Hegel, dwellers in the european house of being know themselves to be connected in a "collective spirit of homeliness." Cf. Hegel's *Philosophy of Right*... Only after the catastrophe of ontological homelessness can the ambivalence of being-in as security *and* captivity be appreciated; now, Nietzsche can say of existence in the disenchanted cosmos: "the world—an open/shut thousand deserts mute and cold." That the Enlightenment also remains committed to the attempt to end the political chaos and to erect a cosmopolitical homeland for all members of the species, reveals itself not least in Kant's idea of natural purposiveness: "a collective *cosmopolitan condition,* as the castle wherein all the native dispositions of the human species are developed" (cf. Kant, *Idea for a Universal History with Cosmopolitan Intent,* §8, end). According to this, the world war is an index of a condition in which the political world does not sufficiently fulfill nature's mission of enabling womb-transitions.

28. Let it be noted that the bipolarity of microcosmic mother-womb and macrocosmic world-womb is exaggerated here because for simplicity's sake we refrain from discussing the "mesocosmic" phenomena with womb-characteristics, namely, groups, society, culture.

29. Watsuji Tetsuro, *Fudo—Wind und Erde* [*The Interrelation of Climate and Culture*].

30. Cf. Peter Sloterdijk, *The Mystical Imperative: Remarks on the Changing Shape of Religion in the Modern Age*.

31. Nowhere in the world is this made clearer than in the teachings of the Zen master Banke Eitaku (1622-1693). "Not one of you who have assembled here is unenlightened. Even now you all sit as Buddhas before me. Each of you received the Buddha-mind—and nothing else—from your mother, when you were born. This inherited Buddha-mind is without any doubt unborn and carries a wondrously clear, enlightened wisdom. In the Buddha-mind all things are consummately dissolved. Of this I can give you my guarantee. If you, facing me, eavesdrop on my words, and behind you a crow caws, or a sparrow chirps, or any other sound is made, you know without listening that it is a crow or a sparrow, because this hearing occurs by virtue of the unborn." *Die Zen-Lehre vom Ungeborenen*, Norman Waddell, Bern, 1988, p. 38.

32. Quoted from *The Enlightened Mind. An Anthology of Sacred Prose*, ed. Stephen Mitchell, New York, 1991, p. 82, translated to German by the author.

33. I would like to remark that from these considerations one reaches an overview of the oscillation in Heidegger's thought between the heroic and the mystic. Only in his late writings did Heidegger become a master of diving, whose instructions were halfway reliable. In his early and middle periods, he made mistakes typical of behavior in suction. When—in a tone of decisionistic agitation—he conjured up the restitution of the subject into being, he obeyed mechanisms of suction of which he understood just as little as his enthusiastic disciples. He misunderstood the act of diving as a commitment to taking over the destiny of being [*Seinsgeschick*], without acknowledging that this amounted to an ontologization of masochism. What pretended to be a freedom of letting oneself be used by a politically colored order of being was in reality an obsessive application to the enjoyment of the gigantic by fusing with historical power. In this, Heidegger was a political Empedocles who threw himself into the crater of fascism to prove himself an elemental thinker. His silence after 1945 could after all be understood as a gesture of Empedoclean shame; when the crater of sages doesn't devour you, but spits you out and condemns you to survival in shame, then the subject carries away its crucial lesson, but the humiliation reaches too deep for the lesson of the crater to be discussed in public. Only at the edge of the crater does the meaning of the sentence "thinking greatly entails erring greatly" light up.

34. Paul Valery, *Herr Teste* [English version: *Monsieur Teste*, trans. Jackson Mathews, New York, Alfred A. Knopf, 1948].

35. That it will always remain hard to differentiate the two from each other is one of the ambivalences of the spiritual field. As an example among many see the pretty anecdote "Strib bevor du stirbst," in Reshad Field: *Das atmende Leben. Wege zum Bewußtsein*, Munich, 1989, 135–36.

36. Among the younger works in this direction ought to be mentioned Jean-Louis Tristani, *Le stade du respir,* Paris, 1978; Luce Irigaray, *L'oubli de l'air chez Heidegger,* Paris, 1983; François-Bernard Michel, *Le souffle coupé—Respirer et écrire,* Paris, 1984.

37. Enlightening in this context: Klaus Heinrich, *Versuch über die Schwierigkeit nein zu sagen,* Frankfurt, 1964.

Chapter 2

1. This expression comes up in a rich orchestration for another time in Socrates' speech to the acquitting among his judges after death verdict; cf. *Apology,* 40c.

2. Cf. Peter Sloterdijk, "A Brief History of Authentic Time," in Peter Sloterdijk and Thomas H. Macho, *Weltrevolution der Seele. Ein Lese- und Arbeitsbuch der Gnosis von der Spätantike bis zur Gegenwart,* Munich, 1991, 1:38–46.

3. ["das Eine, das Not tut"; the single necessity, also the one that asserts a state of emergency.]

4. Cited from *Pètite Philocalie de la prière du cœur: Traduite et présentée par Jean Gouillard,* Paris, 1979, 85. Translation by the author [Sloterdijk].

5. It's obvious why the anachoretic critics of the world are no philosophers; for the place of the latter remains the city, in spite of all the caveats they might want to assert against the given urban livelihoods; even the cynics that seem to some like anachorets remain entirely urban characters. The idealistic thinkers are fully and thoroughly committed to the city—insofar as the city is the political symbol for the reconciling and integrating force of society and thought; the basic concept of philosophy, inasmuch as she is a logic of urban synthesis, is therefore Reconciliation. Anachoretic radicalism, in contrast, begins where the synthetic force of urban life and thinking ends. Worldlessness, from a social perspective, means citylessness. Were hermits philosophers, the basic concept of their teaching would be irreconcilability or nonsettlement: the city is fraud, the world is false appearance. From this perspective one has good reason to ask oneself whether the individualist anarchism of the nineteenth and early twentieth century does not signify a new takeoff [*Aufbruch*] of anachoretic motifs in the middle of bourgeois society [*bürgerlichen Gesellschaft*]. Even in the urban cultures of early bourgeois modernity a paradoxical rediscovery of anachoreticism took place: in painting. The cabinet was flooded with paintings, prints and engravings that showed the saints Hieronymus, Onophrius, or Antonius studying or in ascesis and prayer—on the background of city silhouettes that could indicate Antwerp, Nuremberg, or Florence. While the cloisters lost their attraction, especially in the Reformed countries, something in the bourgeoisie dreams of the Egyptian desert. The fifteenth and sixteenth century discovers, along with melancholy, the dominion of Saturn, of the world-distant, cool, brilliant star. In the eighteenth century the rough Thebaïs transforms into

an elegant solitude—there the best of man is supposed to be at home far from the manor and the city. The nineteenth century, in contrast, detects in the desertedness the passion for alienation: "What a fatuous desire / Drives me into the wastelands" (Franz Schubert/ Wilhelm Müller). In the twentieth century finally the overloaded human comes into view—as the being that needs recovery. Vacations, distractions, illusions, regressions come into view as functions of an immunological interpretation of the *condition humaine*: absence—as it were, an existence-switch turned to Off—is the immune protection of adaptive systems against a reality overload.

6. Aurelius Augustinus, *Soliloquies*, I.7.

7. Eusebius of Caesarea says in his *Demonstratio evangelica* I.8: "Those who have converted to this way of life are as if dead to the traditional way of life and live on the earth with only their bodies, because their soul has in a secret way already entered heaven." Cited in Karl Suso Frank, introduction to *Early Monkdom in the Occident*, vol. 1, *Lifeforms*, Zürich, 1975, 9. Eucherius of Lyon writes in his *Praise of the Hermit*: "The desert is the infinite temple of God; because God dwells in stillness and is pleased by the hidden life. Paradise was almost too beautiful to the first human, it contributed to his fall: that is why the lord has sent us to the desert. He who loves it, loves life. In graceful landscapes/areas one walks easily toward death. All of the saints of the old world up to Christ have known this well and therefore choose loneliness, in order to be closer, in it, to heaven" Cited in Walter Tritsch, *Einführung in die Mystik,* Augsburg, 1990, 63.

8. Therefore all demands for a renunciation of growth and procreation ultimately articulate themselves in a religious lineage—up to the eco-monastic zero-growth theses of contemporary radicals.

9. [English in original.]

10. With respect to the role of the desert in the imaginary of Egyptian Christians of the fourth century, there can of course be no talk of an emptiness in the sense of a vacuum of meaning, considering the survival of the old-Egyptian geographies of the afterlife, according to which the authenticity of life lies yonder. Besides, for the Copts of this time a Jewish semantic probably comes into play as well; it is the ritual chamber [*Klausurraum*] for marital encounters between the chosen people and their god.

11. Quoted in *Frühes Mönchtum im Abendland*, vol. 1, *Lebensformen*, Zurich and Munich 1975, p. 123.

12. It can be argued that the idea of *koinos bios*, which has underpinned monastic community life since Pachomian times, became one of the most powerful ideas of social cohesion in the Western cultural sphere, along with the Greek *polis*-idea and the various concepts of folk synthesis; no wonder, that in the revolutionary restructurings of the nineteenth and twentieth centuries—those times without social synthesis—the cloister-communistic models, transvested by anarchism, proletarianism and council-communism, became active again.

13. [The pejorative *escapism* is the usual translation of the more ambivalent *Weltflucht*.]

14. This does not deny the presence of important monastic existences, but their ability to represent their era; Pachomius, Macarius, John Climacus are, precisely in their eccentricity, typical representatives of their time; who would say the same of Charles de Foucauld, Père Roger, or Mother Teresa?

15. Therefore, so-called secularization does not lead straight to quasi neo-antique cosmocentric conditions but to a constructivist subjectivism wherein surrealism becomes a realism. Hannah Arendt is insofar right to say: "The worldlessness which begins with the modern age is indeed unparalleled." Of course, as I show in this book, worldlessness does not "set in" in modern times—since it must always already be in play as a world foil or negative when the world as a whole comes into the picture; in modern times, however, it becomes possible to translate the dimension of worldlessness from metaphysics, where it was imagined as heaven, pleroma, or uncreatedness, into anthropology, where it means "sleep," the night of system, retreat, and pause.

16. [English in original.]

17. Ilya Kabakow and Boris Groys, *Die Kunst des Fliehens,* Munich, 1991, 119–20.

18. Cf. *Die Gnosis*, vol. 3, *Der Manichäismus*, ed. Alexander Böhlig, Zürich, 1980, 107–8.

Chapter 3

1. [English in original.]

2. J. G. Fichte, *Die Bestimmung des Menschen,* Hamburg, p. 105.

3. Cicero remarks in *De inventione* that it is important not to judge an object *temere atque arroganter,* blindly and arrogantly.

4. Something of the secret of this distinction appears most recently in German idealism, which works with the opposition between epiphanic synopsis and argumentative sequence.

5. By writing *Old* with a capital letter, I want to indicate that it is used here as a psychohistorical epochal term, like the Old Stone Age or the Old Kingdom [of Egypt; *Altes Reich*]. To represent the history of the psychic [*des Seelischen*] as the history of mediumism or as the structural transformation of possession as such, would today probably be the most important desideratum of a philosophically intended cultural history. This would above all have to make clear that so-called high cultures, i.e. the period of monotheistic laws of ego formation [*Ich-Bildungsgesetze*], must be understood as the world-age of Middle Mediumism; this is the time in which humans were only allowed to be possessed by One. From the decomposition of this structure emerges postmodern neomediumism.

6. Ernst Jünger, *Annäherungen*, Stuttgart 1978, 44. [The entire passage reads: "Just as Goethe considered colors to be one of the adventures of light, we should consider intoxication [*Rausch*] as a triumphal parade of the plants in their passage through our minds.]

7. [English translation by Wendy Doniger O'Flaherty, *The Rig Veda: An Anthology*, Penguin Books, 1981. Translation slightly modified to reflect the German version Sloterdijk uses.]

8. Cf. Charles Malamoud, *Cuire le monde: Rite et pensèe dans l'Inde ancienne*, Paris, 1984, 55–56.

9. [Adapted from a translation by Steven Slater, published in the *Entheogen Review*, 2000, 9 (1–2): 34–36.]

10. Cf. Klaus Schneider, *Die schweigenden Götter. Eine Studie zur Gottesvorstellung des religiösen Platonismus*, Hildesheim, 1966.

11. Cf. J.J., *Der Ursprung des Bewußtseins durch den Zusammenbruch der bikameralen Psyche*, Hamburg, 1988.

12. Cf. Ulrich Sonnemann, *Zeit ist Anhörungsform. Über Wesen und Wirkung einer kantischen Verkennung des Ohrs*, in *Tunnelstiche. Reden, Aufzeichnungen und Essays*, Frankfurt, 1987; Thomas H. Macho, *Musik und Politik in der Moderne*, in *Die Wiener Schule und das Hakenkreuz*, Vienna, 1990; *Was denkt? Einige Überlegungen zu den philosophiehistorischen Wurzeln der Psychoanalyse*, in *Philosophie und Psychoanalyze*, Frankfurt, 1990.

13. Cf. Hans Blumenberg, *Paradigmen zu einer Metaphorologie*, Bonn, 1960; Ernesto Grassi, *Die Macht der Phantasie*, Munich, 1979.

14. On the other hand it is unmistakable that the current disturbances on the front of paranormal research contribute to the softening of restrictive reality-concepts; these can lead to a relativizing of the still-hegemonic contemporary antiepiphanism. Still, the idea that theology can be gradually raised to the rank of a science of experience by a professionally constructed paranormalism appears sectarian to me.

15. Theology therefore is under pressure to positivize the nonappearance of god. Cf. Raimon Pannikar, *Gottes Schweigen. Die Antwort des Buddha für unsere Zeit*, Munich, 1992; also Martin Buber, *Gottesfinsternis*, Zurich, 1953.

16. Observations of this kind are shared by the most varied commentators in a strange unanimity. Jacques Derrida remarks: "Since the heaven of transcendence became depopulated, a fatal rhetoric has moved into this void, that is, toxico-manic fetishism" (*The Rhetoric of Drugs*, in *1-800-Magazine*, no. 2, 1991, 36). Cardinal Ratzinger writes: "The drug results from the despair of a world that is felt to be a prison of facts that man cannot permanently withstand.... The drug is the pseudomysticism of a world that does not believe, but also cannot shake off the soul's longing for paradise." In Cardinal Joseph Ratzinger, *Turning Point for Europe? The Church in the Modern World: Assessment and Forecast*, Freiburg, 1991 [translator's

note: Sloterdijk translates Derrida's phrase *toxicomaniaque* somewhat idiosyncratically as *toxikomanische*].

17. That there are just as many types of sublation of reality as there are types of cultural reality-settlements has been seen clearly by Vilém Flusser: "Always and everywhere, inebriants have mirrored the cultural structure which they serve to negate. Thus the opiates of the far east mirror the structure of Buddhism, namely, negative enlightenment [*negative Erleuchtung*]. An analysis of the fact that Islam permits Hashish and forbids alcohol, while for us the opposite is the case, would bring to light a similar mirroring. The same goes for Mexican mushrooms, although in Mexico, as far as we can tell, intoxication plays a different role than in the other cultures known by us. The aim of Mexican culture—and perhaps of Amerindian cultures more generally—seems to be its own negation through intoxication. Therefore we are presently fascinated by these cultures." In V.F., *Nachgeschichten. Essays, Vorträge, Glossen,* Düsseldorf, 1990, 146–47.

18. [This is a reference to the title of Arthur Koestler's autobiography.]

19. Approaches to this can be found at first in the "Tractatus psychologico-philosophicus" from *Der Zauberbaum,* Frankfurt, 1985, 281–92; the idea is explicitly developed in the two books: *Zur Welt kommen—Zur Sprache kommen, Frankfurter Vorlesungen,* Frankfurt, 1988; *Eurotaoismus—Zur Kritik der politischen Kinetik,* Frankfurt, 1989.

20. [Lacan: the aim of analysis is to produce an incurable subject (1968); Joyce is L's example.]

21. As far as I know, the only attempts are those of the philosophical theology of later Schelling as well as the early work of Alexandre Kojève; cf. Dominique Auffret, A. Kojève—*La philosophie, l'Etat; la fin de l'histoire,* Paris 1990.

22. [*Vorzeichen*—connotes musical key signature.]

23. The first person to acknowledge this was, as far as we know, the theologian and disciple of Hegel Ferdinand Christian Baur, in his epoch-making book *Die christliche Gnosis oder die christliche Religionsphilosophie,* Tübingen (Osiander), 1835, 56–64. The decisive passage was republished in *Weltrevolution der Seele. Ein Lese- und Arbeitsbuch der Gnosis von der Spätantike bis zur Gegenwart,* ed. P. Sloterdijk and Thomas H. Macho, Munich, 1991, 308ff.

24. [English in the original.]

Chapter 4

1. [*Will to Power* §822.]

2. As evidence for a perception of nihilistic consequences of the principle of making-conscious one could quote the study *Consciousness as Doom* (1924), by the suicide Alfred Seidel. Attached to a new edition of this work (Edition Subversion, no year) a desperate anti-Freudian note can be found: "Towards a psychoanalysis

of psychoanalysis (sick-healthy): since one capable of living can *only* have illusion as his worldview [*Weltbild*], thus the one who destroys these illusions, the sadist of truth, as such incapable of living, a suicidal type without instincts, a psychopath in the usual sense."

3. The comparability of psychoanalysis and Christianity results not, ultimately, from the fact that both are continuations of Judaism by other means. This is one of the consequences that can be drawn from Yosef Hayim Yerushalmis' book *Freud's Moses: Judaism Terminable and Interminable*, New Haven, 1991.

4. Freud recognized the connection between his speculations and the teachings of Schopenhauer, but was of the opinion that he was presenting something qualitatively completely different than an obscure metaphysics of the will in his metapsychology.

5. [G. M. A. Grube translation.]

6. Modern variants of thinking away the world as a method of extracting an acosmic residue are offered by Descartes in his famous doubt experiment.

7. Concerning the poetry and metaphysics of exhaustion, the German *Liedmusik* of the nineteenth century—from Schubert to Brahms—offers a singular culmination even by world-cultural measures. It is the counterpart of the metaphysization of the climax of the Neoplatonic hierarchical system.

8. This ironically also holds true for Buddhism, which with its negative thesis about the soul, the doctrine of *anatman*, elicited exceedingly intense animation-effects. A panoramic view on the state of reflections concerning the "soul" in post-psychological and (according to our thesis) ipso facto post-psychical time offer the volume *Die erloschene Seele, Disziplin, Geschichte, Kunst, Mythos*, ed. Dietmar Kamper und Christoph Wulf, Berlin, 1988.

9. Cf. Sloterdijk, *Critique of Cynical Reason*, 508–10. In this context, the theses of Franz Borkenau concerning the high religions' psychohistorical task, to contain the rising tide of death-paranoia, becomes especially concerning. Cf. Frank Borkenau, *Ende und Anfang. Von den Generationen der Hochkulturen und von der Entstehung des Abendlandes*, ed. and introduced by R. Löwenthal, Stuttgart, 1991.

10. [English in original.]

11. But not only by them. Even the medieval *imitatio*-teachings and schools of loving god make clear the deathward-directed dimension of the apostolic succession. Cf. Ramon Lull, *Das Buch vom Freunde und vom Geliebten*, ed. and trans. Erika Lorenz, Freiburg, 1992, 68: "One asked the friend what sign the flag of his beloved bore. He answers: that of a dead man.—Why such a sign, one asked. He answered: because he was crucified and tied, and because those who glorify themselves by loving him may follow in his footsteps."

12. Cf. the elaborations by Jochen Hörisch concerning Hölderlin's hymn "The Only One," in *Brot und Wein. Die Poesie des Abendmahls*, Frankfurt, 1992, 201–2.

13. One of the miseries of modernity is that in its anti-metaphysical turn it almost always succumbed to the temptation to discard the principle of the apex along with eschatological and finalistic thought. But therewith the task of post-metaphysical thought is necessarily missed: to dissolve the alloy of apex in ending that was almost indissoluble in the metaphysical imaginary to facilitate a free-floating, non-final, apexicality of life.

14. This is not the final word of philosophical psychology, since the main dispute between (fascinating) Indian and (defascinating) Judeo-Christian psychologies is no way finished.

15. One of the most extreme examples of water language that I know of can be found can be found in the book *Autobiography of an Enlightened Creature*, copyright Victor Langheld, 1991, a German-Irish mystic who calls himself Aquarius: "Wherever water appears, there I pulsate. Wherever a feeling of wetness comes about, there I weep. Where there is only a presentiment of moisture, of liquidity, I am near, ready to respond.... Every time someone falls on a slippery surface into the ground of becoming and thereby understands reality anew, there I have fulfilled my true task" (translation by the author; I owe this hint to Martin Frischknecht.) [The text referred to seems to be unpublished.]

16. Concerning the meaning of "father," cf. *The Antichrist*, no. 34.... "Before sunrise" is also published in Peter Sloterdijk and Thomas H. Macho, *Weltrevolution der Seele. Ein Lese- und Arbeitsbuch der Gnosis von der Spätantike bis zur Gegenwart*, Munich, 2:710–13. In this context Nietzsche's text first attains its full power; although not gnostically oriented in a narrower sense, here is represented the manifesto of a rediscovered psycho-uranic consciousness of space.

17. [English in original.]

Chapter 5

1. This remark is of course only valid for the secular and humanistic fractions of the modern world in its academic and journalistic control rooms. Besides, it is undeniable how a neo-metaphysical, or better, neomediumistic, wave rolls over the entire West.

2. On this activism of reversal, cf. Maxime Rodinson, *De Pythagore a Lénine: Des activismes idéologiques*, Paris, 1993.

3. Probably one must reckon cultural-historically with a double genesis of "great" metaphysics: they spring from the imperial rationalism of grand "political" unities *and* the soteriological rationalism of psycho-cosmo-therapeutics. Since these two rationalities are never fully secured, high-cultural historicity is always marked by latent and manifest antitheses of the type "Power and Spirit," "State Reason and Salvation," "Actuality and Truth."

4. Cf. in this volume the chapter "How do we stir the sleep of the world," where I interpret what is here called "ground"—in contrast to "figure"—as pause or discrete nothingness—in contrast to phenomenal presence or positive image. Totality can be placed before a "background" in two different ways: as physical world before a spirit- or idea-world, [or] as unconcealed being before a concealing nothingness or "beyng."

5. Cf. Sloterdijk, *Zur Welt kommen—Zur Sprache kommen. Frankfurter Vorlesungen*, Frankfurt, 1988, chap. 3, "Die sokratische Maieutik und die Geburtsvergessenheit der Metaphysik," 60–98 [not translated into English.]

6. [Here a wordplay emerges around the word *Fall*, which means both a "case" or a "fall." One falls into the world out of the absolute; thus one's life is a "case" of the absolute. See the Latin *casus*.]

7. Cf. John D. Caputo, *Radical Hermeneutics, Repetition, Deconstruction and the Hermeneutic Project*, Indiana University Press, 1987.

8. Thomas H. Macho, *Musik und Politik in der Moderne*, in *Die Wiener Schule und das Hakenkreuz*, Vienna, 1990, 134.

9. Cf. M. Heidegger, *Contributions to Philosophy (from the Event)*.

Chapter 6

1. The anthropological difference between the concept and the reality of the rational being has its predecessor in the theological difference between man as *imago Dei* and as "sinful" dissident of God.

2. On the emergence of hypnotic, magnetopathic, and fluidistic early forms of modern depth psychology, cf. Sloterdijk, *Der Zauberbaum: Die Entstehung der Psychoanalyse im Jahr 1785*, Frankfurt, 1985.

3. That it can no longer be a matter of heroic or saintly-ascetic but only aesthetic and civil education is shown in the most important anthropological text that was written under the impression of Kant's exposition of the problem: Schiller's Letters on the Aesthetic Education of Man. A good characterization of Kant's transitional anthropology is given by Manfred Sommer in *Identität im Übergang: Kant*, Frankfurt, 1988.

4. The juridification of existential goods opens views onto legal paradoxes. The federal court is currently hearing the suit of a young woman, who wanted to become a photo model, against her mother, accusing her of taking the risk of bequeathing to her child the nasal structure of her father, thus having neglected her due diligence toward the child by a suboptimal choice of partner.

5. Where this approval is explicitly withheld, hard oaths become possible, like Oswald Spengler's: "A human as incapable of love as our mother should not have been permitted to marry. Therein she accrues a great guilt." Quoted in A. M. Koktanek, *Oswald Spengler in seiner Zeit*, Munich, 1968, 11.

6. Something of this kind is hinted at in Nietzsche's deduction of the oldest religiosity, albeit not regarding individuals but peoples: "One is grateful for oneself: therefore one needs a God." *The Antichrist* §14.

7. Wrongly: first of all because there is not a single but rather sequences of primal scenes; second, because the Freudian scene in this sequence is not an early one, let alone the first, but rather comes later.

8. The theory of sexual perversions deals with this awayness of the subject and with the eroticization of other settings and objects.

9. Concerning the questions of fetal psychoacoustics cf. A. Tomatis, *Der Klang der Lebens,* Reinbek, 1987; the psychogenetic dimension of intrauterine acoustic and other stimulations are discussed by Ludwig Janus, *Wie die Seele entsteht,* Hamburg, 1991.

10. Informative in this context are Lloyd de Mause, *Grundlagen der Psychohistorie,* Frankfurt, 1989; Thomas H. Macho, *Zeichen aus der Dunkelheit: Notizen zu einer Theorie der Psychose,* in R. Heinz, D. Kamper, and U. Sonnemann, eds., *Wahnwelten im Zusammenstoß—Die Psychose als Spiegel der Zeit,* Berlin, 1993.

11. The title of Graber's early major work, Vienna 1924.

12. Cf. Emil M. Cioran, *De l'inconvénient d'être né,* Paris, 1973.

13. Graber, *Die Ambivalenz des Kindes,* Vienna, 1924, 23.

14. Ibid., 27.

15. Graber, *Die Ambivalenz des Kindes,* 27.

16. Ibid., 28

17. Graber, *Die Ambivalenz des Kindes,* 29.

18. The useful absurdity of the confusion between things and media appears prototypically in Freud's equation, breast = object. One may ask whether the healing effect of psychoanalysis necessarily stops where this category error comes into play, that is, with all pre-objective entanglements. Cf. the conflict over the right degree of intimacy between therapist and client in pre-Oedipal disorders, grown acute since the days of Sandor Ferenczi [see *Thalassa: A Theory of Genitality,* 1924, English translation 1938].

Chapter 7

1. The manner in which occidental optimism gets behind itself and in its self-reflection even prepares its own self-restriction is indicated in publications such as Jürgen Manthey, *Wenn Blicke zeugen könnten. Eine psychohistorische Studie über das Sehen in Literatur und Philosophie,* Munich, 1983; Jonathan Crary, *Techniques of the Observer: On Vision and Modernity in the Nineteenth Century,* Cambridge, MA, 1990; Thomas Kleinspehn, *Der flüchtige Blick. Sehen und Identität in der Kultur der Neuzeit,* Reinbek, 1991.

2. Part of which is realized in the author's works; under the title *Critique of Cynical Reason* lies an implicit metaphysics of the banal; in the Frankfurt Lectures as well as in the *Versuch zur politischen Kinetik* and in the present Studies in Discrete Acosmology, outlines of an anthropology of absence appear.

3. E. Kästner, *Die Stundentrommel von heiligen Berg Athos,* Frankfurt, 1974, 83.

4. E. Cioran, *Tears and Saints,* Chicago, University of Chicago Press, 1998, 38.

5. [A city famous for New Music since the 1920s, featured in Thomas Mann's 1947 *Dr. Faustus.*]

6. The most important contemporary theory of the unhappy ear, Adorno's philosophy of music, is thoroughly based on a double bind: according to it, regression is always simultaneously forbidden (because musical technique must orient itself toward the frontmost lines of the historically possible) and demanded (because great music always testifies to a homesickness for what is worldly impossible).

7. Cf. Sloterdijk, *Die wahre Irrelehre. Über die Weltreligions der Weltlosigkeit,* in P. Sl. and Thomas H. Macho, eds., *Weltrevolution der Seele, Eine Lese- und Arbeitsbuch zur Gnosis von der Spätantike bis zur Gegenwart,* Zurich, 1991, 1:38–46.

8. René Descartes, *Meditations on First Philosophy* [translation of John Cottingham, Cambridge University Press, modified to match the German text used here:] A. Buchenau, Hamburg, 1954, 16–20.

9. It is not certain that the "realist philosophies," materialisms, or heterologies that have emerged since the nineteenth century are still philosophical in a traditionally acceptable sense. Perhaps the reintroduction of what was previously thought away abolishes philosophy as such. The post-Hegelian gesture of thinking about reality, that is, the anti-Platonism of hard factual, machine-, code- and system-consciousness, has an ipso facto antiphilosophical effect. What remains is the question: how is post-philosophical wisdom possible? How a non-salvation-oriented *bios theoretikos?* How a non-foundationalist behavior vis-à-vis macro-problematics?

10. The habit of securing a self-certain interiority by cognitively subtracting the dispensable exterior extends to Immanuel Kant, in whose metaphysical lectures the following amputation-fantasy is found: "A person whose body has been torn open can see his intestines and all his interior parts; therefore this interior a mere bodily being, and entirely distinct from the thinking being. A person can lose many of his limbs, but he remains, and can say, 'I am.' The foot belongs to him. But if it is severed, he looks at it as at any other thing that he can no longer use, like an old boot that he must throw away. But he himself remains unchanged, and his thinking ego loses nothing. Thus it is evident to everyone, even the most vulgar understanding, that he has a soul that is distinct from the body" (I. Kant, *Lectures on Metaphysics,* Darmstadt, 1964, 132). That the *I-think* can represent the soul immediately: this naïveté was revised in Kant's critical work.

11. G. W. F. Hegel, *Philosophy of Spirit* (Hegel's Encyclopedia of the Philosophical Sciences, vol. 3, trans. W. Wallace, 1971).

12. Cf. Sloterdijk's *Der Zauberbaum, Die Entstehung der Psychoanalyse im Jahr 1785*, Frankfurt, 1985. With Mesmer, a possible end of high-cultural monotheistic (apostolic) mediumism announces itself; in fact, ever since the nineteenth century in Western civilization a "post-modern," post-monotheistic neomediumism has been in the air.

13. In Thomas Mann's novel *Mario and the Magician* this shiver reached its apex: the abuse of the rapport appears as the psychological condition of possibility of fascism.

14. Martin Heidegger, "What Is Metaphysics?," in *Pathmarks*, 87–88.

15. Here I am suggesting, analogous to the distinction in natural philosophy between *natura naturans* and *natura naturata*, a depth-musicological distinction between *musica musicans* and *musica musicata*.

16. Heidegger, "What Is Metaphysics?," 93.

17. Ibid., 88, 90, 89 [translation modified: *silence* instead of *stillness* for *Stille*].

Cultural Memory in the Present

Christopher J. Wild, *Descartes' Meditative Turn: The Practice of Thought*
Eli Friedlander, *Walter Benjamin and the Idea of Natural History*
Helmut Puff, *The Antechamber: Toward a History of Waiting*
Raúl E. Zegarra, *A Revolutionary Faith: Liberation Theology Between Public Religion and Public Reason*
David Simpson, *Engaging Violence: Civility and the Reach of Literature*
Michael P. Steinberg, *The Afterlife of Moses: Exile, Democracy, Renewal*
Alain Badiou, *Badiou by Badiou*, translated by Bruno Bosteels
Eric B. Song, *Love against Substitution: Seventeenth-Century English Literature and the Meaning of Marriage*
Niklaus Largier, *Figures of Possibility: Aesthetic Experience, Mysticism, and the Play of the Senses*
Mihaela Mihai, *Political Memory and the Aesthetics of Care: The Art of Complicity and Resistance*
Ethan Kleinberg, *Emmanuel Levinas's Talmudic Turn: Philosophy and Jewish Thought*
Willemien Otten, *Thinking Nature and the Nature of Thinking: From Eriugena to Emerson*
Michael Rothberg, *The Implicated Subject: Beyond Victims and Perpetrators*
Hans Ruin, *Being with the Dead: Burial, Ancestral Politics, and the Roots of Historical Consciousness*
Eric Oberle, *Theodor Adorno and the Century of Negative Identity*
David Marriott, *Whither Fanon? Studies in the Blackness of Being*
Reinhart Koselleck, *Sediments of Time: On Possible Histories*, translated and edited by Sean Franzel and Stefan-Ludwig Hoffmann
Devin Singh, *Divine Currency: The Theological Power of Money in the West*
Stefanos Geroulanos, *Transparency in Postwar France: A Critical History of the Present*
Sari Nusseibeh, *The Story of Reason in Islam*
Olivia C. Harrison, *Transcolonial Maghreb: Imagining Palestine in the Era of Decolonialization*
Barbara Vinken, *Flaubert Postsecular: Modernity Crossed Out*
Aishwary Kumar, *Radical Equality: Ambedkar, Gandhi, and the Problem of Democracy*
Simona Forti, *New Demons: Rethinking Power and Evil Today*
Joseph Vogl, *The Specter of Capital*
Hans Joas, *Faith as an Option*

Michael Gubser, *The Far Reaches: Ethics, Phenomenology, and the Call for Social Renewal in Twentieth-Century Central Europe*

Françoise Davoine, *Mother Folly: A Tale*

Knox Peden, *Spinoza Contra Phenomenology: French Rationalism from Cavaillès to Deleuze*

Elizabeth A. Pritchard, *Locke's Political Theology: Public Religion and Sacred Rights*

Ankhi Mukherjee, *What Is a Classic? Postcolonial Rewriting and Invention of the Canon*

Jean-Pierre Dupuy, *The Mark of the Sacred*

Henri Atlan, *Fraud: The World of Ona'ah*

Niklas Luhmann, *Theory of Society, Volume 2*

Ilit Ferber, *Philosophy and Melancholy: Benjamin's Early Reflections on Theater and Language*

Alexandre Lefebvre, *Human Rights as a Way of Life: On Bergson's Political Philosophy*

Theodore W. Jennings, Jr., *Outlaw Justice: The Messianic Politics of Paul*

Alexander Etkind, *Warped Mourning: Stories of the Undead in the Land of the Unburied*

Denis Guénoun, *About Europe: Philosophical Hypotheses*

Maria Boletsi, *Barbarism and Its Discontents*

Sigrid Weigel, *Walter Benjamin: Images, the Creaturely, and the Holy*

Roberto Esposito, *Living Thought: The Origins and Actuality of Italian Philosophy*

Henri Atlan, *The Sparks of Randomness, Volume 2: The Atheism of Scripture*

Rüdiger Campe, *The Game of Probability: Literature and Calculation from Pascal to Kleist*

Niklas Luhmann, *A Systems Theory of Religion*

Jean-Luc Marion, *In the Self's Place: The Approach of Saint Augustine*

Rodolphe Gasché, *Georges Bataille: Phenomenology and Phantasmatology*

Niklas Luhmann, *Theory of Society, Volume 1*

Alessia Ricciardi, *After La Dolce Vita: A Cultural Prehistory of Berlusconi's Italy*

Daniel Innerarity, *The Future and Its Enemies: In Defense of Political Hope*

Patricia Pisters, *The Neuro-Image: A Deleuzian Film-Philosophy of Digital Screen Culture*

François-David Sebbah, *Testing the Limit: Derrida, Henry, Levinas, and the Phenomenological Tradition*

Erik Peterson, *Theological Tractates*, edited by Michael J. Hollerich

Feisal G. Mohamed, *Milton and the Post-Secular Present: Ethics, Politics, Terrorism*

Pierre Hadot, *The Present Alone Is Our Happiness, Second Edition: Conversations with Jeannie Carlier and Arnold I. Davidson*

for a complete listing of titles in this series, visit the Stanford University Press website, sup.org

The authorized representative in the EU for product safety and compliance is:
Mare Nostrum Group
B.V Doelen 72
4831 GR Breda
The Netherlands

www.ingramcontent.com/pod-product-compliance
Lightning Source LLC
Chambersburg PA
CBHW032057230426
43662CB00035B/584